SPEECHES ON FOREIGN POLICY

BY

VISCOUNT HALIFAX

SPEECHES ON FOREIGN POLICY

BY

VISCOUNT HALIFAX

(Edward Frederick Lindley Wood Halifax)

Edited by

H. H. E. CRASTER

Essay Index Reprint Series

BOOKS FOR LIBRARIES PRESS
FREEPORT, NEW YORK

First Published 1940
Reprinted 1971

INTERNATIONAL STANDARD BOOK NUMBER:
0-8369-2401-0

LIBRARY OF CONGRESS CATALOG CARD NUMBER:
72-156658

PRINTED IN THE UNITED STATES OF AMERICA

EDITOR'S PREFACE

ONE evening last November two of my friends were listening with me to a broadcast by Lord Halifax. The voice ceased and we sat for a moment in silence, which I broke by saying that I had good reason for remembering an epigram he had quoted, for it had been chosen as the subject for an essay in the College Fellowship Examination for which he and I had entered just thirty-six years before. So we fell to talking of the distinction which marks his speeches and one of my friends spoke of their philosophic quality. We were led presently to the conclusion that, if it were found possible, his principal speeches should be collected and published; and before we broke up I had been pitched upon to serve as editor.

Lord Halifax readily consented to the proposal when it was made to him, and it was arranged that a volume should be published by the Oxford University Press under the auspices of the Royal Institute of International Affairs. I would not have been able to undertake the editorship—having other work to do—without the patient and judicious assistance of Mr. Stephen Wright, under-secretary of the Bodleian Library. To him especially but also to certain members of the Foreign Office staff and of the staff of Chatham House my best thanks are due for the help which they have rendered.

The choice of speeches was left to my discretion. Those speeches which Lord Irwin—as he then was—made during his tenure of the office of Viceroy of India (1925–31) had been printed in two volumes in the Government Press at Simla, and the chief of them had been published in 1932 by Messrs. Allen and Unwin under the title *Indian Problems: Speeches by Lord Irwin*. These have been excluded; and it has been thought best, in order to give unity to the collection, to confine this volume to speeches on Foreign Affairs and on principles of British Policy. A single exception has been made in favour of the address delivered at the unveiling of the memorial to Colonel T. E. Lawrence in St. Paul's Cathedral, an address published at the time of its delivery by the Oxford University Press. Although Lord Halifax did not become Foreign Secretary until February 1938, he had been closely concerned with foreign affairs for some years before. The collection therefore begins in 1934. It closes in 1940 with a memorable oration delivered to the University of Oxford on a February evening in the full-thronged Theatre of the Sheldonian.

The majority of the speeches were made in the House of Lords, and are printed from Hansard's *Parliamentary Debates*. Some are written statements that were given in similar terms by the Prime Minister to the House of Commons, but more are debating speeches. These were delivered extempore; as a rule they wound up debates; and they not only touched on many points of passing interest, but they were liberally sprinkled with references to previous speakers—to this argument used by 'the noble marquis' or to that remark made by 'the noble lord who has just sat down'. When such speeches are isolated from the debates in which they were spoken and put into a volume intended for reading in the study, it is obvious that they cannot be reproduced verbatim. Personal references must be deleted. Parentheses, repetitions, and superfluous phrases must be eliminated. Long passages must be excised and their omission—unless they occur at the opening of a speech—indicated by asterisks.

Non-parliamentary speeches are of different quality. As a rule they are carefully prepared in advance; but their editing—apart from broadcasts which are here reproduced from *The Listener* and the Geneva speeches which are printed from the *Official Journal* of the League of Nations—requires a distinct method of treatment. It is true that where a full text is at hand in the typescript used by the speaker no difficulty arises. But this is not the case with the earlier speeches in this volume, some of which have had to be put together from imperfect reports and from the speaker's typed notes—here a passage written out in full, there the framework of a sentence, and there again an isolated phrase. Here the editor has a more difficult task. Faced with variants he always chooses the longer text. In reconstructing a sentence he attaches more weight to cadence than to strict syntactical construction. He is on his guard against the pitfalls set by faulty reporting, realizing that this may result equally from mishearing and from misinterpretation of shorthand notes. An unskilful reporter may unwittingly set some pretty problems in textual criticism.

An editor's task is not over with the establishment of a text. The speaker thinks in sentences, but the reader requires paragraphs, and good paragraphing is therefore of high importance. So also is punctuation; and where a dash in his manuscript leaps more readily to the speaker's eye the reader will look for commas and semicolons—trifling details which it is dangerous to neglect.

The prefatory notes given to each speech are intended to give the minimum of information necessary to acquaint the reader with the circumstances in which the speech was delivered and to explain allusions contained therein. Each prefatory note assumes the reader's familiarity with preceding notes.

The speeches have been chosen with the object of giving a more or less connected narrative of the events which led up to the present war and of illustrating the slow change in the British attitude towards Germany. They reflect the reliance placed at the outset upon the League of Nations as an instrument of peace and upon the collective security which it was considered to afford. Then, as disarmament changes to rearmament, doubts are felt as to the efficacy of the Covenant and its reform is debated. Regional pacts are sought to buttress the tottering fabric of the League. Insistence that war is not inevitable presages approaching calamity. And so the current of events floods onward with increasing pace towards the cataract of war.

Yet not for this, perhaps, will these speeches be best remembered, but for that philosophic quality of which I said, at the outset, that my friend spoke; for their defence of the ideals of democratic government, and of the aim of democracy—the free development of human personality. The antithesis of democracy is despotism, and as despotism develops its counter-philosophy of aggression, and veils under the name of *Lebensraum* its ambitions for the material aggrandisement of a single nation, so these speeches reveal, growing in intensity, the spirit of democracy, which is Liberty—the Liberty that regards other men's liberties; the Liberty not of a race but of the individual soul; that invincible Liberty, prized above life because deemed immortal.

CONTENTS

1

THE LEAGUE OF NATIONS AND DISARMAMENT

6 February 1934

[The World Disarmament Conference held its first meeting on February 2nd, 1932. In July Germany refused to continue participation in the work of the Conference unless her claim to equality were accepted by the other Powers. A period of stalemate was ended on December 11th by a declaration on the part of five participant Powers recognizing Germany's equality of rights in matters relating to armaments, but there still remained the difficulty of reconciling the German demand for equality with the French insistence on security. Herr Hitler's advent to power as Chancellor of the Reich on January 30th, 1933, intensified the demands of German nationalism for practical equality in armaments with France and French unwillingness to consider armament reduction. In the hope of ending the deadlock the British Prime Minister, Mr. Ramsay MacDonald, submitted to the Conference on March 16th a draft convention which was eventually accepted as a basis for discussion. Attempts followed to settle outstanding difficulties by negotiations outside the Conference, and eventually on October 14th the Foreign Secretary, Sir John Simon, outlined the alterations found to be needful in the draft convention as the result of conversations between the five principal Powers other than Germany. The principal feature of the new plan was a proposal for the carrying out of disarmament in two stages. The first would be a period of supervision and of the standardization of continental armies; the second would be a period of substantial disarmament. The effect of the statement was instantaneous, though not in the direction desired. That same afternoon Herr Hitler announced the withdrawal of Germany alike from the Disarmament Conference and from the League of Nations.

It was against this background of failure that the League of Nations Union organized a demonstration in the Albert Hall in February 1934. A resolution that the meeting recorded its profound conviction that only through the collective system embodied in the League of Nations could war be averted and civilization saved was moved by Lord Halifax. The text of the speech is taken from his notes and from *The Times* report.]

THERE is no need for anyone to disguise the anxiety that we all feel with regard to the present state of affairs and the future state of affairs in the world as they affect the League of Nations. There are large States in the world that have not yet joined it. There are other large States that have felt impelled to signify their intention of leaving it. Yet when we look dispassionately at the state of affairs and reflect upon it, it seems to me that the growing conviction throughout the world is that the world's problems can only be solved by international co-operation. I see no cause for undue depression and alarm. It all depends surely upon what is the real foundation of our faith in the great instrument that humanity has invented—the League of Nations. All thinking people are disturbed to-day at the state of the world. It is no matter for surprise that through repeated disappointment and disillusionments many men and women are in danger of becoming cynics.

The remedies suggested for the present state of affairs differ naturally enough according to men's philosophy. There is one set of minds that ascribe all the failures to the very attempt to train the world to think in terms of unity, and which would accordingly seek refuge by a return to a narrowly restricted nationalism. From this source spring the demands with which we are familiar enough—that we should find salvation in isolation; and from this source also springs a belief in an alleged immutable antagonism between the international order of the League of Nations and the national or quasi-national unit of the British Empire. Surely one of the greatest lessons the War taught was that as science extends its field, and as the economic life of the world becomes more interlocked, the preservation of a lofty and splendid isolation becomes very much more difficult. Those who preach the gospel of behaviour like that of Diogenes, retiring into his tub and disinteresting himself from the affairs of the world outside, are living in a dreamland of their own creation. And especially have we learnt that economic ties are so close that if one member of the world's commonwealth suffers, all members suffer with it. The economic organization of the world is so delicate that no single section of it can be rudely shaken without causing dislocation of all.

As to the argument that there exists an immutable antagonism between the international order of the League and the national order of the British Empire, it might as well be argued that the devotion of a man to his own family was incompatible with the wider loyalty that he owed by virtue of citizenship to the State. The truth is exactly the opposite; we all know that that man is the best citizen who does his best for his own family. Vice versa, that man will be the best father or brother or son who is most conscious of his responsibilities as a citizen. Human life is built upon a series of mutually supporting loyalties; each tends to become stunted and atrophied if it is content to be merely self-regarding. A man's personality shrivels if he seeks to develop it in isolation, and remains regardless of other claims upon his service and love. Loyalty to family, to town, to county, will fade, unless it is balanced by the ideal of wider obligation to the country of which all these form part. The same principle holds good of every unit of the British Empire in relation to the whole, and the same principle holds true of the British Empire in its relation to the wider family of nations which we call the world. And it was this, perhaps, that Nurse Cavell, who made the highest sacrifice any human being can make for patriotism, had in mind when she said 'Patriotism is not enough'. Therefore, so far from there being any mutual antipathy between the League of Nations and the British Empire, I would say that a sane national spirit was the only foundation for the international structure, and that this structure is the natural, and the only complete, fulfilment of all national loyalty.

It is reasons such as these—consciously or unconsciously accepted—which have impelled the great bulk of British people, and every Government which they have called to power, to lend their full support to the League of Nations, and to the principles and purposes of which the League is the outward and visible expression. It is not the fault of the British people, nor of His Majesty's Government—and certainly not the fault of the League itself—if the League of Nations should have been unable to find a solution for any and every problem that disturbed the world's peace. No doubt the League is not perfect—what human creation is?—and perhaps it can be improved. The League is no super-State, and has no power beyond that which it may derive from its constituent members under the Covenant; and powerful as is its main instrument—that of appeal to moral force and conscience—both the League and the individual members of it must and can only seek to promote their ends by the achievement of agreements.

On no subject have the difficulties of achieving agreement been more obstinate than upon disarmament; and on no subject is it more vital for the future of our civilization that difficulties should be resolved. To no subject have His Majesty's Government, and Sir John Simon in particular, devoted more continuous thought and effort. The difficulties are familiar enough. No country can be legitimately asked to disarm below the level of security unless other countries do the same, and, from the point of view of France and Germany, no Englishman who honestly tries to look at the problem with the eyes of the son of France or the son of Germany, but would admit that, were his country in their position, he would feel much the same. And yet all persons concerned are bound to remember that the fears and conflicting claims, from which spring the present difficulties, are only one part of the problem, and have to be set in relation to what must surely be something like the certainty of disaster, if all the efforts to regulate armaments were to fail, and if the world is to be left to the sinister consequences of unregulated armament competition.

His Majesty's Government, therefore, thought it right to make their considered contribution; and in determining what that contribution should be they faced the facts, as is revealed by their recent conversations. Some will say that the contribution was made too late, others that it was made too soon; others again will criticize this point or that among the suggestions made. I readily admit that if the British Government had only their own views to consider they might in some respects have framed the suggestion they made differently; but our business is to secure agreement, and I cannot myself doubt that if a substantial advance could be made by agreement, even if it were less than many of us would have hoped to see, yet that advance would operate as a real reassurance to a distracted world, and would be eloquent of the world's determination to tread the paths of peace. Just as surely, a failure to achieve agreement would give rein to all the dreads and doubts that are to-day distorting the equal judgement upon which secure peace must rest. And therefore you may rest assured that His Majesty's Government will leave nothing undone that may help to secure agreement, and I am convinced that further progress in that direction can be made.

The fundamental point, here as elsewhere, is that we believe that the only way to salvation lies through co-operative effort. It is sometimes said that the League of Nations is mere idealism—that it is a tiresome encumbrance in a practical working world. I have said enough to show that even on the most practical grounds we ought to have learnt that co-operation is essential if a world which is daily contracting before our eyes is to survive. Victory clearly does not suffice to protect the victors from economic distress and loss. But even if the League was less securely founded upon practical necessity, and was predominantly idealistic, that would not be a reason for failing to support and strengthen it.

If we read our own history we find that many of the greatest things recorded in its pages have been done by faith. It was by faith that Wilberforce secured the abolition of the slave trade, which has been described as 'one of the transcendent events in the history of mankind'. All logic, all material interest, all custom and customary thought were against him, yet Wilberforce secured his countrymen's assent, by the sheer moral force of his cause, and by the disinterested conviction with which he pursued it. That page in our history should serve constantly to remind us of the power that conviction in a great moral cause can exert upon the fortunes of the world.

2
THE WORLD AND DEMOCRACY

27 September 1934

[On August 2nd, 1934, President Hindenburg died. Herr Hitler assumed the title of Führer of the German Reich in addition to that of Chancellor, and obtained confirmation of his appointment in a plebiscite held on August 19th. Authoritarian rule had become established in Germany. Its implications were beginning to be realized when Lord Halifax, at that time President of the Board of Education, delivered a lecture at the inaugural meeting of the educational section of Messrs. Rowntree's factory at York, choosing for his subject 'The World and Democracy'. The text of the address is based on a report supplied by Messrs. Rowntree, supplemented by *The Times* report and by Lord Halifax's own notes.]

'THE World and Democracy' is a subject which gives rise to a great many considerations which, in one way or another, are going to be very dominant in the public thought of our country for many years to come, and which are of considerable significance and importance to all of us at the present time. One of the most impressive slogans ever invented to encourage flagging spirits during the War was that the purpose of the War was to 'make the world safe for Democracy'. We were all too busy in the days when the phrase was coined to have time to think what it meant, and the years that have passed since then have been in many respects years of disillusionment. The world as a whole has evidently not been totally regenerated in the purging fire of war. If we look across Europe to-day it is quite evident that the world has not in fact been 'made safe for Democracy' as we in this country understand it. In a good many quarters there are signs of impatience and disappointment, something akin to a sense of betrayal; people feel that something has gone and is going wrong and are not certain what.

What did we mean by that slogan? The peace of the world and the stability of the world had been proved by the War to be of immense personal importance to the millions of common folk who have to live in it. We wished to secure ourselves against a disturbance of that peace by any nation, dynasty, group, or interest that might, for whatever reason, wish again to promote disturbance of it. We felt that the democracies of the world—the millions of common folk all over the world—would readily accept those principles, and would combine for their support. That philosophy presupposes, wrongly as I think and against much of the teaching of history, that the common folk, the ordinary citizens, were at once balanced enough, clever enough, far-sighted enough, and disinterested enough to be unaffected by all those impulses, whether of nationalism, economic pressure, or what might be called false patriotism, that in the past, all through history, have been responsible for war. It presupposes that they would be sufficiently alert to take trouble to watch events and make their judgement felt in the direction that they might desire. In other words, it presupposes that democracy would be more successful than any other form of government in overcoming all those forces that have made it impossible for nations to live separately from one another and very difficult for them to live together. It also presupposes that the world at large would be content with the *status quo* imposed by the Peace Treaties after the War and would bend all its energies to the task—not anticipated to be a very difficult one—of preventing any local disturbances of it. In nearly every particular of this philosophy and of these expectations hopes have been falsified.

It is easy to blame the makers of the peace, and not very profitable; but in justice to them we must cast our minds back to the atmosphere of that time and recollect the catastrophic effect upon history of the failure of President Wilson to carry the opinion of the United States with him in what he tried to do in Paris: we must reflect on how different European history in the past five or seven years would have been if Herr Stresemann's life had not been so tragically cut short. And we must, in fairness, try to place ourselves in the position of our great neighbour—France. It is most certainly true that the circumstances of all the several nations have made it very much more difficult for them, or any one of them, to pursue a disinterested policy, than some of the authors of the League Covenant had perhaps anticipated.

We in this country may indeed claim that we have been able to take a more detached view than some others, but we must always remember that our position in Europe makes it a good deal easier for us than for others. The most astonishing thing of all for English people to watch has been the way in which we have seen great blocks of Europe brought to the point where—sometimes under cruel compulsion, as in Russia, or sometimes with what looks like amazing enthusiasm, as in Germany and Italy—the judgement of the common folk is completely surrendered and is placed in commission. Russia is perhaps a case apart. There, the revolutionary transfer of government to a minority has been employed as a weapon in order to secure a field of operation for new economic theories. A great deal of German recent history can be attributed to Germany's disappointment arising from German defeat—a state of affairs not always wisely handled by other Powers and culminating in the hearts of many people in a feeling akin to despair. In general, the revolutionary changes on the Continent may be said to have been due to causes that in greater or less degree seem to threaten democracy everywhere—the development of social conscience, the belief in short cuts due to the effect of war experience, the readiness to accept quack remedies, impatience with and distrust of old leadership, and intolerance of those who disagree with one's own view.

As against these natural but disruptive impulses we must remind ourselves of the things that lie at the foundation of our democratic faith. The ultimate object of all government in the broadest sense is not merely the production of a State efficiently administered and orderly conducted; that is the means to an end—very important, but still the means to an end. The end itself is the fuller and freer development of human life so that each person may be enabled to make the most of his or her personality. Civics, politics—the regulation of the mutual relations of man to man in society—are the highest ways in which that development may be reached. It is permissible for those of us who believe in the moral government of the world by a conscious and personal Power whom we call God, to ponder the way in which He sees fit to govern the world. If we believe in His person and reality, we are surely driven to admit, as we contemplate His willingness to work for the good of the world through the agency of His men and women, whom He has endowed with the power of choice and free will, taking every chance of things going wrong by our failing to use our free will aright, that this is a unique example of patience and willingness to take risks that we cannot measure or understand. All that risk seems to be taken for the one purpose—to achieve, through man's right direction of his free will, the fulfilment of human personality. Therefore it is against all our experience and against such understanding of moral order as we can reach to expect that the way of salvation in our own difficulties, comparatively small, is going to be through the surrender of our private will and private judgement to some outside authority. That is not the way in which the moral government of the world is carried on. If we approach the problem of government from that angle, we do see that we may be sacrificing something of infinitely greater value if through impatience, or for any such reason, we give up the attempt ourselves to find the way over our obstacles and hand over all our natural rights to judgement and responsibility of judgement to another. Taking a long view, a far better result may be expected from encouraging everybody to put their minds into the common stock than by the establishment of some authority which forcibly, or even by consent, may impose what might appear to be a more perfect plan.

In the true democracy, where the highest value attaches to individual personality, the minority is able broadly to trust the general purpose of a majority, on whose forbearance in use of power also it will be able to rely, because both will know they hold in common the fundamental object of government—the development of personality. Similarly, the citizens of a truly democratic State will consciously accept the responsibilities of their birthright and will do their best always to bring a trained, informed, and ordered judgement to bear upon the public affairs of their country. They will have the qualities of tolerance, compromise, and a sense of personal responsibility. And this is and must be the object, in its widest sense, of all education, from primary school to university, or technical college or adult education—to develop the mind and the spirit and the character of your citizens so as to enable them to pay that back in ordered judgement for the benefit of the State.

There are many questions still unanswered, which the lover of democracy must constantly ask himself. Can a democracy, for instance, be relied upon to conduct a foreign policy upon consistent lines? Can it be relied upon not to be swayed by plausible arguments, by face values? Is it able to take long views? Will a democracy be able to conduct the affairs of a great empire, recognizing the limitations upon its own knowledge—always a difficult thing to do? Will it be willing to give and maintain its confidence in those who serve it at the ends of the earth, and mindful of the inevitable divergences of view that must often emerge between itself and the other governing democracies within the Imperial society? When a democracy has been able to accomplish what has generally been the motive purpose of bringing the democracy into existence, namely, the securing of a standard of life requisite for the satisfaction of its own daily necessities, will it be willing and able to keep alive with enthusiasm and vigour its interests in general, national, and world problems? Are we as a nation going to take our part intelligently and informedly in big world problems? To these questions history gives no answer. But of this I am certain. The answer depends upon the type and general quality of the education that we may try to give and on which we may try to found our citizenship.

It has been said that countries get the Governments they deserve. Perhaps this is slightly truer than most aphorisms of this kind, and it is more true of democracies than of any other form of government, because the remedy lies to a great extent in their own hands. Those who can serve their State in public affairs, local or central, should regard it as an honour and a duty, and those who cannot give that kind of service should always have present in their minds the knowledge that what the individual man and woman thinks matters a great deal, because they form the public opinion of the nation and on that public opinion the character of the Government and of the nation ultimately depends.

There are several reasons why a great responsibility seems to rest on the British nation in these matters. To a great extent Britain may be termed a 'bridge' state. We are close to the Continent of Europe but not a continental Power; we have contacts with Europe but are just outside it. Even to-day, in spite of the development of the air, we are able to take a slightly different point of view from any continental nation. We are a European Power with unique and exceptional contacts with America—contacts of history, family relationship, language, tradition, and culture. We are the natural bridge across the Atlantic between Europe and North America. We are a Western Power with innumerable contacts all over the world with other civilizations, with coloured and with backward and primitive peoples; and most especially does our relationship with India place us in the position of acting as interpreter of the West to the East, and it is here that a great deal of our responsibility lies. We can all imagine the importance of the 'bridge' position in these days, how much it influences policy, economics, culture, and, the greatest thing of all, racial understanding. We certainly have no excuse for being under any delusion as to the greatness of the contribution we ought to have it in our power to make. English people as a whole have extraordinary qualities of steadiness, poise, judgement, and, if they are told the truth, determination and great courage. It is no exaggeration to say that in these days, with our standards of thought and our code of international dealing, the future of the world in a very great measure depends upon us.

3

HITLER'S OFFER OF MAY, 1935

22 May 1935

[On March 9th, 1935, came an official announcement by Germany of the creation of the German Air Force which it had for some time been building up in secret. The announcement was followed a week later by the promulgation of a law in Germany reintroducing conscription in contravention of Part V of the Treaty of Versailles. Anxiety began to spread in Great Britain over the growth of the German air arm, and on May 22nd Lord Lloyd called attention in the House of Lords to the situation with regard to Imperial defence, in particular defence by air. On the eve of the debate Herr Hitler had made an important speech in the Reichstag upon foreign policy. In this he stated that the German Government would respect unconditionally the articles of the Treaty of Versailles other than those which it had just violated, that it would observe the territorial provisions of the Treaty and would follow no other road than that of peaceful understanding in bringing about revision; that he would scrupulously respect every treaty voluntarily concluded, including those concluded before his advent to power and, in particular, the Pact of Locarno; that he was ready at any time to participate in a system of collective co-operation for the safeguarding of European peace; that he was ready to assume commitments binding him to non-aggression and to non-assistance to other aggressors; that he was ready to supplement the Locarno Pact by an air agreement; that he was prepared to limit German armaments to any extent that was equally adopted by the other States; that he was willing to enter into an agreement to renounce bombing of civilians and to renounce the use of heavy weapons such as heavy artillery and tanks; and that he was willing to accept an all-round qualitative limitation of armaments on land and sea.

In winding up the debate in the House of Lords Lord Halifax spoke as follows.]

MY LORDS, I do not believe that any of your Lordships would think it either right or reasonable to go into the detailed proposals and suggestions made in the speech, admittedly of immense importance, by Herr Hitler yesterday, which we had the first opportunity of reading at an early hour this morning. I am quite free to admit that that speech is perhaps the most important speech that has been made in Europe for many months, if not years. It was a remarkable speech, I think, in itself; it was remarkable in the circumstances in which it was delivered, and it was remarkable, in my judgement, also for this reason, that it was a notable response to the invitation addressed to the maker of the speech by the Prime Minister of this country a week or two ago in another place. Therefore, I have no hesitation at all in saying, on behalf of His Majesty's Government, that that speech, all it contains and its implications, will most certainly receive, as it deserves, full and sympathetic and careful consideration at their hands.

But if your Lordships follow me that far you will, I am quite sure, also agree that it is impossible to discuss it in detail to-day; and, indeed, I do not think that it would be profitable for those who can speak for this country, or for any other single country, to pronounce upon it until the statesmen of Europe all together have had an opportunity of considering it and of realizing what may be the possibilities contained in it. Certainly no one of us need be under any misapprehension, and no member of His Majesty's Government is under any illusions, as to the gravity of the state of Europe to-day; nor are they likely to be unmindful of the fact that, each time that an opportunity of advancing the cause of peace by winning through to greater understanding is lost, the difficulty of recapturing the ground that has been lost is indefinitely magnified. I would like to record my own judgement, which is also, I have no doubt, the judgement of everyone of His Majesty's Government, that there is very little hope of progress in Europe to-day if, every time an effort is made by a responsible Leader in another country, at once those elsewhere are tempted to give free rein to all the suspicions that the least worthy among their fellow countrymen would be tempted to hold.

As I conceive it, this Government, or any other Government, have always two dominant duties. They have a dual policy—the dual policy of peace and of defence; and it is, I think, wholly misleading to suggest that these are incompatible, or to say that parity has nothing to do with peace and that we should only follow a conciliatory policy. Are we only to follow a conciliatory policy and let our material means of defence be anything or nothing? That is the unilateral plan of which we have found the results to be singularly unfruitful. I would urge noble Lords opposite, in so far as they have influence in the country, to educate those behind them in what they themselves know to be true, that you have got to do both things—to have adequate measures of defence and all the time pursue a constructive policy for peace.

These proposals are made not because we are warmongers but because we believe it is the best way to secure the cause of peace, that being the other half of the plan we seek to promote. Nor are our proposals made because we have given up hope of limitation; but limitation, I would remind your Lordships, must be on figures that every country can accept as reasonably satisfactory for their own security. It is exactly the same for Herr Hitler as for us. He has not yet limited his Air Force and we have not yet limited our Air Force. If he offers limitation, and agreement can be reached, it is as open to us as to him at any moment to reduce and decelerate and arrive at agreement on any lower level that may be reached. But I profoundly agree that the best way to reach a lower level is to let it be known to the world that you are able and willing to maintain yourselves at a level wherever in default of agreement that level may be put.

. . . .

I can assure your Lordships that in this matter the Government are very much alive to the necessity of placing themselves in a position to discharge the obligations they have taken on their shoulders. It is not so much a question of taking new obligations as of convincing the world that we can discharge the obligations that we have taken. I have always for myself been chary of assuming obligations for this country, but even more chary of seeing this country default on obligations that it had assumed. Therefore, our duty is to see that this country is able to make its contribution to the peace of the world by making it plain that we have sufficient force to act as a real deterrent to anyone who would disturb the world's peace. The outlook in the world is uncertain, and defence provisions must depend upon considerations that have been mentioned in this debate—greater vulnerability of this country, political stability, and the like. Your Lordships may feel assured that, if the clouds lift and the situation improves, no one will more readily respond to the possibility of easement of these provisions and this programme than will His Majesty's Government. On the other hand, the Government cannot divorce themselves from the plain responsibility, however zealously and strongly they wish to pursue the paths of peace, of seeing that they leave no stone unturned to discharge what the noble Lord who moved this Motion rightly said was their primary responsibility, to secure to the utmost of their power the adequate defence of the citizens of this country.

4

ITALY AND ABYSSINIA
THE HOARE-LAVAL PROPOSALS

19 December 1935

[On September 5th, 1935, the Council of the League of Nations appointed a Committee of Five to seek a pacific settlement of the Italo-Abyssinian conflict. The Committee presented proposals for the administrative reorganization of the Abyssinian Empire, but these, though accepted as a basis for negotiation by Abyssinia, were rejected by the Italian Government. On October 3rd Italian troops invaded Abyssinia, and two days later the League Council unanimously resolved that Italy had resorted to war in disregard of Articles 12, 13, or 15 of the Covenant. Economic sanctions were put into force against Italy by the League on November 18th. Meanwhile a suggestion had been made by M. van Zeeland in the League Assembly that the responsible leaders of France and Great Britain should be entrusted with the mission of seeking the elements of a peaceful solution. Sir Samuel Hoare, the British Foreign Secretary, and M. Laval, Premier and Foreign Minister of France, consequently met in Paris on December 7th–8th and formulated peace proposals which involved the cession to Italy of portions of Abyssinia, and the formation in Southern Abyssinia of a zone of economic expansion and settlement for Italy. The peace plan was accepted by the British Cabinet and submitted by it to the interested parties; but it was in effect rejected both by Abyssinia and by Italy; it found no favour with the League, and its publication roused a storm of protest in this country. Sir Samuel Hoare resigned office on December 18th. On the following day Lord Davies moved in the House of Lords a resolution that the House would not assent to any settlement which was inconsistent with the principles of equity and fair dealing and with British obligations under the Covenant of the League of Nations. Lord Halifax, who had become Leader of the House after the general election held in the preceding month, made immediate reply.]

MY LORDS, I think it is in the public interest and from every point of view desirable that I should take the earliest opportunity open to me in this House of making as plain as I can the position of His Majesty's Government with regard to the matters that no doubt are principally in your Lordships' minds. When the noble Lord first put his Motion on the Paper he put it down in circumstances very different from those with which we are to-day concerned. I am quite certain that every one of your Lordships, in whichever quarter of the House you sit, will not disagree with me in saying that no one standing in my place could fail to be conscious of the particular difficulty attaching to this debate, held as it is at this particular moment, with which I am obliged to deal. I think I can best overcome that difficulty if I attempt to give to your Lordships a plain statement of the facts of the case, and, so far as I may, explain how the situation in which we stand has arisen, and what are the lessons that I, speaking for His Majesty's Government, am disposed to draw from it.

The noble Lord referred in some of the observations that he made to what is and has been always present to the minds of all of us—namely, the situation that has been created by the determination of the League of Nations to pursue simultaneously the dual policy of imposing and enforcing sanctions upon a nation declared an aggressor and, at the same time to the utmost of its ability, the task of conciliation in the dispute. It was, let me remind your Lordships, by the League that the French Government and ourselves were charged with a moral mandate for that business of conciliation.

. . . .

There is, I think, no substantial difference between the noble Lord and myself on that point, because I am prepared to go the whole way in agreeing that no more thankless task could ever have been placed on the shoulders of any nation than was placed on our shoulders when we accepted the responsibility, along with France, of trying to evolve a scheme of conciliation. It was thankless not only for the reasons the noble Lord gave, but because, looking back on it, I think we can all see how readily those who accepted such a task were likely to expose themselves to misunderstandings in the world at large. It was almost sure to be said when they came to their scheme of conciliation, or even when they were preparing it, that they were going behind the backs of the League; and it was almost sure to be said, when they produced any scheme of conciliation, that they had, to some extent, forfeited their liberty of action in events that might follow the rejection, on such a hypothesis, of the scheme that they had produced. That, however, is in the realm of history and perhaps not very relevant. What is more relevant is that we should try to have in our minds the background of general considerations that were present to the mind of His Majesty's Government when they were attempting to discharge the task so laid upon them.

There was, first of all, the consideration that while they were pursuing the task of conciliation they, as a Member of the League, and the League itself, were also pursuing as energetically as they could the collective policy in regard to sanctions, with all the possible repercussions that that policy might evoke. It was also present to our minds always that the League, after all, is an instrument for peace and exists for peace. I have never been one of those—and I do not think there are many in this House, though there may be some—who have thought that it was any part in this dispute of the League to try to stop a war in Africa by starting a war in Europe; and that for this reason, that the end of such an extension of the area of hostilities, were it ever to be brought about, is quite impossible for any man sitting in this House to-day to foresee.

Thirdly, this was present to our minds—that however you might assess, high or low, the danger of such an extension of the area of hostilities, it was essential, if there was any risk of it at all, that that risk should be secured against in advance by ensuring that it would be collectively met. I say that not because I believe that, if this country were ever the object of isolated attack, the result would be very different from that of all military operations in which we have been unhappily engaged at different periods in our history. But I say it for this reason, that if this country ever found itself involved in a single-handed war in the cause of the League, it would mean the disbandment of the League itself, since it would be the clearest evidence that the collective system had broken down, and since, if I know the people of this country at all, they would never stand for membership in a League of Nations that was liable to land them into a single-handed war. The last consideration that I think is worth while your

Lordships having in mind, as it was in our minds, is that the League of Nations itself had never denied that there was a case to be met from the Italian side, just as my right honourable friend, Sir Samuel Hoare, had himself quite frankly stated in more than one of his speeches on the subject.

That was, as I see it, the framework against which the thought of those concerned in conciliation had to be set; and it was while, with public knowledge, the discussions in that field of conciliation were proceeding that Sir Samuel Hoare was imperatively ordered by his doctors to seek rest and health abroad; and how urgently that rest and recuperation of health were needed those who were working closest with him are in the best position to judge. On his way abroad he went to Paris. There was very little pre-designed about it. He was passing through Paris, and it was natural that he should meet the French Prime Minister. He did not go there to discuss terms of conciliation; he went to discuss matters, quite other, connected with the Italo-Abyssinian dispute, and consequently he went with no instructions as to possible terms of conciliation from his colleagues in His Majesty's Government. When he got to Paris he found the French Government urgently anxious to make progress as rapid as might be with the proposals for conciliation and, at great personal sacrifice of convenience and health, he agreed to take a personal part with M. Laval. In that, indeed, I think, he could hardly help himself and, as the House knows, he extended his stay in Paris by an extra day in order to continue to prosecute this task to which, at that moment, M. Laval was attaching exceptional urgency and importance.

That task concluded, he left Paris, if I remember aright, on the Sunday night, and the result of his labours reached His Majesty's Government on the Monday. Meanwhile there had been published in Paris a communiqué bearing the authority of the French Prime Minister and the Foreign Secretary, in which mutual satisfaction was expressed at the result of their joint labours, and also, on the Monday morning, twelve hours after the Foreign Secretary had left Paris, a pretty full publication of the whole so-called terms of peace was broadcast in the French Press. It was under circumstances like those that His Majesty's Government found themselves pledged to take a decision on the Monday evening. The noble Lord asked me whether I could tell him on that point whether the Dominions had been consulted, and I can tell him, as was stated in an answer made in another place a day or two ago, that, for reasons I shall make plain, they were not consulted but they were immediately informed.

I want the House to observe the dilemma in which at that point His Majesty's Government were placed. I make no secret of the fact that when they read the terms they did not like them, though I am bound to add, in justice, that the terms in my judgement are not so bad as the noble Lord or as much public opinion outside has represented them to be. If it were relevant and the time permitted I do not think it would be at all an impossible task to show, in one or two material directions at least, how these terms are definitely better from the League of Nations point of view than were the proposals of the Committee of Five. It is not irrelevant to add this, if it be any test in any man's mind of the merits or demerits of those terms, that so far as I have been able to glean information it does not appear that the Government of Italy regard them as unduly generous or are particularly enamoured of them. This at least is quite clear for anybody to judge for himself, that they offer to Italy vastly less than has been officially claimed by the Head of the Italian Government. It was quite clear that the Government could never refuse assent on that Monday night at the price of repudiating their Foreign Secretary, a colleague who was absent and who would have been unheard.

I want your Lordships to appreciate quite clearly the position in which we were placed, for the other possible course that may be in some of your Lordships' minds, that we might have delayed the session until such time as we could invite the Foreign Secretary to return to us and to discuss his work with us, was in fact absolutely estopped for us by the fact of the premature publication in Paris and the immediate repercussions all over the world.

It was open to the Government to support a colleague who had deserved and was deserving of their trust, who had done more for the League of Nations than almost any man in public life in any country to-day, who had brought the League of Nations into the forefront of European politics, and who, if any man had a right to claim it, had a right to claim title to loyalty to the League of Nations for which he had laboured. After all, the terms themselves were based upon exactly identical principles (however those principles were extended) with those that had actuated the work of the Committee of Five at Geneva. The principles that underlay the work of the Committee of Five were an exchange of territory between Italy and Ethiopia, League assistance to Abyssinia, and the recognition of special economic interests to Italy in Abyssinian development. Therefore we were entitled to think, whatever might be said about the precise application of the principles in question, that there was nothing fundamentally different between the principles that had inspired the work of the Committee of Five and those that were behind the work that the Foreign Secretary had done in Paris. That, therefore, was the first course: to support a colleague who, naturally, enjoyed the fullest measure of trust of His Majesty's Government.

The other course was to repudiate him, unheard, unable to plead his own case before his colleagues, and to leave it as the fact that His Majesty's Government, acting on their immediate and individual judgement, had felt unable to support the work that he had done.

In passing it is perhaps worth while to interpose that there was never any question, as the noble Lord suggested, of penalizing Ethiopia if she did not see her way to accept. It has always been made abundantly clear throughout by the Government, that the settlement that they desired, difficult though the condition of attaining it may be, should be one that was clearly accepted by the three parties concerned; and it is quite untrue to suggest that we did not, when weighing these matters, give great weight to the compensation that the Emperor would enjoy by securing that which Abyssinia has never had—namely, an outlet to the sea.

Now, my Lords, I say quite frankly that, placed in a position such as that, with the necessity of immediate decision, most of us are liable to be tempted, perhaps, to allow undue influence to the great trust and regard that we may have had for the comradeship that has bound close colleagues together through times as difficult as any that most of us in this House have known. I do not hesitate to say that that sense of comradeship was reinforced in all our minds—certainly in my own—by an immense feeling of gratitude to Sir Samuel Hoare for the unwearying labour that he had spent in the cause of the country's service and for the contribution that he had personally made to the raising of the prestige of the nation high among the nations of the world.

And if we erred, as we did, in giving approval under such conditions to those proposals, I venture to think that we erred for motives that will be appreciated by all who know how close are the bonds of trust that bind colleagues and how essentially those bonds of comradeship are the foundation of all that is best in the political life of a free nation; they will understand the extent to which we erred and will perhaps not think that the motives of our mistake were undeserving of some respect. I am quite prepared to admit that we made a mistake—not the mistake that is commonly imputed to us, but the mistake of not appreciating the damage that, rightly or wrongly, these terms would be held by public opinion to inflict upon the cause that we were pledged to serve. Accordingly, we share to the full the responsibility for the mistake that was made.

Now, as your Lordships know, Sir Samuel Hoare, with characteristic courage and generosity, realizing that his action, through circumstances only partially within his control, had caused embarrassment to his colleagues and to the purposes that he had designed to further, has placed his resignation in the Prime Minister's hands; and your Lordships will not misunderstand me if I say that I fancy that it may be harder for the Prime Minister to accept that resignation or for his colleagues to learn of it than it was for Sir Samuel Hoare to proffer it. The way of peacemakers is a hard one, and mistakes exact very heavy penalties. The penalty in the case of my right honourable friend has been plain, immediate, and direct. The penalty for His Majesty's Government has been the loss of a colleague whose responsibility they share; and every member of that Government, if it had been possible, would have been willing to pay the same price for their common mistake as his official position exacted of him. And the public service has paid a penalty in the fact of being deprived—not, I hope, permanently—of one who had made the reputation of this country to stand high and who had accounted no sacrifice too great in the discharge of the successive duties that the country had laid upon him.

This effort towards peace, rightly or wrongly, is dead, and it is no time yet to appraise the consequences to this country and the world of what I confess to many of us is a tragic episode. There are many misunderstandings, many ignorances, and many misconceptions to be cleared, before true judgement will emerge. But even now some things stand out and may be held to deserve the consideration of your Lordships' House, and they are greater than any private or lesser interests. The first, though it is not fundamental, is one which has been mentioned before in your Lordships' House but to which I think these events may be held to lend new significance. That is the danger that may attach to direct meetings between responsible Foreign Ministers, other than at Geneva, and the embarrassment that it must often cause to the individuals themselves. The second thing which stands out is much more important, and has left an indelible mark on most of our minds. It is the rallying of opinion here, in the Dominions, and all over the world to the support of the cause of the League of Nations that, rightly or wrongly, they thought was in danger of damage. That is very significant. You may or you may not think it wise or good or anything else, but of the fact there can be, I suggest, very little doubt. But such a rallying of opinion as that demands, in my judgement, that those so feeling should everywhere face the realities. If the League of Nations had been universal, and if all Members of the League had been and were prepared always to fulfil all their obligations, the power of the League would be overwhelming, war would be impossible, and I venture to make bold to state that this war would never have been begun.

My Lords, the world in which we are living is different. We do ourselves no good by forgetting that it is different. When large nations remain outside the League of Nations, and when other nations who are within the League are not prepared to go to war for any cause irrespective of what they conceive to be their national interests, it really does behove all men of common sense to recognize both the risks and the limitations that are involved in pursuit of League ideas.

May I say a word about the risks. The existence of risks is responsible for the breed of isolationists who seek to avoid risks by enclosing themselves inside the insecure barrier of isolation. I record my confident conviction that no salvation lies along that path. It is impossible—the world is too closely knit, and our interests are too widely spread. Nor does salvation come from the other kind of isolationists who would be prepared to see one nation alone pursue its ideals irrespective of the action of others. Both those sets of isolationists are equally dangerous and obstructive to true progress. Therefore you are forced back upon the best and greatest measure of collective action that you can obtain; and that will not serve the cause of peace unless in the last resort those who profess loyalty to it are both prepared and ready—I emphasize those words 'prepared and ready'—to use their strength in the cause of peace to which they pay lip service.

That with regard to the risks. A word about the limitations. It is quite easy to speak about no reward being given to aggressors, and intellectually and morally my mind and conscience go with every word that the noble Lord has said; but I hope that I remember the necessity, when you are using language like that in this imperfect world, of being honest with the facts as with ourselves. What are the facts? The noble Lord spoke of only partial sanctions and of the imperfect operation of Article 16.[1] He reminded us of the limita-

[1] 'Should any member of the League resort to war in disregard of its covenants under Articles 12, 13, or 15, it shall *ipso facto* be deemed to have committed an act of war against all other members of the League, which hereby undertake immediately to subject it to the severance of all trade or financial relations, the prohibition of all intercourse between their nationals and the

tions, the handicaps under which the League had worked in the Far East with regard to which the noble Earl, Lord Lytton, was so directly connected. What is the meaning of that? Take the scheme of the Committee of Five that has been under reference this afternoon. That scheme of the Committee of Five was produced, not, indeed, when actual force, actual war was going on, but, as everybody in your Lordships' House knows, under the direct threat of force, when war was imminent; and whatever the technicalities of the Covenant, there is no such profound difference of principle between force prospective and force actual as the noble Lord might, I think, be inclined to suggest. We may deplore it, but it is a fact that both in such a case as the Committee of Five and in any other it is force that is the instrument by which all world policy to-day is directly and vitally affected. We deplore it. It cuts right across the ideals of the Covenant. But it is not more in my judgement than a reflection of the difference in another sphere that prevails between the Covenant as it was conceived in the minds of those who planned it and the League of Nations as in fact it exists in a still imperfect world.

The Foreign Secretary goes, but the League remains, and remains the basis of international endeavour. With the failure of these peace proposals, the position reverts to what it was before the proposals were made. His Majesty's Government will continue to support the League in all actions that the other Members of it may, with ourselves, think it right, appropriate, and possible to take. I am quite prepared on behalf of the Government, therefore, to accept the Motion that the noble Lord has moved, adding only one rider by way of interpretation to it—that it is the League of Nations rather than this House that must be the ultimate judge of whether the conditions that he lays down as to equity and conformity with the Covenant of the League are or are not satisfied.

nationals of the covenant-breaking State, and the prevention of all financial, commercial, or personal intercourse between the nationals of the covenant-breaking State and the nationals of any other State, whether a member of the League or not.'

I do not for a moment pretend that events such as those which have passed in the last week can fail to have grave results. Of those results, though many of us feel it the most immediate, the personal result is the least important. During recent months this country has attained in rather a remarkable fashion to a position of great moral leadership in the world. These things are mysterious and belong to the imponderables about which men feel but can hardly reason. It is inevitable that, that having been so and the events of the last week having been what they have been, much of the opinion so formed should be temporarily uncertain and confused, for Governments, more than anybody else, have to try to be—though they do not always succeed in being—like Caesar's wife. From the broad point of view the greatest service that my right honourable friend, Sir Samuel Hoare, has done by his act of resignation may be to strengthen afresh the moral leadership of this country before the world—a leadership which he as much as any other man in recent years has been responsible for creating. Yet, speaking as I have to while these feelings are fresh in one's mind, I cannot altogether help feeling that in the long run these events may perhaps serve to win a new loyalty to the better international order that we seek to create, and a loyalty more powerful, surrendering no part of its ideals, and yet able to realize with truer knowledge the sternness of the conditions upon which the future peace of the world, certainly in our lifetime, will depend.

5

LAWRENCE OF ARABIA

29 January 1936

[A memorial tablet to Colonel T. E. Lawrence, the work of Mr. Eric Kennington, was unveiled in St. Paul's Cathedral on January 29th, 1936. Lawrence was an Oxford man, educated at the City of Oxford High School and at Jesus College. He received his archaeological training under Dr. David Hogarth, Keeper of the Ashmolean Museum, and, after the Great War, he held for a time a Fellowship at All Souls College. Speaking as Chancellor of the University of Oxford, Lord Halifax delivered the following address, which forms a separate publication of the Oxford University Press.]

I TAKE it as an honour paid to the University of Oxford that her Chancellor should have been selected to perform this ceremony, and to say something about one of the most remarkable of Oxford's sons. It is my misfortune that it never fell to me to enjoy that close friendship with him, the memory of which is the possession of many here, so it cannot be of their Lawrence that I must principally try to speak. Rather from a standpoint more detached must I make some attempt to appraise the character and performance which we here commemorate.

It is significant how strongly the personality of Lawrence has gripped the imagination of his countrymen! To comparatively few was he intimately known; his fame rested upon achievement in distant corners of the world; to the vast majority he was a figure legendary, elusive, whose master motives lay far outside their cognizance. So true it is that men often admire most what they are least able to understand.

There has been no character in our generation which has more deeply impressed itself upon the mind of youth. Many of us can remember when we began to be told stories how impatiently we used to ask the teller if it was really true; and Lawrence's life is better than any fairy story. As we hear it we are transported back to the days of medieval chivalry, and then we remember that these things happened not yet twenty years ago, and were mainly due to a force present in one man, that we acknowledge under the title of personality.

To Lawrence in an especial sense Oxford played the part of understanding guardian. Trained of old to discern the signs, she readily knew in him the divine spark that men call genius, tended and breathed upon it, until, self-taught, it kindled into flame. And it is perhaps not untrue to say that the discovery by Lawrence himself of his own powers and destiny was in no small measure due to their earlier recognition at Oxford by Dr. Hogarth, whom he was accustomed to describe as a great man and the best friend he ever had. So, with the stamp of her approval, Lawrence set forth from Oxford eastwards, a crusader of the twentieth century on behalf of peoples and causes which must remain for ever associated with his name.

It was an accident that this phase of Lawrence's life should have synchronized with that most searching trial of his country which was the occasion of his rendering her such signal service. He had long dreamed of the restoration to freedom of the inhabitants of Palestine and Arabia, and it was through the reactions of the Great War upon those lands that the chance came to realize his dreams. Others worked with him through the perils of the strangest warfare that those years witnessed, and share with him the glory of achievement. But he, as his collaborators were first to own, was the inspiration and fiery soul of the revolt which shattered Turkish misrule and made freemen of the children of the desert.

In 1914 Lawrence was barely twenty-six, known only to Oxford and the small circle of his friends; when the War ended his name was on the lips of all the world. For nearly three years he had organized and directed against the enemy a race of nomadic tribesmen, difficult of combination in sustained military effort, and, great captain that he was, had turned what might have seemed their chief disadvantage to the invention of a new strategy. Conscious that he had at last found a cause to which he could consecrate all his energies, privation and physical danger became only incidents in the attainment of the great end of his endeavour. By true gift of leadership he was able to communicate to others his own standard of achievement. Each man who looked to Lawrence for instructions knew that he was asked to undertake no duty that his leader would not, and could not better, discharge himself. Small wonder that he could count upon a devoted loyalty almost unique in the annals of military adventure, a loyalty which over and over again carried forlorn hopes to complete success.

The campaign ended, Lawrence found himself engaged in what was for him the more arduous struggle of the peace. Even before the war ended, questions to which for him only one answer could be given were being caught up in cross-currents of international policy and rival national interests. The mark that these days left upon him was deep and ineffaceable. The strain of their anxieties was heightened by the strain of writing his own record of events, to which at whatever cost he felt impelled by historical necessity.

Even at Oxford, where he sought in All Souls to find the rest that the University offers to her returning sons, he found himself unable to escape the burden that pressed upon his soul. Relentless his fame pursued him, forced him from Oxford, made him fly even from himself, to find in change of name, scene, and occupation that loss of identity through which he hoped to win reprieve from his distress.

Thus he came to join the humblest ranks of the Royal Air Force, the youngest of the Services. The future lay with youth, and here for Lawrence was the very embodiment of youth, with all its life before it. His imagination became suddenly on fire with the thought of what the air should be. Sharing its fortunes on terms of simple comradeship, he might inspire the young Service upon whose quality he felt that some day the safety of his country might depend. He called the conquest of the air the one big thing left for our generation to do. It is not without significance that the bulk of the contributions for the memorial unveiled to-day has come from shillings and sixpences given by the ranks of the Royal Air Force. To his decision we owe it that he was able to put into final form the narrative of those desert days, in prose which will live so long as men read the English language, and give Lawrence yet another claim to immortality.

These years from 1922 to 1934 among the unnamed rank and file were perhaps the happiest of his life. Both his mechanical and creative sense were satisfied in the work of perfecting the new speed-boats for the Air Force, and when he returned to private life it was a man restored, desiring yet doubting the taste of leisure, who went to make a quiet home for himself deep in the land of Wessex, beloved of that other master of the English tongue whom he so much revered. Here it was that after a few brief weeks he met catastrophe in what seems to have been characteristic sacrifice of self to avoid collision, and a week later died.

So passed Lawrence of Arabia, leaving behind him a memory and an example. For he always maintained that he was no more than the average of his time; what he could do another might, granted the will and the opportunity.

What was the secret of the almost mesmeric power that he exerted? So different was he from other men that they could often only catch part of his singularly complex personality, and it is perhaps just in this difficulty of judging the man whole that lies the true evidence and measure of his greatness. Nor, with his strain of puckishness, was Lawrence himself averse from deepening a mystery, at times not less baffling to himself than to many of his friends. No one can read his private letters, in some ways the most arresting of his literary work, without being conscious of sharply alternating moods, almost the conflict of competing personalities.

But, this said, there are certain fixed points that hold firm in contemporary judgement. All those who knew him agree that he possessed some quality to be best described as mastery over life. While, like all men, he owed much to the influence of heredity and environment, he, more than most men, had or acquired the capacity to mould life instead of lending himself to be moulded by it. Here lay the secret of his command over affairs, over others, and last, but not least, over himself. It is seldom that the direction of world events can be so clearly attributed to the dynamic force of a single individual. He saw a vision which to the ordinary man would have seemed like fantasy, and by the sheer force of his character made it real. From his fellows he drew without exertion an allegiance unquestioning and absolute. Most men when they are asked to give are tempted, like Ananias, to keep something back, but Lawrence asked everything, and, because of the authority with which the demand was made, everything was given. Many elements contributed to the acceptance of this superiority, unchallenged and unsought—great powers of intellect, of imagination, of intuitive understanding of other men's thought; but above all else must rank the overwhelming conviction that he gave of moral purpose.

It was not merely that he brought to bear upon life the concentrated strength of all his being, but that this faculty was eloquent of victory in the stern struggle for self-conquest. All the things that clog—ambition, the competitive race, possessions, the appetites of the natural man—all must give way if real freedom is to be won. Life—free, unhampered, unalloyed—alone deserves the name. As he said: 'The gospel of bareness in materials is a good one.'

I cannot tell what fed the consuming fire that made him so different from the common run of men. It has been said of him that no man was ever more faithful at any cost to the inner voice of conscience. Everything he did fell under the lash of his own self-criticism, and the praise of men was unsatisfying and distasteful. But I cannot doubt some deep religious impulse moved him; not, I suppose, that which for others is interpreted through systems of belief and practice, but rather some craving for the perfect synthesis of thought and action which alone could satisfy his test of ultimate truth and his conception of life's purpose.

Strange how he loved the naked places of the earth, which seemed to match the austerity of life as he thought that it should be lived. And so he loved the desert where wide spaces are lost in distance, and, wanderer himself, found natural kinship with the wandering peoples of his adopted home.

His was the cry of Paracelsus:

> I am a wanderer: I remember well
> One journey, how I feared the track was missed,
> So long the city I desired to reach
> Lay hid; when suddenly its spires afar
> Flashed through the circling clouds; you may conceive
> My transport. Soon the vapours closed again,
> But I had seen the city, and one such glance
> No darkness could obscure.

Yet side by side with this craving to accomplish ran another strand of feeling that lifts the veil from the inner struggle which I suppose grew harder in his later years. In August 1934 he was writing to a friend about his own disquiet: 'I think it is in part because I am sorry to be dropped out. One of the sorest things in life is to come to realize that one is just not good enough. Better perhaps than some, than many almost. But I do not care for relatives, for matching myself against my kind. There is an ideal standard somewhere, and only that matters, and I cannot find it. . . .'

There we must leave it, for the waters of genius run too deep for human measure.

Lawrence himself was never free from the challenge of his nature's secret. Perhaps he came nearer to the answer during those last days when he lay in the uncharted land between life and death, and saw his life no longer in part, but whole before him. Once more, it may be, he visited the Norman castles which first in boyhood had excited his romantic sense, or walked again amid the ancient works of Palestine. Or there came back to him the vision of the endless desert, rocking in the mirage of the fierce heat of noontide, and once more he trod the dusty ways of Akaba, Azrak, and the city of the Caliphs, and, last of all, of his beloved Damascus, with her green gardens by the river, these fading in turn before the places of his spiritual hermitage, Henlow, Bovington, Cranwell, and the Air Force stations of India—Peshawar, Miranshah, Karachi. And before the end came, I like to think that he saw again the spires of Oxford, unearthly in their beauty, set in the misty blue of early May, until at last he reached no earthly city, but that city of his vision where he might see no longer as in a glass darkly, and know at length as he was known.

6

GERMAN MILITARY REOCCUPATION OF THE RHINELAND

23 March 1936

[On March 7th, 1936, German troops reoccupied the demilitarized zone of the Rhineland in violation of Article 43 of the Treaty of Versailles. The German Government simultaneously denounced the Treaty of Locarno, but declared itself ready to conclude new agreements for the creation of a system of security for Europe on the basis of certain proposals, of which the chief were the conclusion of a non-aggression pact of twenty-five years' duration between Germany, France, and Belgium, and the conclusion of a western air-pact. Three days later representatives of the Locarno Powers other than Germany met in Paris to discuss the changed situation, the representatives of Great Britain being Lord Halifax and the Foreign Secretary, Mr. Anthony Eden. The meeting, resumed in London, ended on March 19th in the adoption of draft proposals which were approved that same evening by the British Cabinet and submitted on the following day to the Council of the League of Nations, then also sitting in London. The proposals included a declaration that nothing that had happened could be considered as having freed the signatories of Locarno from any of their obligations or guarantees; an invitation to the German Government to subscribe to certain provisional arrangements for what came to be known as the interim period; and a further invitation to Germany to take part in negotiations on the basis of the German proposals of March 7th, for a revision of the status of the Rhineland, and for the drawing up of pacts for mutual assistance. Great Britain accompanied its approval of these proposals by an undertaking, in return for reciprocal assurances, to take measures for ensuring the security of France and Belgium against unprovoked aggression, and for that purpose to establish contact between the General Staffs of the countries concerned.

Although Germany's provisional reply to the invitation was not received until the day following the one on which Lord Halifax made his speech at Bristol, it was already clear that Germany would reject the provisional arrangements upon which subsequent negotiations were to be conditional. The speech is here printed from Lord Halifax's notes, supplemented by *The Times* report.]

DURING the last fortnight we have realized how vitally and how directly the life of all of us may be affected by the cross-currents of international affairs and the developments which spring from them, and it has been the single desire of the whole country, instinctively aware of the danger so suddenly arising, to use its full influence for the preservation of European peace, and to build this peace upon the only possible foundations, namely, respect for treaties freely made, and mutual understanding between nations. That in its simplest terms is the very essence of our foreign policy to-day. And it has been the knowledge that Mr. Eden was working whole-heartedly to secure this end that has, I think, given him the assurance of nation-wide support.

It has been repeatedly said that the choice here, as elsewhere, for the conduct of foreign policy lies between three possible courses. First, there is that of a return to the old system of alliances. But the war-scarred history of Europe during the past 300 years, during which a policy of this sort—the Balance of Power—was invariably pursued, gives no encouragement to hope that war would not again result from a renewal of that same policy to-day. Secondly, there is the policy recommended in certain quarters that we should seek salvation through isolation. But those who urge this policy upon us seem to me entirely to disregard the fact that with our widespread Empire, our commitments in every part of the world, and the vast network of our foreign trade, we cannot isolate ourselves. As a matter of history, isolation has never been a practical foreign policy since William the Conqueror, and it is still less practicable to-day. Indeed, isolation is a dream to which, as an island people, we may be particularly subject, but which, at the same time, for obvious reasons we have never been privileged to put into practice. We cannot be both of the world and out of it. Lastly, there is the policy, which in my view alone affords any real hope for the future, by which this country has stood faithfully ever since the War, and which is the basis on which we have tried to build all our international effort, namely, loyalty to the League of Nations and acceptance of the collective obligations of the Covenant.

I do not know whether we here realize to the full how great a shock to confidence has been caused not only by the method that Germany employed in the reoccupation of the Rhineland and denunciation of the Treaty of Locarno, but also, and not less, by the genuine surprise with which German public opinion is reported to have received the protests of the other co-signatory Powers to the Locarno agreement. There is no more delicate plant than that of confidence in the international field, and none that shrivels and fades more quickly if its roots are rudely disturbed by careless hands. And when, therefore, a treaty that the head of the German Government had expressly accepted as having been negotiated in full freedom by Germany was openly violated, it was quite unavoidable that the repercussions should be immediate and far-reaching.

I do not overlook the case that Germany can make and the force of argument with which she can support it. It was presented last week to the Council of the League of Nations by the Special Envoy of the German Government. It is not difficult to understand the German claim to establish full sovereignty over German soil, nor the need as it may well appear to German eyes to secure in all circumstances that her capacity for self-defence should not be prejudiced, nor again the insistence of the leaders of Germany upon the absolute equality of her treatment by and with the other nations of the world. There is much in such a case that must command sympathy in many quarters. But the better the case, the stronger is the argument for presenting it to the world by reason and not by force; and whatever sympathy Englishmen had with the broad claims that Germany was making, their instinctive respect for law will always make them condemn action that is taken in direct violation of it.

And if we recognize the German case, let us not fail to recognize the particular position of France and Belgium. The demilitarized zone was devised for their direct protection after they had been disappointed by the failure of other security proposals. Wounds leave deep scars upon the minds of nations as they do upon the bodies of men, and if we would make our own the feeling of France and Belgium, we must picture what would have been our own reactions if we had had a land frontier, say where the English Channel meets the south coast of England, across which we had been time after time invaded, and along which for our protection a narrow strip of quasi-neutral zone had been established, and if in a night this zone had been reoccupied by the very troops by whom our soil had been invaded not twenty years ago. No one who heard it a few days ago could fail to have been moved by the plea of the Belgian Prime Minister to the League of Nations when he pointed out that, whatever complaint Germany might have, be it ill or well founded, against France for her signature of her pact with Russia, against Belgium no ground whatever of such complaint existed. There is no reason, therefore, for surprise at the anxiety and resentment caused to France and Belgium, and at the effect that this feeling had in creating a situation not without real danger to European peace.

The position of this country was somewhat different. Though we were signatories and guarantors of Locarno, bound by all its obligations, in some respects more onerous than many people have appreciated, and justly enjoy the reputation the world over of never defaulting on our solemn undertakings, we were by history and by situation disposed to view the problem from a somewhat different angle, and to judge rather differently of the action most appropriate to meet it.

No great powers of imagination are required to picture what might have been the consequences to Europe if peace had once been disturbed. If whatever danger there was of such an issue has, as I believe, now passed, it has been due to two things—first to the restraint of France and Belgium, as anxious for peace as we ourselves, and secondly to the untiring efforts of Mr. Eden, who, while receding from none of our obligations, has laboured for better understanding between Germany on one side and France and Belgium on the other, by which better understanding alone the structure of peace may be made proof against the strains and stresses that it may at any time be called to bear.

The results of these efforts in the shape of the agreed proposals of France, Belgium, Italy, and this country are before you; and our countrymen can judge them for themselves. Three main elements find place in them—the first, the assertion of the rights and sanctity of international law; the second, proposals by way of temporary measures to deal with the present situation, and to enable us to get on with the third, namely, the examination of the larger issues, those propounded by the German Chancellor, together with others recognized as fundamental to a durable settlement.

Of most immediate importance are the proposals for the transitional period which is the essential preliminary of the larger work. In these, France, Belgium, and this country, which through their Governments have accepted the proposals, have all made a large contribution. How great is the contribution of France and Belgium, those who were charged with the duty of conversations from the first are in the best position to know.

As regards this country, we have declared our complete adherence to the obligations of the Treaty of Locarno, and have expressed our willingness to reinforce the security of France and Belgium on a reciprocal basis with ourselves, by practical discussions, in advance, of the means by which this country could lend its aid if these countries were victims of unprovoked aggression. I believe this to be a real contribution to the cause of peace, because it is a real contribution to the creation of an atmosphere in which the things that make for peace can be dispassionately discussed.

And we look forward to the completion of these guarantees for peace by the establishment of non-aggression pacts, as contemplated by the German Chancellor, these pacts being supported and strengthened by such promises of mutual assistance as would in time to come act as powerful deterrents on any would-be aggressor. And I should hope that into these arrangements Germany would be willing to enter on equal and mutual terms, in order that these instruments of peace may be practical examples of the organization of peace on a truly collective basis.

We want no encirclement of Germany. We want no exclusive alliances. We want to build a partnership in European society in which Germany can freely join with us and play the part of good Europeans for European welfare. I have never concealed from myself that in asking what we did from Germany we asked a hard thing. But, after all,

Germany has created the conditions in which the stability of Europe has been shaken, and it was not too much to ask her in the circumstances to make a contribution that was admittedly a hard one. Indeed, I would have been prepared to say that, just because it was so hard a contribution, it placed it within the power of Germany to do something that, more than anything else, would have restored European confidence and have placed her in the position of making the greatest contribution of us all to the future of European peace.

But I read reports in the Press that Germany will not be able to accept at least one of the invitations addressed to her by the Locarno Powers. If that is correct, I should feel that, while these proposals were never intended to be anything in the nature of an ultimatum which Germany had to sign as they stood, we should hope that from Germany, if she does not accept our proposals, would come other proposals, counter-proposals, that would not be less effectual than ours to represent a solid and substantial German contribution to the remaking of the European structure of confidence that is to-day shaken. So far as His Majesty's Government is concerned, whatever serious counter-proposals may emerge from Germany are assured, as they are bound to receive, the most careful and most anxious consideration.

There is another thought which I should like to place before this great audience so closely in touch, as it must be, with the spiritual side of the nation's life. During the last dozen years the world has had many covenants, pacts, treaties, guarantees. Some, no doubt, have been better than others and some have been very good, and yet at the end of it all, suspicions, fears, misunderstandings still cast dark shadows across the hearts of men, and block the path to the temple of peace where we desire to enter and to be at rest. And this is because with all its anxieties and preoccupations the world as a whole has not yet called clearly enough to its aid the old cardinal qualities on which all life is based, the qualities of Faith and Hope and Charity. And to-day, while we are bound to make provision for the necessities of national defence, because in the present state of the world to fail to do so would be disloyalty to the ideals and purposes which we have made our own, yet I would have us, in whatever sphere we work, hold firm to the faith that can remove mountains; the hope that will not be denied; and the charity that seeks always to think and to find the best, and not the worst, in other people.

Let us remember that while we labour and have to deal with a difficult world as we find it, our greatest and most compelling task is to make it better—that we may make it indeed a truer counterpart of that Kingdom which is above: which great men have seen in vision, and for which we daily pray.

7

THE BRITISH EMPIRE

25 March 1936

[At a farewell dinner to Lord Linlithgow, Viceroy-designate of India, given by the combined Empire Societies at the Hotel Victoria in London, and presided over by Lord Zetland, Secretary of State for India, Lord Halifax, himself an ex-Viceroy, proposed the health of the Empire Societies. His speech is printed in full in *United Empire, the Journal of the Royal Empire Society*, vol. xxvii, pp. 245–6.]

THE main object, I suppose, of the Empire Societies is to afford an opportunity to men and women of no doubt very differing points of view to record together their belief, their continued belief, in the value of the British Empire. There are those to-day who are tempted to apologize for the British Empire and are sometimes tempted to give away parts of it to other people. I must confess that I do not belong to any of those groups. At the same time I do admit to myself that the British Empire is the strangest phenomenon on which the eyes of men have ever rested, and if any of us were to try to translate into language the terms in which, in our mind's eye, we visualize the British Empire, we should no doubt do it very differently. I might do it differently from Lord Linlithgow, because I come from a different part of the country from his. Some no doubt would visualize it in terms of place. It is commonly said, for example, that he who returns from travelling in France is accustomed to visualize England through the fields and orchards of Kent. Some might visualize it in terms of the great public servants of the past who have made the British Empire what it is. Some again might visualize it in terms of the purposes of the future to which the efforts of the British Empire and those who believe in it will continually be directed.

And it is perhaps the greatest compliment to the British Empire as a whole that it is able to act as a focus of all those different and various loyalties and gather them all together in a single point of allegiance, to which we are all proud to give our faith and our service. I am told that the British

Empire is a continual bewilderment to men and women of foreign lands. They have never been able to understand whether the British Empire is to be more truly conceived of as an alliance between independent States, or a unitary State, or something akin to a federation. It is, in truth, none of these things and it is more than all of them. In that lies one of the fairest hopes of the future of the world. And it is also significant that this strange British Empire's pre-eminent characteristic, from another angle, is that it is founded upon the most successful reconciliation of unity and diversity, through the alchemy of liberty, that the world has ever seen. We of the British Empire are one, not because we must, but because we will. It is sometimes said by those who scan anxiously the horizons of the world that there is no future hope for the world unless it can erect some super-State, invested with independent sovereignty and independent force to compel allegiance to that sovereignty; and yet, when I hear such gospel preached, I am tempted to feel that if that be the only hope of the world, hope is indeed far off, and I am tempted to despair. Then I fall back upon the reflection that nearer home, in the British Empire, we have at our doors an example of how men, differing in nearly everything that concerns the foundations of life—race, culture, religion, traditions, colour—have yet managed to do a thing that 150 years ago would have seemed inconceivable, namely to decide insensibly and yet irrevocably that they will never summon force as a solvent of any disputes or differences that may arise between them; and I wonder, when one ponders upon how great has been the passage of thought in that last 150 years, whether it is in fact as impossible as some to-day would be tempted to think, to look forward to the future where men, belonging to different nations, with all the differences that persist in the British Empire, may yet come in the fullness of time and under the guidance of Providence to learn the same lesson that the British Empire has learnt, that reason based on liberty is the greatest solvent of differences and disputes which arise between sections of the human race.

8

BRITAIN'S OBLIGATIONS TO FRANCE AND BELGIUM

8 April 1936

[The German counter-proposals, which were being awaited when Lord Halifax made his speech at Bristol on March 23rd, were delivered on March 31st. They contained an assurance that the German Government would not reinforce its troops in the Rhineland for a period of four months, and an offer to enter into discussions for the conclusion of a twenty-five years' non-aggression pact between France and Belgium on the one hand and Germany on the other, to assume obligations to render military assistance arising out of such an agreement, and to invite the States on the German south-eastern and north-eastern frontiers to conclude non-aggression pacts with Germany. They contained no response to the proposals made by the Locarno Powers on March 19th for the creation of an international police force or for abstention from building fortifications in the Rhineland zone. As a contribution to the restoration of confidence they were held to be unsatisfactory, and on April 3rd Mr. Eden informed the House of Commons that the British Government had sent a letter of guarantee to France and Belgium on the previous day in regard to action to be taken if negotiations for a new settlement should fail, and had expressed their willingness to institute conversations between the General Staffs of the countries concerned. On April 8th Lord Snell, Leader of His Majesty's Opposition in the House of Lords, invited the Government to make a statement on the European situation. Lord Halifax made the following immediate reply.]

MY LORDS, in respect of the main matter to which the noble Lord has directed our attention I find great identity of purpose in everything that was contained in his speech with that which I find in my own mind. We both have the common purpose of trying to the best of our ability to contribute to European peace. It has been frequently said that peace is the greatest British interest. It is far more than that. It is the only interest of the whole world that is worth fighting for, because in the interests of peace nearly everything else is contained and by it subserved. The promotion of peace has been the constant end to which all the efforts of my right honourable friend the Foreign Secretary and His Majesty's Government have been continuously directed. And I do not find in the speech of the noble Lord any great difference as to the method by which we have sought to ensure that end.

When we speak of peace, what do we, in fact, mean by it? It is sometimes spoken of as if it meant merely abstention from open warfare, but I think peace that was merely that would deserve the name of peace as little as a system of morality would be entitled to claim our loyalty that aimed no higher than the avoidance of open ill-doing, and I think it would be as insecure. Indeed, I believe that one of the contributory causes of 1914 was the fact that our policy of that day was not sufficiently positive. Peace is no mere negative thing, because in this great struggle—the great struggle of the world and of human nature—the forces of good that make for peace and the forces of evil that make for war are perpetually ranged against each other. In that warfare there can be no armistice and no neutrality. If we want peace we have to work always for the understanding which may make possible the adjustment of differences, and also may give vitality to any terms of settlement. And I venture to think that, so long as the path is blocked by fears and by resentments and by mistrust, progress is at the best uncertain and at the worst impossible.

The world to-day is standing at the cross-roads, and a hundred years hence, if the world survives, we shall all be judged by the direction that we now take; for upon the choice that we make depends much more than the issue of our immediate difficulties, and the price of wrong judgement will be a very high one. Though the cross-roads have long been in sight, it is true to say that the world has been brought right up to them by the recent action of Germany and by the inevitable reactions from it. The history of those events is fresh in our minds, and I do not recapitulate it. It is quite undeniable that the method chosen by Germany to force her claims upon the world's attention has dealt a wounding and very far-reaching blow at all the foundations on which the international order has to be reared. Germany has justified her action on the plea of past grievances, and there will be, no doubt, a general desire that what I may call this era of grievances should be closed. But if and when that can be done and has been done, we must be sure that in future, as there will be no justification so there will be no intention in any circumstances to resort to that method again; and there will be no hope whatsoever of a settlement unless we can be positively and absolutely sure of that.

I need not remind your Lordships that confidence in the observance of international undertakings is as vital to the life of nations as confidence in the observance of contracts is to the conduct of their business and economic life. Therefore, the first thing that my right honourable friend had to do was to re-establish the foundations before he or anyone else could set to work at building the new house which we all desire to see. I have seen it suggested that the fact that my right honourable friend laid great stress upon the importance of what he has often called this interim period implied that he was unduly obsessed by the technical spirit, and was not sufficiently alive to the greater project of the building of permanent peace. But that is quite untrue, because the due liquidation of this interim period was the essential condition of getting on to the permanent work which we all desire to see undertaken. And it was for that reason that the efforts of His Majesty's Government infallibly fell into two compartments: first of all, the attempt to devise conditions for the period intervening before the negotiations on larger issues could be undertaken; and, in the second place, the direct preparation for the time when, if the earlier difficulties could be overcome, the larger work should be taken in hand.

It was with that double object that the Locarno Powers worked some three weeks ago. It was evident that unless by some means some measure of confidence could be re-created in the period antecedent to that when it was hoped to reach discussions on the main questions, there was no chance of establishing a sufficient background of confidence to permit any hope of the larger negotiations being brought to a successful issue, even if it were possible ever to get them begun. It is at that point that we feel that the German Government might have given us greater help. We have made it quite plain that our proposals of March 19, whatever their merits or demerits, were not of the nature of an ultimatum. But we had also the correlative right to expect that if the German Government were unable to accept any or all of the proposals we made, they would have made alternative proposals of equivalent value for the purpose to which ours had been directed. As the noble Lord knows, my right honourable friend will be holding discussions, in which I shall also be associated, with representatives of the Locarno Powers during the next day or two, when one or two of the other matters that he mentioned will no doubt come under review, and therefore he will perhaps excuse me from saying more at this stage about them than that. But the fact that the German Government have been unable to make such a contribution as we had asked from them to this interim stage seemed to His Majesty's Government to reinforce the obligations that they had accepted in the earlier conversations to do what they could to reassure their co-signatories of Locarno—France and Belgium.

I was very glad to hear what the noble Lord said at the end of his speech when he invited us to place ourselves in the position of those countries. Those countries had lost, literally in a night, a security to which they attached great importance, and they had lost it in a way that seemed to them, as to us, to strike at the root of international stability. Therefore, quite apart from the fact that we were bound by our signature to very precise obligations under the very Treaty which Germany had unilaterally denounced, it was abundantly plain to those who were engaged in these negotiations of three weeks ago that those countries could only be induced to take their just share in the task of reconstruction if, meanwhile, they could be reassured as to their own security. The Staff conversations, of which the noble Lord spoke with some anxiety, and the letter that my right honourable friend sent a week or so ago to France and Belgium, were the contribution of His Majesty's Government to the creation of conditions which might make negotiations possible—in my judgement a contribution that it was quite essential to make.

I must say a word or two upon the Staff conversations.

It is not necessary to emphasize again that these Staff conversations are concerned only with the discharge of our existing obligations in the event, which we hope will not occur, of unprovoked aggression. My right honourable friend gave the further assurance in the House of Commons on April 3, to Mr. Lloyd George, that

> 'it is not contemplated to put any of these military plans into operation in the unfortunate event of the failure of these negotiations unless'—

I would ask noble Lords to mark these words—

> 'there is an unprovoked attack by Germany on Belgian or French soil—an actual invasion of either France or Belgium.'

Nor will your Lordships have failed to observe the precise conditions my right honourable friend attached to these conversations in his letter to the Ambassadors on April 1—namely, that

> 'this contact between the General Staffs cannot give rise, in respect of either Government, to any political undertaking, nor to any obligation regarding the organisation of national defence.'

In view of these explicit statements, I hope your Lordships will be satisfied that no danger can rightly be held to attach to them of involving this country in unspecified commitments. They are not the assumption of new obligations. They are only an examination of the technical steps that would be necessary to fulfil obligations by which we are already bound, and it is perhaps worth while to remind your Lordships that these obligations correspond exactly with the vital interests of this country, recognized as such for many centuries. There was, as was said in another place, nothing new in Locarno, and there is nothing new about its maintenance. Moreover, if the conditions postulated in the letter in the White Paper ever came to prevail, the condition of our assistance to France and Belgium against unprovoked aggression, for which this Staff contact may be continued, would for the first time be on the basis of reciprocity. I can imagine that when no conditions are laid down as those in which one country would undertake to help another, it might be possible that Staff conversations might give rise to expectations that the event might prove unfounded, but that cannot arise when both the obligations and the means of discharging them have been the subject of exact definition.

With all respect for Mr. Lloyd George, I cannot myself see that there is any foundation at all for suggesting that the existence of such carefully circumscribed obligations or contacts would be likely of themselves, in any degree whatever, to make war more probable. The noble Marquess, Lord Lothian, has often talked in this connexion about the time-table beginning to operate; about the action of one country leading by mechanical consequence to counter-action by another, until the inevitable drift is set up towards that steep slope at the foot of which lies war. I believe he would agree that that against which he has warned the country is the result of something quite different—namely, the division of Europe into opposing blocks of nations bound to one another by close alliances; and no one could feel more strongly than I do that against any such issue from our present anxieties all our statesmanship must be directed. I do not think that Europe can ever hope to win peace by a return to the pre-War system of alliances; but I do think, definitely, that in any attempt to organize collective security for an area about which we feel able to anticipate with reasonable assurance the judgement of our fellow countrymen, it is a real guarantee of peace that it should be plainly stated in advance that this country would resist with all the means at its disposal any wanton disturbance of the peace.

I fully share the sense of the importance of precision. 'Unprovoked aggression', under Locarno and under these Papers, means what it says. It does not mean, if I may repeat the words that my right honourable friend used in another place:

> 'a situation when, owing to obligations elsewhere, our neighbours may become involved in conflict and may call for help in a quarrel that is not ours.'

These undertakings, therefore, have no wider scope than the original obligations deriving from the Treaty of Locarno which they are designed to implement.

That brings me to say something about the relation of Locarno, and what flows from it, to the wider instrument of the Covenant of the League, subject to which the Treaty of Locarno was drawn. It has been a criticism of the Locarno Treaty—as of any other limited and specific undertakings—that it *pro tanto* weakened the prestige and position of the Covenant. The argument is plain enough. If the Covenant was what it has pretended to be, there is really no need for these other reinsurances which are only taken out because you do not feel certain that on the day the Covenant will be able to meet the claim. That is the broad argument in colloquial language, and I would readily admit that argumentatively the position is a strong one and can be sustained; but, as so often happens with human affairs, though the argument is excellent I am convinced the truth lies on the other side. I believe that these regional and specific guarantees, so far from weakening, supplement and reinforce the Covenant and help it with its main job which, I would like some of our warmongers constantly to remember, is peace.

And that I think for two reasons. First of all, because of the difference between the original conception and the actual conditions in working practice of the Covenant to-day; and, secondly, because it is essential in these matters, however much we may seek to set our gaze on the stars, that we should be realists and keep our feet on firm ground. I believe that British public opinion is prepared to accept particular and antecedent obligations to support France and Belgium against unprovoked aggression, firstly, because it thinks that this is a real contribution to the steadying of the European situation; and, secondly, because it feels by instinct that, as it has always acted for generations, so, given the compelling circumstances, it would infallibly act again.

But this attitude should not be interpreted to mean that because we have assumed more specific obligations in the west which we were not prepared to repeat for the east of Europe, therefore we disinterested ourselves from all events and issues arising outside what perhaps I may call the Locarno area. In my view such an attitude would be quite impossible, partly because peace is indivisible, and it is very hard for me to imagine that if the east of Europe were really aflame you could feel any confidence that the flames would not spread across to the west; but also because of our obligations under the Covenant, which are obligations by which we abide and which we intend to implement to the utmost of our power. Therefore it is with the single object of trying to strengthen the forces of real peace, and with some such conception as I have tried to lay before your Lordships as to how it can be achieved, that we shall examine the latest German Note and any proposals coming from any other quarter that may be laid before us.

The plan of which I have seen reports in the newspapers as likely to be submitted by the French Government has not yet reached the hands of His Majesty's Government and therefore I can say nothing about it. The Secretary of State has already said that, while he regretted that the German Government had been unwilling to give us greater help in the immediate problem, he yet, along with His Majesty's Government, recognized the importance of many of the proposals that the German Government had made and, taken together, they obviously constitute a body of material which must be carefully sifted and examined. On that task of sifting and examining those proposals His Majesty's Government are already engaged in the hope that means may be found by which the Governments with whom His Majesty's Government have been working may be associated with them in their examination. The German proposals range over ground much wider than the Rhineland or the position of the signatories of the Locarno Treaty. On that ground, as indeed on others, there is a good deal to be said for so extending the scope of the preparatory discussions as to make the League of Nations a party to them, and I hope that we may secure a general agreement for that course.

Your Lordships, therefore, will not expect me to make detailed observations upon particular points of the German Note to-day, but one or two general observations may not be out of place. In all human relations, and particularly in such a case as this, when the attempt is made to compose differences, the vital thing is that all parties should be so inspired by the common purpose that that which they have in common is really deeper and stronger than all the things by which they appear to be divided. And where that condition prevails agreement can be won, and, agreement having been won, such understanding can be established as is likely to give that agreement the quality of permanence. We are all only too well aware of how gravely and how disastrously the efforts of the last years in Europe to find this true basis of peace have been prejudiced by all the complex of conflicting emotions to which the nations of Europe have been very naturally subject. We all see the problems in different perspective so that it is extremely difficult for one nation to see that which seems plain necessity or simple equity to another, and it is from that that in part comes the failure up to now in reconciling what always must be the two dominant paramount necessities of Europe which must be reconciled if the peace of Europe is to be any more than an uneasy and insecure neutrality; and those two paramount necessities are the equality of Germany and the security of European States.

I would hope, for example, that to-day France and Belgium would be not less willing than ourselves to give full recognition to the rightful claims of Germany in the sphere of equality provided that they can be satisfied that the German Government will in fact recognize the duties towards all Europe that such equal rights entail. In other words, if I may use perfectly plain and frank speech, Europe needs to be satisfied that the peace project of Herr Hitler is sincerely meant, and that the fact that certain countries find no specific mention in it does not imply that they have no place in the peace vision of the German Chancellor. No one can deny that, whatever faults there may have been on the other side, the German Government, by the procedure of the *fait accompli* and by the proclaimed philosophy of the overriding justification of State necessity, have gravely shaken international confidence. And confidence is a plant of painfully slow growth. Yet, if progress is to be made, it is to the future rather than to the past that our hopes must turn. So far as this country is concerned our policy will be to stand steadfastly by all who seek peace, and to oppose all who would betray the cause of peace. Every opening must be put to a fair and dispassionate test—the test of time and practice. By that proof alone can the genuine character of the nature of such opportunities for settlement be ultimately judged.

I do not think that for practical statesmanship there is any other way of determination. Meanwhile, we shall neglect no effort to reach a land of peace; but we will relax no precaution on the road. Nor, finally, can I doubt that, if ever the hopes of peace that we all cherish are to be more than dreams that pass, the nations of the world must call to their aid forces of which they have made insufficient use. Trust begets trust, and I see little hope of European peace, even if we are able to gather the nations to the business of negotiation, unless those concerned can bring to the Council table that quality which will then impel them to see the best and not the worst in what each may have there to contribute, above all remembering that they are perforce and in truth, by the common fact of their humanity, common partners in the enterprise of securing the conditions by which alone the future of the human race can be preserved.

9

REFORM OF THE COVENANT OF THE LEAGUE OF NATIONS

29 July 1936

[The German Government's offer to re-enter the League of Nations, contained in their memorandum of March 7th and repeated in their counter-proposals of March 31st, helped to bring to the front the question of the reform of the Covenant; for it was argued that Germany could not be expected to renew her membership until it was known on what lines the League would be reformed. On July 4th the Assembly of the League issued invitations to Member States to send in proposals for reform. Two opposing views, each of which had considerable support in Great Britain, were expressed in motions made in the House of Lords on July 29th. One, moved by Lord Ponsonby, was to the effect that the Government should put forward a proposal for the elimination from the Articles of the Covenant of any obligation on the part of Members of the League to use military force. The other, standing in the name of Lord Allen of Hurtwood, was in favour of setting up the necessary machinery to implement the existing Articles of the Covenant, so that they might be used to remedy grievances, provide economic advantages to States Members, and strengthen the procedure for the collective maintenance of the Covenant in its entirety and particularly for steady collective resistance to all acts of unprovoked aggression. Lord Halifax replied at the end of a general discussion which had covered the ground of both motions.]

MY LORDS, the course of the debate seems to me to have been typical of a very sharp divergence of opinion. . . . There is, if I may take it in inverse order to that in which it has been presented to us this afternoon, first of all the attitude which would maintain that in order to ensure peace, and in order to maintain the League as a reality, it is necessary to make the obligations of Articles 10 and 16[1] much more

[1] Article 10: 'The Members of the League undertake to respect and preserve as against external aggression the territorial integrity and existing political independence of all Members of the League. In case of any such aggression or in case of any threat or danger of such aggression the Council shall advise upon the means by which this obligation shall be fulfilled.' Article 16: 'Should any Member of the League resort to war in disregard of its covenants under Articles 12, 13 or 15, it shall *ipso facto* be deemed to have committed an act of war against all other Members of the League, which hereby undertake immediately to subject it to the severance of all trade or financial relations, the prohibition of all intercourse between their nationals and the nationals of

precise, or, at least, to make much more clear the will of all nations to give these Articles their full opportunity.

It would not be untrue to say that to the collective system, in this view, there might be applied what the late Mr. Chesterton once said of Christianity—that Christianity had not failed because it had never been tried. Those who hold that view believe quite honestly that if a strong enough lead were given by some great Power along the lines of asserting their unqualified willingness to resort to all measures in the exercise of force for Covenant purposes, all other nations would follow their lead, all would be well, and the way to disarmament would be clear, for the reason that in future the threat of general war against all invasions of the Covenant would be so intimidating that there would in fact be no such invasions and that, consequently, the threat of general war everywhere would be a great security against a real war anywhere.

I think that is not an unfair statement of their view. At the same time I think the more thoughtful representatives of that school would recognize that there is difficulty in the plan, because, as other noble Lords have said, nations may be unwilling to fight, or to risk having to fight, in causes outside what they conceive to be causes involving their honour or national interest. That is, as we have all seen in the last few months, a very real limitation. . . . There would have been no unanimity among the principal nations concerned at any time during the last six or twelve months upon the pursuit of a policy that was likely in fact to lead to a European war.

But there is another reason why I think this extreme philosophy requires modification, and that is in what to my mind is always an even profounder difficulty arising out of the nature of the constitution of the League itself. There is sometimes academic debate as to whether it is the principal purpose of the League to secure peace or to secure justice. It is quite evident that these two things need not be identical, and I think it is true to say that under the present

the covenant-breaking State, and the prevention of all financial, commercial, or personal intercourse between the nationals of the covenant-breaking State and the nationals of any other State, whether a Member of the League or not.'

League constitution the emphasis rests rather upon the avoidance of war and the preservation of peace. As things are, the League is pledged to protect peace, but without any corresponding power to secure the removal of conditions that may threaten the preservation of peace. It is quite true that Article 19[1] is in the Covenant, but the League has no power to give effect to Article 19 against the will of any one of its States Members, and in that respect, therefore, I do not think it is untrue to say that the League is in the somewhat unenviable position of responsibility without power; and if and when the cause of peace might, for any such reasons as those, appear to conflict with the cause of prudence or justice, it is not certain that world opinion would in all cases be prepared to use force to enforce peace. Those are some of the difficulties which confront the most stringent application of the coercive Articles.

Now the opposite view is not unfamiliar—'Above everything, let us in these things be realists.' The ultimate test by which any such general undertakings must be tried is the willingness to fight. The noble Marquess, Lord Crewe, gave, I thought, a remarkably forceful illustration from another sphere, showing how the real support of anything so well established in the world as the Monroe doctrine was consciousness in all quarters that in the last resort there was the willingness to use force for it. And the converse is equally true. The case of Japan and Manchukuo was conclusive proof at that time of what happens when nations are not in the last resort prepared to fight under all conditions, but only when they conceive themselves bound by honour or self-interest to do so.

I think it is unhappily true that in most cases that one can conceive the brunt of military action would in fact fall upon few shoulders, and that, if any general coercive system were to be surely counted on to function successfully in all cases, it would have to be on the conditions contemplated when

[1] Article 19: 'The Assembly may from time to time advise the reconsideration by Members of the League of treaties which have become inapplicable and the consideration of international conditions whose continuance might endanger the peace of the world.'

the Covenant was framed—that is to say, that all nations should be in, and that all nations should be disarmed. I believe that to be true, and I believe, therefore, that the most loyal supporter of the League may readily admit that it is impossible to give full application to such a theory—the original theory of the League—when the circumstances of its operation to-day are so radically different from those in which it was conceived. Those who would hold that view would say that it was better to re-design your structure, to cut out these coercive elements and to open the door to the great Powers whose participation in the League is essential but who perhaps will never give it to a League invested with and pledged to use coercive force. Thus we should avoid the danger of misleading any who might be mistakenly relying upon a greater measure of support than in fact would be in the power of the League to give them, and by that means only could we look forward to a system that could properly enjoy the title of collective.

Now, as my right honourable friend the Foreign Secretary said a few days ago in another place, I do not believe there is any chance whatever of securing agreement either in this country or at Geneva on either of these extremes—that is to say, on either the system of automatic and universal coercion, or of such an evisceration of the Covenant as to leave it merely a body for consultation and conciliation. . . . What then is to be the attitude of His Majesty's Government and of this country? As I see it, for various reasons this country has been in a position somewhat different from many others, and for that reason alone it must be our duty to try to find a solution as between these two extremes which would command the maximum of support elsewhere. I do not think it is very helpful to make proposals that we know beforehand are not likely to win acceptance.

I think that while keeping our own ideal we must also remember that we have to face real and disagreeably hard facts. . . . Governments who are concerned to try to build up a world system must always take account of the views of other nations which either fall short of or go beyond their own. I would mention in passing that it is very essential that we should take account of what may be the views on these issues of the Dominions, and I would strongly deprecate a definite formulation of views by His Majesty's Government on matters that so vitally affect Imperial policy before there has been opportunity for the fullest consultation with the Dominion Governments. Therefore it is that I look with some suspicion on the plea that is advanced to the effect that it is the duty of this country, or that it would be profitable for this country, to give at this moment a clear lead on these highly controversial and debatable issues in advance of discussion at Geneva.

I think it is probable that the nations will have to try and reach a middle course, and, as your Lordships know, there are several that have been suggested. The object of all of them is to seek to introduce by way of interpretation of Articles 10 and 16 just that principle of variety of obligation according to national circumstances and willingness of nations to undertake precise commitments. Into that general group fall those regional pacts that should be incumbent only on those who specifically for specific purposes make them. Your Lordships will know that, accompanying such a plan as that, the suggestion has been made that there might be a system of general application by which other States Members would bind themselves to take economic action against aggressors. That economic action would range from extreme forms of sanctions—complete severance of financial and commercial intercourse—down to refusal to do such obvious things as supplying arms or lending money.

Whatever may be the middle course on which agreement may ultimately be found, it remains true that conciliation and the round table stand in any case as the first stage, and after that emerges the dominant question to which we have to find, if we can, the right answer. It is this: Is it in the last resort better to preserve on paper a code of general obligation, although you know that when the test comes that code may not in fact be capable of fulfilment, or is it better to recognize facts as they exist and make the best of them, not laying greater burdens on nations than they are willing to sustain, and admitting that, with great nations outside the League, with national feelings and national anxieties still strong everywhere, making progress to disarmament difficult, the conditions for the successful operation of any general coercive plan are only partly present?

Whatever their views, I do beg of all Parties not to blind themselves and not to wear blinkers about the real obstacles that we have to overcome. We have to face the fact that, until the League is universal, many States who are Members of it will never be willing and can hardly be expected to frame their policy and action as if it was universal. . . . I think it is true that unless nations are prepared to forgo a large part of their national sovereignty and accept in advance what the rest of the world by majority may decide; unless nations are prepared to reduce their armed forces; and lastly, unless all nations in fact believe that all their neighbours are certain in all cases to adhere to such self-denying undertakings, I venture to think we should be in some danger of misleading both ourselves and others if we were to pretend that we had overcome the dangers and the difficulties with which we are to-day confronted by the drafting of any League constitution, however widely its provisions might be drawn.

Therefore, my Lords, it is for these reasons, and seeing those things on each side, that I conceive that it will be in the forthcoming discussions the duty of this country to use all its influence for the reconciliation of opinions that will be very sharply opposed to one another, bearing always in mind those principles which were referred to by my right honourable friend in the House of Commons a few days ago. May I put those principles in a slightly different frame? The first, to my mind, is that there must be a collective plan. Without it the world falls back into chaos. On that there is universal agreement, and indeed I think on no point in Europe to-day is there greater agreement than on the opinion that to return to any system that invited, or appeared to invite, the establishment of armed camps ranged in opposition to one another would be to court disaster. The second thing I would say is that in any such system the purpose must be the prevention of war and the deterrence of aggression. There I share the view that there is something to be done—not a great thing but perhaps a valuable thing—by the strengthening of Article 11[1], by which the preventive power of the League will be strengthened, inasmuch as the operation of that Article might no longer be made dependent upon complete unanimity.

The third thing I would say is that I believe that if we are to have real hope of achieving our purpose of discouraging aggression and preventing war, we must devise means more effective than we have at present by which the potential causes of war may be freely brought into the arena of discussion and the pressure of world opinion directed to their remedy. Human life is not static, it is always a changing thing, and nothing is more certain than that an international organization which represents an attempt to encase world affairs in a rigid mould of a particular date carries within itself the seeds of disintegration and decay. In no field is that more true than in the field of economics. It is especially true of the economic maladjustments in the world to-day which reflect themselves directly in the standard of life, and in the outlook consequent upon the standard of life, of many nations. There are few things more urgent than for all countries at the present time to realize how vitally these forces, always in operation and operating with inexorable force, are affecting the future success or failure in the establishment and maintenance of peace.

There are, in these matters, no short cuts. Every day we learn how laborious is the effort for peace and how constantly checkmate attends our best endeavours. But I think it is right to remember that, if these things to which I and others of your Lordships have this afternoon made allusion are against us, there are also powerful influences on the side of peace. I believe that in every European country to-day the masses of the population, and not least that part which

[1] Article 11: 'Any war or threat of war, whether immediately affecting any of the Members of the League or not, is hereby declared a matter of concern to the whole League, and the League shall take any action that may be deemed wise and effectual to safeguard the peace of nations. In case any such emergency should arise, the Secretary General shall on the request of any member of the League forthwith summon a meeting of the Council.'

fought in the Great War, crave for peace, and that most of the irresponsible talk about war to-day is in truth rather the reflection of men's fears than of their expectations, for they know that, if there should be war again in Europe, there would be a ruthless obliteration of the distinction between combatant and non-combatant, and the wound to civilization, on which all their life depends, might possibly be mortal.

Therefore it is the duty of all of us, and it is the constant endeavour of His Majesty's Government, to use every effort that we may to liberate these forces of peace through the promotion of understanding and through the removal between nations of everything that would impede its growth. I believe that in proportion as we can achieve success in this direction we shall at once facilitate our task of devising machinery for the new international order for which we work, and we shall also ensure that this machinery shall truly represent the corporate will of those whom it will be designed to serve.

10

REARMAMENT

19 November 1936

[Throughout the year 1936 the Powers of Europe were rearming. The British Government's plans for rearmament were made public in a White Paper on March 3rd. Although the Opposition came reluctantly to admit the necessity for rearmament, they continued suspicious of the uses to which expanded armaments might be put. On November 17th Lord Strabolgi moved in the House of Lords 'That inasmuch as the extent of the armed forces of the Crown depends mainly upon national policy and the purpose they are designed to serve, this House calls upon His Majesty's Government to furnish full information to Parliament as to what measure of rearmament has already been achieved and as to what is the programme for the immediate future; and at the same time to make an explicit declaration of the policy in relation to the League of Nations and foreign affairs which they are pursuing as a justification for the heavily increased expenditure on armaments'. In winding up a three-days' debate Lord Halifax spoke as follows.]

MY LORDS, no one who casts his mind back over two or three years to when the Disarmament Conference was in being can doubt that since that day public opinion in this country has been undergoing a very necessary and very steady process of education on the whole question which we have to-day in debate. Whether that process of education could have been completed more quickly I do not know. I doubt it. But long before the election proposals were made to Parliament for the first programme of air expansion, and long before that programme was laid before Parliament, the Staffs of all the Services and of the Government Departments affected, not least the Finance Department, had been engaged upon a detailed examination of the plans which it would be for the Government to submit as soon as they could get popular approbation for the plans to be laid before the country. . . .

These things, although they are of the past, do vitally concern the present, and it is because, through the operation of causes for which all Governments since the War have been responsible, we started with considerable handicap, that the scope and speed of the programme were all the more important. That programme is steadily proceeding. Attention has been drawn, to-day and on previous days, to a number of points where deficiencies are not being remedied at the rate which the speakers deem satisfactory. We all know that. We should be the first to admit that that is so. It is impossible for progress to be uniform over the whole programme of repair and expansion. We have spoken frankly about the difficulties in regard to recruiting. We may be a bit forward on one part of the programme and a bit backward on another, but your Lordships may rest assured that the Government know as well as anybody else where the difficulties are making themselves felt, and are losing no time, to the best of their ability, in overcoming them. It is quite impossible to bring these things to what I may call any final test of certainty. We are not dealing in all this business with factors which are easily to be insulated or controlled. The whole problem of national defence is a thing with a hundred heads.

. . . .

From one point of view it might be argued that this country could not, in the present condition of the world, be held safe unless it was at this moment as strong in material armament as any conceivable enemy, and indeed one sometimes hears argument almost on those lines. But it is obviously impossible to state or to decide the problems so simply as that. Much evidently depends upon the foreign policy that you are pursuing, and the ends which you try to encompass and promote. I put to the House as typical of what I have in mind three questions which must present themselves to the thought of every reasonable man. Is the policy that you are pursuing likely to lead you into conflict with others? Is it, so far as you can judge, likely to be to the interests of others to force a conflict with you? And is material armament the only thing you have to consider, and are you not bound also to take account of financial and economic strength?

The problem only has to be stated to show how impossible it is to deal with it regardless of all those other more general considerations. And the weight that has to be given to other variants must vary itself with them. Take the question to which my noble friend the Secretary of State for Air addressed himself on the first day of our debate, and in regard to which I am not going to do more than to say three or four sentences—the question of a Ministry of Supply. He pointed out to your Lordships that the root fact in the problem to-day is that the competition for skilled labour and material is not a competition between Service Departments, but a competition between Service requirements and civil industry, and that therefore, if that is to be tackled, it can only be tackled by a pretty complete system of control such as we knew in the late War, which would involve a pretty free invocation of the Defence of the Realm Regulations and the like. Would you under that system get along any more quickly? I imagine the answer is that after an initial period of dislocation, that would last for some months, you might.

But what is quite certain is that in the process you would gravely dislocate trade, budgets, general finance, and the general credit of the country. Circumstances might arise where you would have no other course, but do not let us be under any illusion as to what it would mean. Therefore, the conclusion that I reach is that prudent men, while making all the practical preparations that are necessary for the immediate turnover in the event of war, would wish before actually adopting such heroic remedies to satisfy themselves that it was the only way to achieve their end. That, therefore, leads you to this question—Are we in fact to judge the question so serious that everything has to give way to the military reconditioning of our Defence Forces? Such a conclusion, in fact, appears to me to rest upon a premise, not only of the inevitability, but of a degree of certainty as to the early imminence of war, which I am not prepared to accept.

Foreign policy and this policy of rearmament all the time act and react upon one another. If we believe, as I think rightly, that a strong England will help the Foreign Secretary in his attempt to secure European peace, it is not less true that, in giving effect to this policy of rearmament, we are bound at the same time to take into account the influence that general policy may exert in the foreign and economic field. On the economic side we hold, as my right honourable friend the Foreign Secretary said the other day, that one of the greatest means of improving international relations would be, if we could, to ease the flow of international trade, and thus diminish these economic difficulties that press upon the world. It would be the abrupt termination of all such hopes as those if we were to begin by introducing new and grave disturbance into the trade and industry of this country, which remains one of the world's best and most receptive markets, and which, I hope, we are not too self-satisfied in regarding as a rallying-point for economic sanity.

As to foreign policy, there are two things that can be and ought to be said. It will, I think, be generally conceded that no country has laboured during these last years more disinterestedly for the cause of peace. Through years that have not been easy His Majesty's Government have consistently, and not without success, pursued a policy of avoidance of the risk of war, and that not from any lower motive than because they felt that once the prairie fire started it was not easy to say where it would stop. The other thing I must say about foreign policy, and which I must develop in rather more than a sentence, is that it is based on the League of Nations, and one of the principal purposes of the measures now being taken is to place us in a position in which, if we so decide, we can throw our weight with others into the scales for preserving peace. But the corollary of that is that, if war ever came, we may reasonably expect not to be alone, and therefore the hypothetical aggressor, when weighing the chances of a speedy and successful issue from military adventure, would not be able to feel any assurance that he might not find himself more deeply and more doubtfully involved.

From several quarters during the debate has come a demand for clear thinking, and that is always a process important and desirable. I would hope that that demand is not made only upon the Government. Some persons argue that it is the duty of the Government here and now, regardless of perhaps vital circumstances, to state their readiness to implement the fullest obligations of what is called collective security, sometimes even going beyond the direct obligations of the Covenant. There are others who plead that our obligations should be strictly limited, and that it is the duty of the Government to be quite clear as to what were vital issues, for which in the last resort it would be prepared to fight. As I conceive it, there is, and there always will be, a firm determination in this country not automatically to be dragged into participation in any war where the vital interests of the country are not involved; and in this connexion I would remind your Lordships, if it were necessary, that the Covenant itself contains no automatic military obligations.

But having said as much as that, may I go on to say this? I think it is very important that we should not in this matter quarrel about words. However zealous we may be to support the League of Nations, we do no service to the League by laying upon it burdens heavier than it can bear. We shall, I hope, so long as our signature stands, continue to honour the obligations that that signature entails; but everybody knows that, in a non-universal League, States Members will not in fact be prepared to accept in every case, in advance, automatic obligations to take coercive action in all circumstances and regardless of what they may consider to be their own vital interests. That is true of foreign nations, it is true of the Dominions, it is true of this country, and we do well, I think, to recognize it. Everybody knows also the difficulty of making even economic action effective in a non-universal League. It will not have escaped notice that M. Litvinov, in July of this year at Geneva, reminded the world that 25 per cent. of the existing Members of the League were not applying all the sanctions that were agreed upon in the last dispute. Therefore I think the noble Lord, Lord Strabolgi, gave us good advice when he said we should face realities.

I would hope that it was not necessary for us to pretend

to think that the attempt to face realities implied any disloyalty to the League or to the League's ideals. It was exactly that reason—a desire to be loyal to the League—that led my right honourable friend to make the concrete proposals that he did at Geneva the other day for the improvement of the working of the Covenant. He spoke, your Lordships will remember, about the better operation of Article 19, on which I do not wish to dwell to-night. He spoke also on the separation of the Covenant from the Treaty of Versailles. Incidentally, when appeals are addressed to the Government to give a lead on this matter, I think I am entitled to say we have already given that lead, and whether that lead is to be followed will depend on the degree of agreement we secure for it when it comes under the consideration of the machinery of the League.

Perhaps the more important proposal was that which has indeed secured a considerable measure of approval from those who have spoken in this debate—namely, the proposal by which the operation of Article 11 should be facilitated and improved. It is important to enable the League to intervene before, instead of after, a war has begun, and, as my right honourable friend pointed out at Geneva, if that can be done you will achieve one of two objects, both desirable. If such an examination shows that the Council feels strongly, and that States Members of the League are evidently prepared to act, that knowledge will be imparted to the hypothetical aggressor before he is too deeply committed to his project. If, on the other hand, they are not prepared so to act, then it is evidently to the advantage of everybody that the facts should be known early so that disappointment subsequently may be avoided.

Besides these drafting proposals, your Lordships will remember the suggestion frequently made for the extension of definite regional pacts. These, as I understand, involve obligations which are not in substitution of, but in addition to, the obligations of the Covenant. I am quite sure, as my right honourable friend the Foreign Secretary stated the other day, that the almost self-evident truth is that the value of agreements for collective action as a deterrent evidently bears largely on the certainty that they will be applied.

His Majesty's Government are not by any means blind to the dangers of the world, especially those that arise from the clash of sharply conflicting ideologies in Europe. Especially would anyone in my position be alive to the dangers of confident prophecy as to what turn the wheel of fate might at very short notice take in these disordered days; and no statesman would be wise to forget the classic example of Mr. Pitt, who, the House will remember, a short time—I think six months only—before Europe was plunged into the revolutionary wars, had the misfortune to assure the House of Commons that there never was a time when from the situation of Europe we might more reasonably expect fifteen years of peace. But, that said, and applying the best judgement that His Majesty's Government can, and putting the matter on the lowest grounds of self-interest, they do not believe that any country to-day is prepared, much less anxious, to take the responsibility of letting loose a war that might spread through Europe and beyond it.

For the last three years certainly, there have not been wanting those who have persistently preached to us of the inevitability of war. Nor is it to be wondered at that the sequence of many events should have frayed many nerves in Europe. We have been witnessing the gradual substitution in Europe of a new order—which in some degree many have long deemed inevitable—for the order constituted by the Treaty of Versailles. For years the attempt was made to find some simultaneous solution for the twin problems of German equality and general security; and, when the simultaneous solution was not found, it was not unnatural that many, still to some extent under the influence of the earlier order of ideas, should feel some doubt whether German equality, unilaterally achieved, would in fact be found compatible with security. It is not given to men to see far into the future, and it were folly for any nation, our own or any other, to close its eyes to possible dangers from whatever quarter they may arise. But it is not less folly for all nations to lose the chance of strengthening the forces of peace by the exaggeration of all the things that make for international suspicion and by failure to remember the words that always live in my mind, the words used by the late Lord Grey when he said that 'Nothing so predisposes men to understand as the consciousness that they are understood'.

11

REGIONAL PACTS

24 February 1937

[Replies to the invitation issued by the Assembly of the League on July 4th, 1936, for proposals for the reform of the League Covenant came before the Assembly when it met again in September. Mr. Eden opened the discussion with a detailed expression of the views of his Government. He proposed that, in order to enable the League to intervene more effectively in the early stages of a dispute, the League Council should have power, under Article 11 of the Covenant, to make recommendations without the consent of the parties concerned, and he stated that the British Government was in favour of regional pacts, provided that they were consistent with the terms of the Covenant. The debate terminated with the setting up of a Committee of Twenty-eight to study all the material collected.

Prolonged but ineffectual efforts were being made to negotiate a general European settlement, and in particular a new Western Pact that would replace the Treaty of Locarno. Isolation of Great Britain from the affairs of Europe, though it had its advocates, was becoming impossible in face of the rising power of an aggressive Germany. On January 30th, 1937, Herr Hitler denounced in the Reichstag the 'War-guilt' clause of the Treaty of Versailles and the provisions of the Reparations agreements regarding the administration of the Reichsbank and the German railways. Popular confidence in collective security had suffered a severe blow through the failure of economic sanctions to bring pressure upon Italy. At the same time the acceleration of the British rearmament programme provoked a desire at home for a clear definition of the purposes for which the new armaments might be used. This was given by Mr. Eden in a speech made at Leamington on November 20th, 1936, the day following that on which Lord Halifax had spoken in the House of Lords (no. 10 in this collection).

Lord Halifax surveyed the situation in two speeches which he made three months later, one at a meeting of the League of Nations Union held in Southampton, and the other in the House of Lords. The text here given of the first of these is based on a report supplied through the League of Nations Union, supplemented by the reports given of it in *The Morning Post* and in *The Times*]

IT is an inevitable and great weakness of the League of Nations that it should not embrace all the nations of the world within its membership. It is also true that it is the existence of the minatory clauses of the Covenant—sanctions—which is in great part responsible for the League of Nations not being universal to-day. There is a strong body of opinion for the abolition of sanctions, but there is a volume of opinion also in many countries that a League of Nations from which all sanctions had been withdrawn would be too light a thing to perform the duties that mankind expects of it. I fancy that, as often, the truth probably lies between the two extremes. When I was at Geneva the other day I listened to the Dominion of New Zealand stating the full sanctions case, Canada stating a kind of middle case, and some other nation stating the kind of case we have heard put forward to-night. It does seem that if we are to obtain unanimity it will have to be by a middle course between the two extreme views.

Mr. Eden has stated the views of the Government at Geneva recently. His two salient points were these. First, in the view of the Government the peace front might be immensely strengthened by a system of what have come to be known as regional pacts—a system whereby certain countries in certain areas of the world, sharing a direct and common interest in peace in that area, pledge to combine themselves in a pact to do more than the Covenant imposes—namely, to say in advance that if peace were disturbed in that area they would all be prepared to fight to preserve it. If that were possible, and if by that means a series of strong points could be established on the peace front, I do not think it would encounter the criticism that the general system of sanctions not unnaturally excites among a great many people whose opinion is deserving of regard. On the other hand, it would have the effect of making it quite plain to potential aggressors that, if they disturbed the peace, they would be able to count in advance on the opposition of the other people bound by the pact to preserve peace. Mr. Eden suggested as his second point that a reform of Article 11 of the Covenant would be valuable in enabling the League of Nations to intervene at an earlier stage than when the act of aggression had actually been committed.

There is no interest that compares for intensity in any of

our minds with the interest we all have in the preservation of peace and the avoidance of war. It is because we hope and believe that the League of Nations can be the instrument of peace that we wish to strengthen it to the utmost of our capacity. There are a great many causes to-day that compel us to search our thoughts rather closely. All over the world you see nations disquieted, uneasy, and anxious, and they are everywhere rearming. Everywhere there is concern to achieve security as great as possible. They are laying great economic and financial burdens upon the people by armaments—burdens which, unless they are eased, are likely to prove in the course of time almost intolerable. You see almost everywhere ideas of economic nationalism driving nations along courses which are insane and, in the ultimate analysis, suicidal.

It is true that everywhere there is a great clash between what we want to see and what we do see; but do not let us be unduly disturbed about that. Many years ago a wise philosopher saint said that every action of man partook of man's nature in that, like man, it had a soul and a body. The soul of the action was the purpose by which it was inspired, and the body was the outward expression in action of that purpose. There are, in fact, always the ideal, and the actual. I conceive that for us human beings it is above all things essential always to hold our faith firm in the ideal, because ideals are the nourishment of the soul of man, and without that nourishment the soul of man starves, and the best of man's achievement becomes impossible.

That need not blind us to the fact that there will always be a great gulf between the theoretical and the practicable. We do not, for example, despair in our own domestic society in England because the actual fact does not come up to our ideal—because we look forward to, and would like to see, a State in which the law was never violated. But our ideal at the same time does not absolve us from keeping a police force as a deterrent to those who are not law-abiding. It is the same all over the world. There may come to be, and it is our great ambition to see, a time in which the reign of law will be established, and in which the nations will discuss their differences instead of fighting about them. Until we are certain that the law is safe and inviolate we cannot be absolved from the obligation to defend the law-abiding and deter the law-breakers.

One of the greatest troubles and difficulties that beset the League of Nations to-day is that we are asking the League to do more than human nature in all the countries of the world is prepared to implement and accept. The present weaknesses of the League are apparent to us all. They are, first, that the League of Nations is not universal; second, that it is set in the midst of an armed world. When the League of Nations was devised at the Paris Conference it was assumed by those who devised it that all nations would be in it, and that all nations would be disarmed. It is obvious that, so long as present conditions hold, the great nations are bound to have regard to the attitude of nations outside the League as well as to those inside the League. It is not reasonable for any man to complain that a ten-ton lorry is not able to carry smoothly and efficiently a twenty-ton load; but that is exactly what you are asking the League of Nations to do.

It has been suggested that the Government's rearmament programme implies some disloyalty to the League and to the ideas for which it was founded. Exactly the reverse of that is true: it is undertaken in defence of loyalty to the League. Nobody who has had anything to do with the League of Nations in the last ten or twelve years can say that he has not often heard it brought as a charge against our country that since the war we have been trying, first of all through France and next through the League of Nations, to get our security on the cheap. It is not a very nice thing to have said to anyone. I do not hesitate to say this: it would be flagrantly dishonest of this country to sign pacts or undertake obligations arising out of them unless we knew we were in a position to be able to carry them out should the necessity arise. Quite frankly I say that we have not been in a position to carry them out, and we shall not be in a position to carry them out until we have re-equipped our defensive forces.

The essence of collective security is that we never wish to go back to a system of exclusive alliances between any one or two Powers against any other one or two Powers, but that we seek to build our foreign policy on a plan more comprehensive than exclusive alliances or precarious balance of power, a plan which invites the co-operation of all nations who are willing to co-operate with us, without any line of exclusion anywhere, in the cause of a better understanding between the nations. We ought to do, and desire to do, that on a basis so broad that no country, however powerful or well equipped, will venture to try to disturb or break the peace. I would not remain a member of any government that had a foreign policy smaller or less broad than that.

If we are to convince the world of the honesty of our intentions and undertakings in the sense of collective security, we must show people that we are in a real position to make a contribution towards achieving collective security, and in a real position to do what we profess ourselves willing to do. I have been responsible at different times for short periods for the Foreign Office, and I have been responsible more than once for the country at Geneva. I challenge anybody to contradict me when I say that there is no loyal member of the League of Nations who would not see in our defence measures the strongest guarantee for the maintenance of European peace to-day.

The first desire of democracies is peace, and democracies are never in any danger of thinking of war as one of the conditions essential to human progress. It is on these foundations that the Government have sought to pursue their policy. The negotiations for a European settlement—and that by means of the maintenance of the authority of the League of Nations, which is in our view the ultimate foundation of the law and practice of peace—afford the means to achieve political appeasement between the nations and a better adjustment of economic difficulties which, if unchecked, are going to make greater difficulties in the future. In all this the re-equipment of our defence forces has its own very definite part to play.

The other day the Foreign Secretary defined for what object the forces of this country exist. He said:

'These forces will never be used for any purpose inconsistent with the

Covenant of the League of Nations, but are designed to enable this country to discharge any obligations resting upon her, or to assist victims of aggression where it would be proper under the provisions of the Covenant of the League of Nations to do so.'

The duty of lovers of peace in these days is difficult: but it is not at all difficult to discern what that duty is.

12

OBLIGATIONS UNDER THE COVENANT

3 March 1937

[The general situation at the time at which this speech was made in the House of Lords has been summarized in the prefatory note to the preceding speech. Lord Halifax wound up a three days' debate on a motion made by Lord Arnold as to the need for a change in British foreign policy which would bring it more into accord with the realities of the existing situation.]

MY LORDS, the main burden of this debate has been the examination of the relationship in which this country ought to stand to the obligations and the theories of the League of Nations. I do not think that this debate, even if that were all that it had produced, would have been unconstructive. It is perfectly natural that those issues, lying alongside the old international obligations, must excite thought and must in many cases give rise to some anxiety; and, in the course of these three days, more than one of your Lordships has examined what are the possible directions in which a course may most wisely be steered over seas that are necessarily stormy.

Pacifism has claimed its advocates, although more than one of them has explained that he does not regard pacifism to-day as practical politics. I do not think there is any subject that needs to be more constantly searched by Christian thought, and, although this is not the place to argue that, if I could see my way to a general pacifist system in which all nations would resolutely and finally abjure war I should be glad, for that is what we all want. But I cannot myself believe that for a single nation, in the conditions of the world to-day, to forgo both the will and the power to defend what it believes to be right, is either politically practicable or morally imperative.

Then some of those who have spoken have referred to the alternative of the automatic invocation of military force against all infractions of the Covenant and of peace. The noble Lord, Lord Arnold, rather unkindly but perhaps not untruly, immortalized certain persons as victims of the bitterest disappointment if there was a war anywhere and they were not in it. If I were quite sure that such an interpretation of collective security would in fact keep the peace I would naturally support it, but I venture to think you cannot be quite sure, and it is because you cannot be quite sure that it is important to define what you are willing to fight for. Otherwise you are participating in a huge *bloc*, and there is a real danger that what might be a local war would become a world war. The most enthusiastic supporter of the League of Nations would not admit that it was any business of the League to promote that end.

The opposite alternative which has been discussed is to say that in no circumstances will you fight unless you are attacked —isolation. In my view it is only small countries that can with any assurance claim the privileges of isolation, and I am quite certain that the centre of a great Commonwealth such as ours, with interests in all parts of the world, could not in fact isolate itself. On the moral side I should certainly feel that no great country has a right, even if it could, to throw away its power and its capacity to exert influence on the problems that lie at its door.

Therefore, having exhausted those possibilities, I come to the position of His Majesty's Government. It has in fact been repeatedly defined by the Foreign Secretary, and I will not weary your Lordships by repeating that definition here.[1] It rests, as you know, upon the drawing of a

[1] 'These arms will never be used in a war of aggression. They will never be used for a purpose inconsistent with the Covenant of the League or the Pact of Paris. They may, and if the occasion arose they would, be used in our own defence and in the defence of the territories of the British Commonwealth of Nations. They may, and if the occasion arose they would, be used in the defence of France and Belgium against unprovoked aggression in accordance with our existing obligations. They may, and if a new Western European settlement can be reached they would, be used in the defence of Germany were she the victim of unprovoked aggression by any of the other signatories of such a settlement.

'These, together with our treaty of alliance with Iraq, and our projected treaty with Egypt, are our definite obligations. In addition, our armaments may be used in bringing help to a victim of aggression in any case where, in our judgement, it would be proper under the provisions of the Covenant to do so. I use the word "may" deliberately, since in such an instance there is no distinction between cases for which arms would certainly be used, and other cases of possible disturbance of peace in which this country would be free to judge of the merits and the circumstances at the time, subject to our Covenant obligations. That is not disloyalty to the League. . . . The future is always and necessarily uncertain, but so far as it is possible to be definite I suggest that His Majesty's Government's policy is crystal clear. I should be prepared to maintain the position that never in the eighteenth or nineteenth century was British policy so clearly defined in advance as it has been by my right honourable friend the Foreign Secretary in recent months.

I know perfectly well, and indeed I largely share, the anxiety to which others have given expression in this debate as to the possibility of what I may for brevity term an Eastern entanglement. I am not oblivious to that, and I am not oblivious to the anxiety of those who see indirect but grave danger to the West of Europe from possible complications in the East, linked as in the judgement of many observers East and West are by the Franco-Soviet Pact. I do not know whether your Lordships have in your minds a question and answer in the House of Commons on February 8 last. Mr. Lambert asked the Secretary of State for Foreign Affairs:

'whether any commitment exists whereby under the Franco-Russian Pact Great Britain could be involved in a European war; and, if none does exist, has this fact been made clear to the French and Russian Governments?'

That question was answered by Viscount Cranborne. He said:

'The answer to the first part of the question is No, Sir. As regards the second part of the question I think the French and Soviet Governments are fully aware of the position.'

I think that is a pretty definite Parliamentary answer to one side of the kind of question that the noble Lord who initiated this debate had in his mind.

I would go a little farther than that, and I would say that

automatic obligation to take military action. It is, moreover, right that this should be so, for nations cannot be expected to incur automatic military obligations save for areas where their vital interests are concerned.'

unless you are prepared on the one hand to say, 'I will fight in every case on behalf of peace, which is one and indivisible', or on the other hand to say, 'I will only fight when I am myself the victim of attack', there is an inevitable no-man's-land of uncertainty lying between, which is quite incapable of antecedent definition. Therefore it is that if we are unable to define beforehand what might be our attitude to a hypothetical complication in Central or Eastern Europe, that is not to say that we disinterest ourselves in the fate of those parts of Europe. We have repeatedly maintained our determination to carry out to the best of our ability our obligations under the Covenant, and, if those obligations are not capable of achievement with precise exactitude, that is a feature—and I venture to think not an accidental feature—of the Covenant itself. If it is right that the League itself is crippled, as indeed it is, by the defection of important Members, that does not mean that this country is without influence and authority which she would use in endeavouring to prevent such a conflict arising. I suggest that that influence and authority will be greatly reinforced by the steps that we have now decided to take in the matter of rearmament.

Lord Allen asked me if I had any views on the question of one regional pact. I followed, of course, what I understood to be his thought—namely, that if you have one regional pact immunizing, isolating, keeping in permanent peace one area, you will be likely to leave to the greater danger of disturbance the other parts of Europe. I hope that what I said a few moments ago will have assured him that that is not the way in which His Majesty's Government see the problem with which we are concerned. The regional pact is not in competition with the League, nor is the pact the instrument to which we should look for the remedy of injustices which we would desire, when opportunity offers, to see remedied. I have seen it suggested that the best guarantee, or a guarantee, against war would be that immediately on the outbreak of war, whatever the merits, the Prime Minister should be hanged, somewhat on the principle by which I understand the Chinaman ceases to pay his doctor when he ceases to be well. I should not greatly mind that being done if everybody conformed, especially if a war synchronized with the advent of a Labour Government to office.

But the real guarantee against war, or against war for any but the clearest and most overwhelming of reasons, is that which the noble Lord, Lord Arnold, referred to in his speech when he said that it was impossible for any democratic Government in these days to make war unless it could count on the overwhelming support of the country behind it in doing so. That is true. And what is not less true is that it would be impossible for any Government in this country to decide on a declaration of war unless they were morally confident that not only this country but also the whole Empire was associated with them, or prepared to associate itself with them, in their decision.

. . . .

I am not one of those who do not think that there is more than one reassuring element in the present situation. I think it is something which we can be pleased to learn that the Chancellor of Germany should have assured us on January 30 last that the era of surprises was over. The second thing that I ponder with some degree of satisfaction is that, so far as I can judge, any nation who wanted it could have had a war any time they liked during the last six months over Spain. They have not had it, though if they had wanted it they could have had it. Therefore I disagree with the statement that rearmament meant that the Government foresaw war as likely. We have no such gloomy anticipations, and I would state my feelings in terms exactly the reverse: that in our view, as in the view of others who have spoken, the programme of rearmament is calculated to make war far less likely. At this stage of international adjustment I do not believe that this statement is capable of challenge—namely, that the stronger this country is the less likelihood there is of war.

I go the whole way with the noble Lords who have deplored the waste of money on armaments. I go the whole way with them when they say that rearmament in itself is no solution. It is only a means to an end. But it may be the only means to an end, and that end is not selfish or aggressive but is the end of securing for this country due weight in European councils, and I do not believe that any loyal Member of the League of Nations anywhere in Europe would disagree with that assessment of the situation to-day. . . .

The prolonged trial that we made of unilateral disarmament had no other result than to convince us of its futility. The one lesson that we have learned has been the impossibility of getting other people to make sacrifices and come down to a low level, when we had already made sacrifices in advance, and had therefore proportionately less inducement to offer to other nations to follow our example. The writer of the fable of the fox and his brush had a great deal of human wisdom stored up.

The time may come, and we hope it will come, when it is possible to negotiate with more success reasonable equilibrium in armaments, and I would emphasize this, at a much lower scale than at present we are being compelled to build. The settlement of all these problems depends on two things: (1) the intrinsic elements in the problems themselves—racial, economic, and political—and (2) the spirit of approach that all countries can make to the problems and the degree of understanding that they can bring to them.

It is too often suggested that *rapprochement* with one country must involve estrangement with another. That is not our conception. A great deal is said about collective security. That, if it means anything, must mean real security, and if it is dangerous to be deluded by phrases that do not correspond to reality, it is not less dangerous to bury our heads in the sands of isolation, which the first gale will blow away. . . . The essence of collective security is that we do not believe in exclusive alliances, which are the only effective alternative before us. We seek always the method of co-operation as opposed to any plan that would divide those whom our whole policy is to bring together.

The noble Lord, Lord Allen, complains that we have never invited Germany to the council table on terms of equality, and he answered in advance the reply that I should naturally make, that that is exactly what we have been seeking to do for the last six or twelve months. He himself would prefer what he called a more constructive approach, not indeed by way of a world-wide conference, but by way, as I understood him, of a small conference in which all questions of possible difference would be brought into the arena of free discussion. But, as he spoke, I said to myself: 'Who would be participating in such a conference? Russia?' He would know well, presumably, the difficulties an invitation of that sort might encounter. There are other people whose interests might be affected, but whatever might be my first judgement about such a proposal as that, I can certainly assure him that any talks at any time that might seem likely to lead to fruitful results or better understanding would always secure the sympathy and the goodwill of His Majesty's Government. That is, indeed, the spirit in which they are constantly seeking to approach European problems, and the same spirit in which we should always welcome the co-operation of the United States.

I want to emphasize the point that though we believe that the cause of peace is in fact one, it may well be that an approach to a general settlement may be advanced by the solution of particular questions, which can be treated separately, although they must ultimately form part of a larger whole. It is for that reason that we have been attempting to bring the five Western Powers together. It is for that reason that we took the initiative in the proposed raw materials inquiry, and it is for that reason that His Majesty's Government would welcome any agreement anywhere that was honestly devised to promote the cause of peace.

I hope I have said enough to show that the policy of His Majesty's Government is not negative, is emphatically not the policy of despair, and is not one which leads us to feel that international goodwill is no more than a futile dream. We still retain our faith in the ideals of the League of Nations and in the possibility of finding means to make those ideals prevail. Whether the world will or will not succeed in that, no one here and now can say, but it is quite certain that we can make no contribution to that end unless we are in a position to play our part. And therefore it is that all the efforts of His Majesty's Government, diplomatic, military, industrial, and all other, will be subordinated to the single aim of endeavouring to build peace upon a foundation of justice, that can alone support a durable structure under which all the nations of the world can be at peace.

13

RESPONSIBILITIES OF EMPIRE

25 June 1937

[A series of broadcasts on the responsibilities of Empire was planned by the British Broadcasting Corporation to coincide with the sittings of an Imperial Conference in London (May 14th–June 15th, 1937). The last contribution to the series was delivered by Lord Halifax from Oxford on the day of the laying of the foundation-stone of the Bodleian New Library Building by Her Majesty Queen Mary, a ceremony over which he had presided as Chancellor of the University.]

I HAVE come from taking part in a ceremony which has particular significance for the British Commonwealth. Only a few hours ago Queen Mary, one of the best loved and most revered figures in our public life, was laying here in Oxford the foundation-stone of the new building of that Library to which Thomas Bodley gave his name more than three hundred years ago. Thus, while those who have shared with me the privilege of speaking to you upon the responsibilities of Empire have, with but one exception, rightly done so from London, which is pre-eminent in that Empire's political and commercial life, it falls to me to give the last of these talks from the oldest British seat of learning—this ancient University of Oxford. Here for centuries have been stored, and here we hope for long centuries to come may be preserved, in trust for the British Empire and for the whole world, many of the most rare treasures of human learning and experience.

It is, therefore, natural that my thoughts should turn back this evening towards that duty of spiritual leadership which Lord Baldwin, in the earliest talk of this series—one of his last public addresses as Prime Minister in His Majesty's Government in the United Kingdom to be broadcast—so strongly impressed upon his listeners. You will remember that he warned us of the danger of allowing the material to outstrip the spiritual, and there is no doubt that if the first of our responsibilities is to give the world a spiritual lead, we must do everything that we can to equip ourselves to fulfil that duty.

I think that it is just in this that Oxford and all our places of learning throughout the Empire have their special contribution to make. It is their responsibility to train the men and women of the Commonwealth to search out and appreciate truth, and to show them how truth may be applied in the affairs of daily life to the service of their fellows. If this task is fairly faced, it will be found wide enough to include everything that may minister to the needs of men. In the field of applied science it will concern itself with all the problems that arise in the satisfaction of material requirements; in the sphere of medicine it will be constantly stimulating research by which war may be waged more efficiently against disease; in the study of art, philosophy, history, and letters this same pursuit of truth will point the way through which men may learn to appreciate the deep forces by which their own life is moved. It is in relation to these things that the worth of any civilization must be judged, and, if the British Empire is to justify its place in history, it must have regard always to the eternal value of this loyalty to truth.

We who have been trained in the British tradition are accustomed to believe that parliamentary government in a democratic system is the best guarantee of freedom and of progress. We are not blind to its difficulties or its dangers. We are not ignorant that, judged from some angles, there are other systems that appear to offer the reward of greater executive efficiency. None the less, the British system, by the emphasis that it lays upon the rights of individuals, appears to us more favourable than any other to that development of personality, without which man cannot achieve the ultimate purpose of his existence.

But if democracy is to succeed it must be the government of itself by an educated people. And by educated I mean a people so trained that it can apply its knowledge in wisdom, for knowledge alone is not wisdom. There is indeed grave reason to think that to-day much of our knowledge—this so-called mastery of the forces of nature that we have acquired over the last 150 years—has failed to assist real progress, because man has not yet learned to apply it properly; his spiritual advance has not kept pace with the march of science. I therefore hope that all our educational institutions throughout the Empire may constantly aim at working in close touch with one another, taking advantage of the special opportunities of each, and all moved by the single purpose of inspiring their students to desire that true learning which alone will make their citizenship worthy of its name. Thus may the minds of sons and daughters of the Empire grow in common understanding, combining the wisdom of age with the enterprise of youth.

This leads me directly to another thought, on which Mr. Casey dwelt in the course of his address. Many from the various nations of the Commonwealth come here to the United Kingdom and feel themselves to be revisiting their old homes, while some of our folk in their turn go out to see their kinsmen in whichever of the Dominions they may have settled. But few from here visit more than one Dominion, and there is all too little exchange of visits between one Dominion and another. For we cannot learn to know one another, nor appreciate one another's problems, unless we meet and experience them ourselves upon the spot. The Empire will be truly one when its citizens are equally at home in each and every part of it, familiar with their surroundings and in full sympathy with their peoples. A commonwealth of peoples so knit together can look out at life steadily and see it whole. Above all it can face the responsibility to which I think every previous speaker has referred, and in particular Mr. Winston Churchill—the supreme responsibility of making the utmost contribution that is within our power to the cause of peace throughout the world.

Peace is the supreme interest of man, and it is a responsibility of the nations and peoples of the Empire, which they share with all the other nations who are partners in our common civilization, to be prepared to prove to the world that peace is not only the better but also the more profitable way. A quarter of the world's surface and a quarter of the world's population standing as one in the cause of peace can exercise an impressive and perhaps a decisive influence. The British Commonwealth presents an example to the nations of the rule of law as opposed to the age-old rule of force in international affairs. It must be at once too strong to tempt the aggressor and too just to allow bitterness to linger in the mind of any other nation, there to develop that dangerous sense of wrong from which so many wars have sprung. On such foundations the interests of the British Commonwealth and of world-peace meet, and thus, if the Commonwealth is true to itself, it may give priceless service to humanity.

Here in this University city, more probably than in any other place, have been formed those standards and that attitude to life which go to make the British character. Freedom, toleration, justice, fair-play, respect for the law, the ability to see the other man's point of view, generosity of spirit to friend and foe—all these are part of that way of living for which the British Empire stands. We do not claim all or any of these virtues as exclusively our own, but it is by the operation of these qualities in just combination that the British Commonwealth lives. By the right admixture of them all, we have been wise enough or lucky enough to find the secret of reconciling the claims to individual freedom of the several parts of the Empire with those of unity. Each constituent member of our Imperial society feels itself to be a true part of the larger whole, and at the same time knows itself to be not less truly free to cast its national life along the lines most suited to its national genius. Therefore it is that, when international relations appear difficult, and the peace of the world seems threatened, the bonds of mutual trust and common interest draw the Empire more closely together for the protection of those liberties of which we have learned to appreciate the value.

No one who had the privilege, that I lately enjoyed, of sharing in the counsels of the Imperial Conference could doubt either the need or the assurance of the common purpose which inspired the attitude of all who were gathered round the Conference table towards the problems of international relations, as they present themselves to-day. That purpose was, first and last, to help in the maintenance of peace through justice and understanding between peoples; and nothing was more significant than the recognition by all parts of the Commonwealth represented that, while the approach might necessarily sometimes differ, we were all seeking the same end. To all who have the imagination to picture to themselves the place that the Great Dominions and India may hold when they have come to their full stature in times to come, there could have been no stronger ground for encouragement and hope.

Let me leave this last thought in the minds of those who are listening to me. The will of a nation and of a commonwealth of nations is in the last analysis the sum of the wills of its individual citizens. We must therefore be ready to put self aside and to work for the common good if we are to realize to the full the ideal of service to mankind for which the British Empire stands.

These talks upon the Responsibilities of Empire are not intended to be mere statements of political theory. It is hoped that they will have a reflection in the increased interest that those who hear them will take in the fulfilment of those duties which the citizenship of the Commonwealth lays upon them, in addition to the privileges which it enables them to enjoy. So only, and in no other way that I can foresee, may our Commonwealth in future fulfil the hope of all its peoples, and help to realize those aspirations after a new world-order upon which men of goodwill everywhere have set their hearts.

14

DEMOCRACY

8 July 1937

[The following address, which has been printed from the speaker's typescript, was delivered by Lord Halifax in the Bonar Law Memorial College at Ashridge to a conference organized by the Association for Education in Citizenship.]

IT is not only a great honour but also a great responsibility to open these proceedings. For this Conference is one of no ordinary kind, as it will deal at no ordinary period in the world's history with a subject of no ordinary importance. During its course, men and women of all parties in the State will discuss, freely and without reserve, the principles and the workings of democracy as we know it. Not the least part of the value of this Conference may be to prove to the world, if indeed the world still needs proof, that the one cause common to all our parties is the determination to maintain that form of government which the experience of a thousand years has taught us to regard, not only as the form of government best suited to the genius of our people, but as the completest example of true democracy.

Our meeting is well timed. Less than twenty years ago mankind was suffering all the agonies of a Great War, in order, as the democratic peoples then persuaded themselves, to make the world safe for democracy. When that struggle ended they fondly imagined that they were on the threshold of the golden age of which mankind had dreamed through history. Great hopes were born for a new ordering of the world in which the nations would live happily together, and justice, not force, would rule. But these high expectations have been disappointed. All over the world men awoke to the fact that there was no ground for believing that the war-to-end-war had, in fact, achieved its purpose. National animosities had evidently not been exorcised, nor had the way of peace been made plain. And to-day we find a world that is not particularly safe for anybody or for anything; quite certainly not one in which the cause of democracy is assured. Parliamentary government is constantly challenged and its suitability for the circumstances of to-day denied. At the same time the claim is made for other systems of government, deriving authority from a totally different philosophy, that they are at once more efficient and no less truly representative of the views of the vast majority of the peoples governed by their systems. These then are the circumstances in which this Conference has been called, and in which we have at once the opportunity and the duty to justify our faith.

We must first be clear in our minds as to what we conceive to be the object of government, in order that we may judge why the system which we call Democracy is best calculated to achieve the results we want.

For various reasons I do not think that many of us are satisfied to-day with the Benthamite definition of the purpose of government as being 'the greatest happiness of the greatest number'. In the first place, we are sceptical of the power of governments to produce happiness by legislation or by administration, but secondly, and more important, such a definition seems to pay insufficient regard to the claims of the individual and to the rights of minorities. The dictum that 'minorities must suffer—it is the badge of their tribe' has never sufficiently reflected our political thought to permit us to use a foundation that appears to admit its truth. The main reason for which modern thought in England has moved away in this respect from Bentham supplies the clue to what more truly at the present time would seem to us the purpose for which government exists. Though in many directions we have travelled far on the road of extending State activities, we have simultaneously been according fuller recognition to the claims of individual personality. The lines we are trying to follow in our educational development, of making the curriculum fit the child; the diminished value that modern opinion is disposed to attach to the authority of tradition and convention; the relations of parents and children—all these in different ways reflect the shifting of opinion from what may be termed the static view of society towards one which emphasizes the right of self-expression through development of personality.

The reasons for this change of direction are sufficiently familiar, and the pace of modern scientific invention has no doubt had much to say to it. In a sense the British character has always been, and I trust will always remain, strongly individualist. And therefore it is—partly due to inherited characteristics, partly to the 'mobility' of the age, partly to the acknowledgement of the claims to self-expression—that we have come primarily to regard government as being the instrument to secure conditions favourable to the fullest possible development of personality. Government therefore —to take the two most elementary examples—establishes a Police Force to secure the individual against internal violence, and Defence Forces to protect him from external aggression. And the whole range of government activity, that we are accustomed to call the social services, is designed to secure the best conditions that it may for the achievement of the main purpose, the growth of personality.

It might be argued, and indeed is argued, that all this function of government can be discharged better by some system other than that of democracy, which I interpret to mean government of the people by itself. It is not necessary to deny the results of the achievements within their own sphere of any other form of government; but the point is that it is exactly the power and the responsibilities of self-government that have so much to contribute to the end we desire—an end moreover that can be produced from no other stock. Once you make your paramount object that of the encouragement of human personality, it is obvious that a community that retains in its own hands the judgement on questions of its own government is in a more favourable position to profit by experience, with all the consequences that this brings, than one which disembarrasses itself of the necessity of forming judgements by entrusting plenipotentiary power to other hands.

At this point too self-government through democracy derives strength from the impact on human thought of

Christian philosophy. From this angle the responsibility placed upon the individual citizen under the democratic system is seen in close analogy with the responsibility vested in him under the moral law. Man is endowed with the gift of free will, of which admittedly he not seldom makes disastrous use. From God's point of view, if we may reverently so speak, these unhappy results of man's free will might have been avoided if man had not been so endowed. But free will, with all the risks of its misuse, is so far as we can judge the deliberate method chosen by God, in order to make possible the great results of the right use of free will which could never be open to man, were he the mere creature of mechanical necessity with no right of choice. And thus, though in the application of these eternal principles to the practical life of man there must always be adjustments and regard to considerations of time and circumstance, I always feel, when I hear people say 'Good government is better than self-government', that that does not appear to be the way that God has chosen to direct the affairs of the human race—affairs of infinitely greater importance than those dealt with by any earthly government. But this is a digression; and I hope that apart from the last consideration, with which you may not all agree, you will be at one with me in giving weight to the responsibility of active citizenship as a vital element in the formation of the personality of citizens.

It is of course no longer possible, as in the ideal Greek City-State, for all the citizens of a nation to exercise directly legislative or administrative functions; and therefore the British people—partly of design and partly fortuitously—have devised through history the representative system that we know to-day. Time was when it was not unknown for constituencies to beg to be excused from sending a representative to Westminster, in order to be spared the cost of maintaining him there, in addition to making financial contribution to the subventions that the Crown demanded. But gradually, as every schoolboy knows, these doubts gave place to the constitutional principle of 'No taxation without representation', which has played so powerful a part in shaping both our own nation and the Commonwealth. It is the operation of that principle which gives the legislature control of the executive, and which, along with the practical application of the doctrine of the equality of all men before the law in a constitution where the legislature and executive are both sharply excluded from interference with the Courts, is the ultimate safeguard of individual liberty.

The present working of our Constitution is familiar enough to us, however unintelligible it may be to foreign students. I heard the other day of a German student who had learnt greatly to admire the British Constitution from his study of its effects in history, and who was sorely puzzled, on asking an Oxford bookseller to supply him with a copy of it, to learn that no such thing existed. The truth is that this strange creature of centuries of evolution is no bad expression of the instinct of a race which naturally mistrusts logic, and habitually subordinates theory to practical result.

The late Lord Balfour hit the nail on the head when he said towards the end of his life:

> 'Many people have dreamed dreams since the war ended. It is partly the fault of the British nation—and of the Americans; we can't exonerate them from blame either—that this idea of "representative government" has got into the heads of nations who haven't the smallest notion of what its basis must be.
>
> 'It is difficult to explain, and the Anglo-Saxon races are bad at exposition. I doubt if you would find it written in any book of the British Constitution that the whole essence of British parliamentary government lies in the *intention to make the thing work*. We take that for granted. We have spent hundreds of years in elaborating a system that rests on that alone. It is so deep in us that we have lost sight of it, but it isn't so obvious to others. They learn about our parliamentary methods of obstruction, but nobody explains to them that, when it comes to the point, all our parliamentary parties are determined that the machinery shan't stop. "The King's Government must go on", as the Duke of Wellington said.'

But a part of the machinery, hardly less vital than His Majesty's Government, is the officially recognized Opposition to His Majesty's Government, to which recently for the first time statutory recognition has been given by the provision to pay a salary to the Leader of the largest party in opposition in the House of Commons. It is perhaps strange that the parliamentary system should rest so largely upon the activities, and presence in adequate numbers, of persons whose principal object in life must be to oppose what another set of persons enjoying the major degree of national confidence desire to do. Yet it is by this method of criticism and attack that the merits or demerits of proposals can be tested, and the best work of Parliament is not done when the Government of the day has only to face a weak Opposition.

It is by the existence and constitutional position of the Opposition party that the country is able to ensure peaceful and orderly succession to the place of government. They are the alternative Government, if public opinion decides to make a change, and the knowledge that they may be called upon in office to implement professions made in opposition no doubt contributes to exert a sobering influence upon irresponsible enthusiasms. Meanwhile, the Opposition in a democratic system such as ours exists to secure that which is of the very essence of democracy, that the just rights of the minority should be respected. When the minority of to-day may be the majority of to-morrow this respect is more readily conceded, and it is precisely in this recognition of the right of the Opposition to oppose, that civil freedom consists. For the ultimate test of the justice or otherwise of the claim of any government, of whatever form, to be free and careful of the liberties of its subjects, is the extent to which it is permissible openly to express views contrary to its own.

One sometimes hears it said that in these days the executive—the Cabinet—is able to enforce its will too easily upon a pliant majority in the House of Commons, and that we are insensibly drifting, in spite of universal suffrage, into something very different from operative democracy. No doubt in the everyday working of Parliament the Cabinet exercises great power, both through the initial decisions that it takes on policy and through its influence on those to whom it looks for support in the House of Commons.

The power to treat questions as matters of confidence is a real one, involving as it may the appeal to the electorate, especially in the light of the modern practice of payment of members and non-payment of election expenses. And it may be admitted that the now accepted custom under which Governments take a serious view of any parliamentary defeat, even on details of their measures, is not without disadvantage. On the other hand, it is not necessary to look far afield to see the inconvenience that arises when Governments are obliged to rely for support upon the shifting combination of different groups, and no one who has ever worked in the Cabinet would support the thesis that Cabinet deliberations were unaffected by the opinions circulating among Private Members in the Lobbies.

From time to time indeed the influence thus exerted is very sharply manifested, and three notable examples in recent times are fresh in the memory of us all. The first Regulations for application of the Means Test were sharply criticized and had to be suspended; the proposals accepted by the Cabinet at the instance of Sir Samuel Hoare in December 1935 induced a parliamentary crisis, culminating in the resignation of the Minister principally concerned; and, most recent of all, the proposals for a National Defence contribution submitted by the present Prime Minister in his last Budget as Chancellor of the Exchequer were so unfavourably received that their author wisely and magnanimously withdrew them. I am not here arguing where in each or any of these matters truth lay: I only quote them as illustrations of the real power on broad and important questions of policy which under our system is exercised by Private Members, on behalf of the corporate body of citizens whom they represent.

There are obvious dangers to which any popular system is naturally exposed. I have only time to mention two or three of the most conspicuous. Twenty years ago the great question that exercised the minds of many political thinkers was whether or not a democracy could run what we then called an Empire. The fear was entertained of attempts at control, based on insufficient appreciation of actual conditions, which might not impossibly repeat the unhappy experience of the eighteenth century. These anxieties have been happily dissipated through the complete surrender of even its titular rights by the democracy in the United Kingdom to its sister democracies overseas, with the result—again often very astonishing to foreign eyes—that the essential unity of the whole is more securely rooted on the new foundations.

To-day there is cause for some misgiving as to the capacity of democracy to handle delicate problems of international relations. The tendency, of which there are signs to-day, to import into our judgements on the issues of foreign policy our likes and dislikes of forms of government elsewhere is full of danger; and it is not necessary to stress the difficulties that can be created for the best Foreign Secretary by injudicious questions in Parliament or by well-intentioned but ill-informed attempts to cut knots that it is often the business of statesmanship painfully to untie. I conceive that in nothing will democracy be more severely tested than by its ability to exercise the restraint that is essential if the country is to exercise its full influence abroad by presenting in that field a united front.

On the domestic side, the vital necessity for the well-being of democracy is that it should learn to distinguish the genuine from the counterfeit in the wares that are submitted for its approval. As long as human nature remains at all like the human nature that we know, there will not be wanting those of all parties who will be tempted to choose the easy way of promising smooth things, and who will endeavour to buy electoral favour by I O U 's, which they can hardly hope to be in a position to redeem. The most indispensable requisite for the democratic State is the capacity of its citizens to establish such standards, both of judgement and conduct, such power of discrimination between policies and persons, that the temptation of this way to the politician may be abated.

But if citizens are to supply such correctives to the weaknesses of politicians, they must themselves resist the temptation to take too much of their thinking ready-made from others. And this means education. In a non-democratic State the lack of educational opportunity will cause great loss in countless ways to individuals, and ultimately to the State; but the stability of the State will not be directly affected. To a democratic State, education is a vital necessity; for without it, it is as if a man were placed in charge of a complicated and rather dangerous piece of machinery, who had no knowledge of how to work it, and whose mistakes would spell wide disaster. As a wise and experienced educationalist once put it to me—'It is surely not a small return for the millions that we spend on education that ideas can be profitably discussed on the banks of the Thames that would cause explosion on the banks of the Volga.' Nor are these dangers the mere figment of timid imaginations. The world to-day is the victim of a system of subtle and ceaseless propaganda—suppressing, exaggerating, distorting; and atmospheres are all the time being created that are subversive of rational thought. A background is established against which identical facts appear so different as to be almost unrecognizable, and the task of finding solutions for difficulties arising is rendered infinitely more complex. On those who supply the news or other material for judgement, whether through the Press or broadcast, the heavy responsibility that must always accompany power must be held to rest; and the work of such a Society as this must be continually to emphasize to the general body of citizens their duty to search out for themselves the matters on which it is the function of citizenship to form opinions and record a verdict.

And lastly, if the representative system is to attract the services of the best men, it is essential that we should never forget some among the wisest words of Edmund Burke—

> 'Certainly, Gentlemen [he was addressing the Electors of Bristol], it ought to be the happiness and glory of a representative to live in the strictest union, the closest correspondence, and the most unreserved communication with his constituents. Their wishes ought to have great weight with him; their opinion high respect; their business unremitted attention. It is his duty to sacrifice his repose, his pleasure, his satisfaction, to theirs—and above all, ever and in all cases, to prefer their interest to his own.
>
> 'But his unbiased opinion, his mature judgement, his enlightened conscience, he ought not to sacrifice to you, to any man, or to any set of men living. . . . Your representative owes you not his industry only, but his judgement; and he betrays, instead of serving you, if he sacrifices it to your opinion.'

It is to the credit of the British constitution or character, or both, that we still regard public service, local or national, as the most honourable occupation to which men and women can devote their energies. Long may it so remain. For it is by this means that we succeed, better as we think than in other countries, in striking the just balance between the claims of the individual and those of the State to which he owes allegiance. That balance is not to be found in adherence to either extreme, whether of liberty for the individual or subordination of individual liberty to the State. It remains as true to-day as when Burke said it—if I may quote him again—'The extreme of liberty obtains nowhere, nor ought to obtain anywhere. Liberty must be limited in order to be possessed.' On the other side, we cannot follow other nations who appear to exalt the claims of the State to a point where the State almost becomes an end in itself, and where loyalty to the State is deemed to involve denial of the loyalty to his own conscience, by which man must ultimately be bound. We have another conception of the endless adventure which is man's journey towards the ideal social order, and that conception I sought to set out earlier, when I defined the principal purpose of government as that of protecting and favouring the development of human personality. A State which stamps all its citizens into a common mould and seeks to unify what Nature has so wonderfully made diverse may gain whatever advantage there may be in singleness of aim in politics. But it will assuredly be the poorer by the loss of that variety of life which the State, jealous in guarding the individuality of its citizens, has to offer.

John Stuart Mill many years ago summed up the whole matter:

> 'The worth of a State, in the long run, is the worth of the individuals composing it; and a State which postpones the interests of *their* mental expansion and elevation, to a little more of administrative skill, or that semblance of it which practice gives, in the details of business; a State which dwarfs its men, in order that they may be more docile instruments in its hands even for beneficial purposes—will find that with small men no great thing can really be accomplished; and that the perfection of machinery to which it has sacrificed everything, will in the end avail it nothing, for want of the vital power which, in order that the machine might work more smoothly, it has preferred to banish.'

There we may well leave it; but, if we agree with Mill, it is well to remember that we can only make his doctrine our own by the fulfilment of the obligations for which such type of citizenship calls. The things that are most worth having are not those most easy to achieve, or when achieved to keep; and great treasure is only in safe custody when there is constant vigilance and the willingness to make sacrifices for its preservation. It is not, for example, a wholesome sign that the exercise of the franchise, for which our predecessors laboured and suffered over centuries, should appear to be losing for some of our people its significance. The right to vote, which is surely the crowning privilege of free men and free women in a free democracy, can hardly be said to be adequately prized when the ballot boxes are half filled.

The centre, as we are, of a world-wide commonwealth of freely associated nations, each under a closely related democratic system, we in this country cannot escape a special responsibility. To-day, as for the past three hundred years, the world still sees in the United Kingdom the example and the champion of free institutions, and it is by the progress of our people under democracy that the strength or weakness of that system of government is appraised. If this Conference serves to awaken our people to the dangers of the neglect of the primary duties of citizenship, it will have more than served its purpose and have done much to ensure for future generations that ordered freedom under which we ourselves are fortunate enough to live.

15

THE CHRISTIAN ATTITUDE TO WAR

11 July 1937

[The following address was delivered at a service of prayer for peace held at St. Martin-in-the-Fields, Trafalgar Square, and was broadcast to the nation.]

THE purpose of our service to-night is to help forward by our prayers the coming of God's Kingdom. Those to whom I speak will think differently about many things, but we are all one in our desire to strengthen the cause of peace.

There can be no one who remembers the past or whose imagination can picture the future who must not long for peace. We shrink from the horror of all the suffering that war, with the accompaniment of modern science, must involve, and from the tragedy of human lives broken and destroyed. We well know the probable consequences for civilized society of the unchaining in war of all the worst of man's disruptive passions. All these feelings are powerful, and in their place right, and we do well to give full weight to them. But for Christian people they cannot come foremost in the reckoning. For they are dictated by consideration of war from the side of man, whereas the principal endeavour of those of us who profess and call ourselves Christians must rather be to judge of peace and war in relation to what we believe is the ultimate purpose of man's existence according to the will of God.

What then ought we to think about the purpose of man's life? Man is endowed by his reason and his intellect with great power over the rest of the animal creation and over the forces of nature. Every day he is extending the boundaries of his knowledge, and of his mastery over the physical conditions of his own life and the physical world by which he is surrounded. Simultaneously he finds himself strangely involved in another and quite different world, which he terms spiritual and of which he knows much less. Of this spiritual world, an outstanding characteristic is that it is constantly confronting him with the necessity of choice between two courses of action, one of which he knows to be right and the other of which he knows to be wrong. It is this faculty of judgement between right and wrong that he calls conscience. However much he may stifle or disobey it, he is constrained to recognize its existence, and to conclude that it reflects a moral law deriving from some authority outside himself. And this authority the Christian calls God.

Moreover, in a way that we cannot exactly rationalize, we become conscious of being so made that human nature at its best can never be satisfied except by something outside and greater than itself, leading to the conclusion that the purpose of man's life is to mould his nature more and more into the fashion of the Divine, in order that he may thus fulfil the end of his existence and—whatever we exactly mean by it—make approach to union with God. This conviction comes to men in countless different ways—all mysterious: through personal experience, through the example of others, through pain, through joy, through sorrow, through art, and through appreciation of nature in all its manifold and wonderful beauty. And unless we are wholly deceiving ourselves about the existence and nature of God, we must believe that it is His purpose that all men everywhere should so come to approach and know and love Him.

If this is so, it is evident that this union with God, for which it is the duty of all human beings to strive, must, in so far as we are able to achieve it, have the effect of bringing us into the most intimate relationship with one another, and the 'Body of Christ' must have a significance wider than that of our own religious society. Quite obviously this intimate union with others in the unity of all with the Divine is imperfectly realized, and frequently interrupted, by reason of the failure of individuals and by the destructive effect of anti-social forces. In the ordinary intercourse of life, we see every day how sorely this harmony is impaired by selfishness and everything that follows from it: and it is this interruption of God's purpose—the union of all men in Himself—that is the gravest consequence of war, and that constitutes war's real condemnation. For this reason we must, I think, feel that war (even when it is, as I believe it may be, entirely justifiable and in certain circumstances inevitable) is yet the ultimate outcome of forces opposed to the will of God, and that only through and in peace can the will of God for man be perfectly fulfilled.

Realizing this, many good people repudiate war altogether as being, by its perversion of the powers of human nature and its degradation of human gifts, wholly and always opposed to the will of God, and would tell us that the only way to convert the world, and to be faithful to God's purpose, is by the refusal in all circumstances to have recourse to the instrument of war.

I respect, but I cannot take this view. There is no Christian who does not feel how great a thing it would be to abolish war and secure the world against its recurrence. But in trying to do this we have to recognize that war is itself only a symptom of a disease deeply seated in human nature—namely, evil—and while we rightly do all in our power to treat the symptom, we must face the fact that there can be no real or permanent cure of the symptom except by eradication of the disease. We are also forced to admit that while war is the product and symptom of evil, it is plainly not the only manifestation of evil in the world, and it may well be that refusal to face war might have the consequence of encouraging in worse forms the evil of which war is the visible outcome. To Christian people, therefore, seeking to bring the world to loyalty to God, the problem must present itself in terms of a comparison of evils; of which war, however deplorable in itself, may legitimately in my view be felt in special circumstances not to be the greatest. It is no doubt this that has led Christian thought through the centuries to hold that in cases of resistance to the major evil it was justifiable for Christian men to take up arms.

It is also necessary to distinguish between what may be the duty of individuals and that of the organized society that we call the nation. For the latter stands in the place of trustee for all its citizens, present and future, and is responsible for their well-being. And it might well be that action justifiable in the case of an individual dealing with his own could not be justified in the case of a trustee acting on behalf of others. Thus, indeed, may we reconcile the seeming contradiction in the New Testament between the injunction to extreme self-surrender in the individual and the commendation of rulers as those entitled to use force for the restraint of evil doers. A careful study of our Lord's words in the New Testament suggests that He was for the most part concerned to assert principles rather than to formulate precise rules of conduct. If His followers could be faithful to the principles, they would naturally translate them into the action that they have to take upon the problems of everyday life as they arise. While warning His disciples that His Kingdom was no temporal Kingdom, He expressly recognized the authority of temporal government—government indeed quite untouched by His teaching. 'Render therefore to Caesar the things that are Caesar's, and to God the things that are God's.' And if He thus recognized the authority of temporal government, it would seem to follow that He could scarcely have intended to condemn vindication of its authority, even in the last resort by force, for ends legitimate to the purpose for which such government exists.

In the sphere both of national and of individual action, it is always the spiritual motive on which judgement has to be passed. We are familiar with this upon the other side: 'Though I bestow all my goods to feed the poor, and though I give my body to be burned and have not charity, it profiteth me nothing.' It is the spirit behind the act that makes or mars its value.

So it is with the application of force. The State, for the assertion of the law and the protection of loyal citizens, enforces its will by the machinery of policemen, law court, and, if need be, punishment. The policeman or private person who is obliged to fight a street bully, who has knocked down a child, will use exactly the same method as the bully used a minute before; but, judged by their motive and spiritual value, the two actions are essentially distinct. I do not believe it possible to argue that force, which is generally admitted to be legitimate in one form, is always wrong in another. It is a question of degree and not of principle, and thus I do not think we can deny that cases may arise in which the use of force in the extreme form of war may be both unavoidable and right. Nor can a clear line be drawn, as some might wish to do, between a defensive war waged for compelling reasons of national self-preservation, and war waged by international effort in pursuance of the ideals that we associate with the League of Nations. For in essence the deciding factor—resistance to injustice—is the same in both, and what matters always is the motive on which resort to the use of force is had.

The physical consequences of resort to force, in the shape of war, are of course infinitely more serious and operate over a wider field than any other; and the motives compelling nations to take so grave a decision are certain to be confused, and therefore need more jealous scrutiny. Moreover, in every case of war there is the danger that the original motive gets overlaid by others less worthy, such as hatred and revenge; and I conceive, therefore, that, however just was the first cause, it would always be the duty of the Christian man to watch for and to check the confusion of the original issue by the emergence of evil passions, and constantly to be searching the possibilities of concluding a righteous peace.

I am therefore led to conclude that the pursuit of peace under all conceivable conditions might mean the acceptance of greater evils even than war, conducted with all the devilish resources of the twentieth century, and might therefore in itself be more reprehensible than war seriously and solemnly undertaken in defence of vital principles that would be denied and betrayed by a refusal to break the peace.

When we think and speak of peace, what do we really mean? We naturally tend to think of it as something negative—not war—and for that reason to be something worthy of all we can do for its preservation. But just as I can imagine individuals confronted by a situation which Christian men and women would feel was worse than death, so I can imagine circumstances for a nation or for human civilization in which immunity from war could be too dearly purchased. The peace, therefore, for which we must work and pray is something greater and deeper than the outward avoidance of physical conflict between nations, greatly as we must long to be spared the horrors that such a clash must mean. And what I suggest we ought to mean by international peace is the establishment between nations of that relationship which ought to obtain between Christian individuals as members of Christ's body. We know on what foundations alone that kind of relationship can be established: mutual respect and mutual trust, unselfishness, the service of others which will come only as we truly love our neighbours as ourselves, and finally the subjection of every part of our being in thought and word and deed to the service of God's will as we may be guided to apprehend it in our daily life. That, and not less, is what we must mean when we think and speak of peace.

The contrast between such an ideal and the present state of the world is the measure of man's failure to do God's will and to fulfil His eternal purpose. And the fact that, nineteen hundred years after God's revelation of Himself in the world, war is still possible between men is the symptom of grave spiritual disease, and of disharmony between God's will and the wills of men. Man has failed to achieve that unity between God and himself which would order his life according to God's way and make war unthinkable. So great a failure constitutes for us all a constant challenge to repentance and to prayer: to repentance for our share in the responsibility for human blindness in not seeing and following God's guiding; and to prayer that all men everywhere may come to make His will the touchstone of all their conduct.

We cannot all be experts in the detailed management of international affairs, and it would probably be unfortunate if we acted as if we were, for more confusion than advantage generally follows from the attempt to do other people's business. Nor is it God's way to show us easy short cuts through difficulties. But there is a great thing that the humblest of us can do, and that may achieve more than the greatest efforts of those we rank as statesmen. We all can and we all should pray for those whose business it is to take decisions, that they may seek to form their judgements in accordance with God's will, and in so doing receive the guidance of His over-ruling wisdom. 'God, who didst teach the hearts of Thy faithful people by the sending to them the light of Thy Holy Spirit, grant to us and to all men to have a right judgement in all things.' In particular we may pray that they may be moved to examine in the spirit of Christian charity all questions that may from time to time appear likely to cause discord between nations, and, so far as we may in a world not yet made perfect, deal with them in accordance with Christian principles. If all nations could be brought so to act, we should indeed have been successful in the establishment of a new and better international order. For how much of the world's disappointment and anxiety is not each one of us directly responsible by the half-heartedness and dullness of our prayer? And how different would be the prospect if all men would realize the full power and privilege of prayer, flowing from hearts filled with the faith that removes mountains, and inspired by a love strong enough to break every barrier that the forces of evil may erect.

Let us indeed resolve so to pray; for ourselves, for those in all countries who have it in their power to mould opinion, by speech or writing, that the temporal kingdoms of this world may come to be the true image of that Kingdom which is eternal and whose foundations are set in charity and peace.

16

SPAIN AND THE FAR EAST

21 October 1937

[The outbreak of civil war in Spain on July 18th, 1936, led almost at once to the adoption by the European States, on French initiative, of a policy of non-intervention, undertaken with the dual object of permitting the Spanish nation to decide its own destiny and of preventing the Spanish conflict from expanding into a war between Great Powers. A committee, known as the Non-Intervention Committee, was appointed to supervise the execution of the non-intervention agreement, the scope of which was extended on February 20th, 1937, to include prohibition of enlistment or dispatch of volunteers to Spain. A series of incidents in the Mediterranean during the following summer resulted in a conference of States with special interests in that sea being held at Nyon on September 10th to devise means of dealing with the menace of piracy, and in the establishment of a system for the protection of non-Spanish merchant ships. England and France had been working since March to secure the withdrawal of volunteers from Spain, and although Italy finally refused, on October 10th, to enter into conversations on the subject in a Three-Power Conference, the British and French Governments accepted the Italian suggestion that the subject should be referred back to the Non-Intervention Committee.

Another storm-centre lay in the Far East. Fighting broke out between Chinese and Japanese troops near Peiping on July 7th, 1937, and spread over northern China. A month later the conflict extended to Shanghai. Attempts were made by the Western Powers to end hostilities. In a speech made at Chicago on October 5th President Roosevelt pledged America to engage actively in the search for peace, and on the following day the League Assembly issued an invitation to those Member-States that were signatories to the Nine-Power Treaty of Washington to meet, as provided for by Article 7 of that Treaty, for consultation.

The following speech was made by Lord Halifax in the House of Lords in answer to a question as to whether the Government was in a position to make a statement on the international situation, with special reference to affairs in the Far East.]

MY LORDS, the first topic on which I would propose to say a word is that of Spain, which is immediately nearest home. Ever since the civil strife in Spain started, the policy of His Majesty's Government has been directed to three objectives that I might perhaps state quite simply: first of all, to try to induce Spaniards not to fight one another in Spain; secondly, to try to induce foreigners not to fight one another anywhere because of the fact that Spaniards were fighting one another in Spain; and thirdly, to try to secure that the issue of the Spanish civil war should not be permitted materially to affect the relations of Mediterranean Powers and their position in the Mediterranean.

I have no doubt whatever in my own mind that the country generally has steadily approved of the non-intervention policy that His Majesty's Government have sought to pursue. That is not to say that the country has had any illusions, either that the non-intervention policy would work perfectly or that it has worked perfectly. But I think your Lordships will agree that that policy has had and to-day still has this quality: that so long as nations continue to accept the policy of non-intervention officially, that fact is a protection against incidents assuming proportions of a menacing international character. We are all aware how greatly recent events have strained both the theory and the practice of non-intervention. We have done our best to make the practice effective and to maintain the theory.

It is not necessary for me to remind your Lordships again of the actual accomplishment which we have seen bearing fruit in the time that has elapsed since the Conference that was held at Nyon. I only remark at this point that I think the willingness of His Majesty's Government and of the French Government to see the matters on which they had thought of a Three-Power Conference again remitted to the Non-Intervention Committee at the suggestion of the Italian Government was a proof of the genuineness of His Majesty's Government's desire to reach a settlement upon them. It is quite true that at that time His Majesty's Government and the French Government were doubtful whether that would in fact be the most fruitful measure of procedure, but I think it is permissible to say that that course has been so far justified by results. I most warmly welcome the Italian initiative which has made further progress possible. It has been a real contribution to the relief of international strain and a great encouragement to those who wish to see that strain removed.

I would ask your Lordships not to underrate the great psychological value of even a token withdrawal of volunteers, if that could be secured. I have been asked this specific question: whether it was in mind that there would be precise guarantees against more troops being sent during the interval that must elapse while these matters were being investigated by the Committee. I think perhaps the best answer is that the Italian representative himself, at the meeting of the Non-Intervention Committee, was concerned to lay great stress upon the perfecting of a system of control as part of a general improvement in the checking of intervention on one side or the other.

. . . .

I think that if this new situation can be developed, it is not unreasonable to hope that it may make it possible to clear up a great many misunderstandings that have arisen out of the difficulties of the Spanish problem, and I can myself look forward—I do not want to be unduly optimistic—to the gradual establishment of a new and healthier atmosphere, in which it would be possible to reach the position where Anglo-Italian conversations might be held. If that stage can be reached, I should myself hope that a great many of the misunderstandings that at present are damaging the relations of what used to be two friendly nations—and the mass of whose people, I think, want to be on friendly terms again—might be removed, to the great advantage of both, and to the great advantage of the peace of Europe, in which both those great nations have a great and constructive part to play.

I turn now to deal with matters that have been raised in connexion with the situation in the Far East. . . . We deplore the pursuit of policy, by Japan or any other nation, by military means and the recourse to force, which are contrary to the spirit of a new relationship between nation and nation, and indeed to the whole order of ideas expressed in the Covenant of the League of Nations, and to ideas, it is relevant to remember, which were brought into practical politics and sponsored by our great sister nation, the United States, and which were wholeheartedly and sincerely adopted by our own country.

Therefore His Majesty's Government wholeheartedly welcome the speech of President Roosevelt at Chicago. So far as I can judge there is no divergence of view between the Government in this country and the Government of the United States as expressed in that speech, and we look forward now to this conference under the Nine-Power Treaty, set in motion indeed by, but not held under, the League, and meeting under the inspiration of the President of the United States. It is quite impossible to anticipate what that Conference will do. It is, however, quite possible to form a clear idea of what methods that Conference will adopt, and what will be its outlook, from the wording of the League resolution which was responsible for the initiative in the matter. Your Lordships will remember that the League resolution expressed the hope that the States concerned (that is, the signatories to the Nine-Power Treaty):

'will be able to associate with their work other States which have special interest in the Far East to seek a method of putting an end to the conflict by agreement.'

I would emphasize those last words 'by agreement', because that seemed to me to be the spirit which pervaded the speech of the President of the United States—not an extension of war, but an endeavour to find an end of war.

Therefore it is that we enter the Conference in a simple fulfilment of our Treaty obligation. We have no intention of putting one party or the other in the dock, but we do intend to proceed in the spirit of Article 7 of the Treaty, that laid down that in such a situation as this there should be 'full and frank communication between the contracting Powers concerned'. It is just that that we hope to achieve, and I earnestly hope that Japan will see her way to be represented there. Even if she is not, I can conceive great influence being exercised by combined co-operation on these lines by the Powers there gathered. I am quite convinced that it is only that attitude of mind which can give any chance of the Conference securing success. It is really no good going to such a Conference as this with the anticipation of failure in your mind. If you go there with failure in your mind you will soon have failure to record, and I would entirely decline on every ground at this stage to attempt to answer questions, in this House or anywhere else, as to what I should do or should not do if that Conference failed to secure the result that I desire.

I only make this observation. I hope that this Conference will decide to proceed in the spirit of the League resolution—but do not let any of us at this stage think that it is necessary to be more royalist than the King—employing whatever methods of peaceful persuasion and conciliation the Conference may deem most useful. And obviously, should the Conference fail, and should the result that we look for show no promise of being achieved, no nation participating has forfeited any of its liberty of action.

May I say one or two general words before I sit down? This is the first debate that we have had on foreign affairs for some months, and we shall no doubt have several more as a new Session proceeds. At the present moment the world is very sadly disordered and awry. The tempers of human beings and of Governments and of peoples are all so strained, and are affected by so many conflicting influences and emotions, that less than ever to-day is it possible in my view to rest on short and easy generalizations. There is really no simple, positive, short-cut answer to the dangerous and complex political problems by which the world to-day is beset; and if anybody attempts to give a short-cut and a simple answer, you may be almost certain that the answer is misleading and wrong.

There is another reflection that I would, with diffidence, offer, and it is this. I think it is always extremely difficult for one nation to be quite sure that it appreciates truly all the forces by which another nation is moved. Whatever the appearances of any question, it may well be that they are in fact making improper allowances for the causes and influences from which the action of other nations flows. At the present moment no doubt all of us look with wistful longing to the League of Nations, and we are all too often and all too sadly conscious of the great gulf that exists between what I may call the spirit of the League and the spirit of man in many parts of the world. And when people here talk about amendment of the Covenant, many people naturally feel that what is more needed is the more fundamental amendment of the spirit of man to bring that spirit into closer harmony. It is indeed not the letter of the Covenant but the spirit which cries out for change.

But while that is all true, and strong as is the desire for peace among our people, and I believe among all the peoples, or most of the peoples, of the world, the desire to strengthen the League is itself based upon the desire for peace; and I venture to think that the condemnation of those who were responsible for getting them into a war which in the broad judgement of the nation might rightly have been avoided, and of which no man could foretell the end, would not be any less severe because it had resulted from some policy which could claim the support of the letter of the Covenant, drawn up under conditions totally different from those which prevail to-day. And therefore my last observation is this. The burden that rests to-day upon those who direct the foreign policy of this country, and who wish to have regard both to this country's obligations as a loyal Member of the League and also this country's real desire for peace, is not an easy one. And yet that double obligation to the best of our ability we have so far sought faithfully to discharge, and we shall continue to do so. And I have not much doubt that along the lines on which we have sought and are seeking to discharge it, we do enjoy, and I hope shall continue to enjoy, the support of the overwhelming majority of the country.

17

THE PURSUIT OF PEACE

17 February 1938

[Since 1936 the reform of the League Covenant had been under discussion by a special Committee of Twenty-eight, sitting at Geneva. A report presented to the Committee on January 31st, 1938, by Lord Cranborne, British Under-Secretary for Foreign Affairs, clearly set out the different conceptions which existed concerning the nature of the League. Some persons put their trust in a coercive League, others in a League which carried no obligation to apply sanctions, and yet others in a League of intermediate type which might use coercion in certain circumstances. Simultaneously with discussions for the reform of the League, attempts were being initiated to bring about an improvement in relations between Great Britain and Italy, and the Government of the latter country pressed with increasing insistency for the immediate opening of conversations. A debate on British foreign policy, particularly in relation to the League of Nations, initiated in the House of Lords by Lord Arnold, was wound up on the second day by Lord Halifax.]

MY LORDS, as so often happens, the Government policy has been the target of criticisms, some friendly, some less friendly, from a variety of different angles. In so far as speeches have been concerned with the League of Nations, there have been those who have found fault with the Government policy for being too weak, and who would wish to go further, and act with far greater firmness in connexion with Article 16[1]. There are others who frankly regard Article 16, and the other Articles connected with it, as dangerous and provocative, and as a genuine hindrance to that international co-operation which they wish to see.

Nearly everybody has a natural tendency to think, and is rather pleased to think, he is either more virtuous or more perspicacious than his neighbours. But the wise man is he who can combine in just measure the qualities of both idealism and realism. Those two attributes, let me say in passing, are not by any means incompatible, and it would be most unfortunate for human life if they were. For most

[1] See page 24, note 1.

human life consists in reconciliations, and the whole of human life would stop unless it were possible for us to make some effective working reconciliation between realities which are often ugly and ideals which, as has been well said to-day, are the foundation on which all progress depends.

The facts as to these so-called coercive Articles of the Covenant are plain enough to see, and it is quite inevitable, in my judgement, that we should draw differing conclusions from them. It is quite possible to recognize disagreeable facts, and yet to doubt whether the right conclusions are drawn from them. If I may give an example, nobody feels more strongly than I do how vulnerable to-day is the position of the League with these coercive Articles, so-called, in the Covenant; and yet one is bound to recognize how limited to-day is the power of the League of Nations to enforce them. The noble Lord, Lord Allen, has said, 'But look how successful was the Nyon Conference; there you had the principle of the League of Nations in operation, with immediate success.' And he said that the reason was that the will to act was there. Exactly; that was the whole point; and it is just when you get a situation in which the will to act is there that the League of Nations principle—collective security—will work. It is just because the will to act is not always there with all nations that it will not always work. We must all be prepared to recognize that fact.

No one is more sensible than His Majesty's Government of the complications caused by the non-universality of the League. I would make great sacrifices to redeem the League from that truncated state. But are we sure there is no ground for the fear that if, moved by those considerations, you were to follow the course of expunging Article 16 from the Covenant, you might find yourselves unwittingly weakening, if not destroying for years to come, the whole conception of international order which the Articles in question were designed to promote? It is quite certain that you would get no agreement upon any such course. My conclusion, as is also that of very many of your Lordships who are much wiser than I, is that the Advisory Committee of the League was wise, having regard to the widely differing views held in the Committee on these matters, when it decided to adjourn and give further opportunity for consideration. I am prepared to say no more at this stage than has already been stated on the subject on behalf of His Majesty's Government. . . .

The noble Lord, Lord Arnold, in the course of his speech yesterday made a statement which I think is sufficiently important to deserve a specific reference. He was arguing the case for isolation in contrast to the Covenant, and he used these words:

'. . . under isolation there is a very good chance of keeping out of the next war, whereas under League policy there is no such chance at all. Under League policy whenever war comes, wherever it is or whatever it is about, Great Britain is bound to be in it—and not only in the next European war, but in all European wars.'

He went on to say:

'I find it difficult myself within the limits of temperate language to find the right adjective for such a policy.'

I almost felt bound to borrow those last words as indicative of my own feeling towards such a statement.

I do not want to weary your Lordships, but I think this is important enough for me to remind your Lordships of how the Foreign Secretary, some fifteen months ago, defined quite clearly—and your Lordships will not have forgotten it—the military obligations of this country in a now not unfamiliar speech at Leamington.[1] I do not know that I need quote his definition to your Lordships, but noble Lords will remember that he there defined them in quite specific terms. I make this assertion with complete precision: that there are no other military commitments of this country, and that in every other case His Majesty's Government would be wholly free to act as they might, in all the circumstances of the time, think right. I do not, however, agree that it is either possible or even always desirable for any country to state precisely when it would or would not feel it right to enter upon armed resistance. I am quite certain that it is not possible. Unless you are prepared to say, 'I will always

[1] See page 75, note 1.

fight when the Covenant is attacked anywhere', or 'I will never fight unless I am directly attacked'—unless you are prepared to take one of those two extreme positions, there is always bound to be ground between them in which His Majesty's Government of the day must judge whether they will advise the country to fight or not. . . .

The policy of isolation is attractive if you think it will work, just as retreat into a monastery has through history offered attraction to anxious souls tormented by the insoluble problems of the world. But those who went into a monastery were at least sure that, when they got there, they were out of the storm. I am not sure that any great nation can feel the same degree of assurance as those early pious and devoted men. Therefore, while I share, as every one of your Lordships shares, repugnance to war and conviction of the need for public opinion being behind any war, I cannot feel that it is either politically practicable or morally justifiable for this country to pretend that it can disinterest itself in what goes on in the great world outside.

There is a not infrequent tendency to think and to speak of international affairs in terms of domestic politics. What I mean is this. In domestic politics the Government are free to reach their decisions and, subject to criticism and attack and possible defeat, to act on their decisions, taking the risk. They can do it. But in international affairs there are only three ways that I know in which things can be settled. There is the way of agreement, there is the way of war, and there is the way of the fear of war. It takes at least two parties to make agreements, and therefore it does not lie with one party alone to enforce that agreement.

During these last years every one of us knows only too well that of the necessity for agreement, and of the fact that advance is only possible by agreement, we have had abundant and all too much evidence. I would only say this about the kind of course that has been more than once pressed on His Majesty's Government for more vigorous action here, there, or elsewhere, that it might or might not have been successful but it certainly would not have been successful by way of agreement. When you rule out the possibility of agreement in international affairs you bring nearer the only alternative we all wish to avoid, which is war. Let us not forget that, whatever be the place in our philosophy we give to the League of Nations, the League of Nations itself is only a great means to the greater end of international peace, and if it is possible to reach agreements which really offer international appeasement through machinery other than the League, I can hardly suppose there would be any Member of the League so shortsighted as to grudge that conclusion. I do not wish to see the world divided into *blocs* of democratic and non-democratic States, and His Majesty's Government have repeatedly made it plain that they earnestly desire world appeasement to which all nations have got to make their contributions and to which, on such conditions, we should be very willing to make ours.

I agree that in such discussions on these subjects as might be undertaken there must be no jealous balancing or bargaining items one against another, for that way, I think, lies only irritation, suspicion, and disappointment. Rather, I think, must these matters be approached from the angle that all nations must be prepared to make a contribution to that which is the common object of each; and His Majesty's Government would hope that all those who are concerned would be prepared to meet, as opportunity offered, in a spirit of willing determination to make the fullest contribution that might rightly lie in their power towards the end that all, I hope, desire to secure—namely, that of a full and peaceful understanding. I hope it is not necessary for any spokesman of His Majesty's Government to say that, in any efforts we may make to reach such understandings, nothing is further from the thought of His Majesty's Government than an attempt to impair the smooth working of the Berlin–Rome axis, any more than in any conversations we might have, or that might be held elsewhere, we should ascribe to Germany or to Italy any Machiavellian project of trying to interrupt the close relations happily existing to-day between ourselves and France.

. . . .

May I sum up what I have tried to say in a few sentences?

The broad purpose of the foreign policy of any Government of this country must be to pursue that which is the greatest of all British interests, namely peace; and if at any time one hundred per cent. success in that pursuit is impossible—and that is not a matter that lies wholly in the hands of any British Government—it will still remain their object, I hope, to protect as much of the cause of peace as they may be able to do. We believe, not less strongly than any one of your Lordships, that the future of the world depends upon its willingness to prefer the way of reason and law in international affairs to the use of force. But inasmuch as the world never stands still, we have to be on our guard to see that the assertion of these principles is not distorted into an attempt to obstruct all change, which is one of the primary laws of all human life. I agree that not the least of the problems that are to-day confronting us is to make provision for the security of peace, which may not exclude peaceful revision and change, where such may be rightly required.

I do not believe, and I have never believed, in the imminence of war, and in more directions than one I believe time to be on the side of peace. Greater progress would in my judgement be made if we could rid our minds of the catastrophic conception of Europe always on the brink of the abyss, which I think is itself largely responsible for maintaining the background which makes the whole picture look so dark. As I see it, the truth is that Europe is not so much dangerous as confused. For years since the War, Europe sought, in appearance at least, to build its policy upon the League; and it is naturally disturbing when that basis is the object of such direct and open challenge as it is to-day. None of these considerations is absent from the mind of His Majesty's Government, and I hope I have said enough to show that we are very sensible to the force of all the arguments that may be urged from all the different angles of this highly complex collection of problems of which the world to-day is made up. I can only say that in face of the sharply conflicting advice that is tendered to His Majesty's Government from many different quarters in this House, representing as it does sharp differences of opinion outside, they will relax no efforts that they are able to make, by whatever machinery seems to them most appropriate, to remove misunderstandings that endanger peace, and to labour in support of those things that may reinforce it.

18

THE AUSTRIAN ANSCHLUSS. I

14 March 1938

[The statement made in the House of Lords by Lord Halifax (who had succeeded on February 25th, 1938, to the post of Secretary of State for Foreign Affairs vacated by the resignation of Mr. Eden) was simultaneously read to the House of Commons by the Prime Minister, Mr. Neville Chamberlain. The narrative of events which it contains starts from the meeting of Dr. Schuschnigg, the Austrian Chancellor, with Herr Hitler at Berchtesgaden on February 12th. At that meeting the Austrian Chancellor found himself confronted with demands for the appointment of three Nazi leaders to Cabinet posts and for the immediate legalization of Nazi activities. To both demands he was compelled to yield under the threat of German invasion. A new Austrian Cabinet was formed in which a Nazi, Herr von Seyss-Inquart, was given the key portfolio of Minister of the Interior.]

Government Statement

MY LORDS, the main sequence of events of the last few days will be familiar to the House, but with the permission of noble Lords I will make a statement upon them in fairly full terms. The results of the meeting at Berchtesgaden on February 12 between the German and Austrian Chancellors was stated by the former to be an extension of the framework of the July, 1936, Agreement. Noble Lords will not need to be reminded that that Agreement provided, *inter alia*, for the recognition of the independence of Austria by Germany and the recognition by Austria of the fact that she was a German State. Whatever, therefore, were the results of the Berchtesgaden meeting, it is clear that the agreement reached was still on the basis of the independence of Austria.

On Wednesday of last week[1] Herr von Schuschnigg decided that the best way to put an end to the uncertainties of the internal situation in his country was to hold a plebiscite under which the people could decide the future of their country, for which provision is made in the Austrian Constitution of 1934. This decision on the part of the Austrian Chancellor was unwelcome to the German Government, as it also was to the Austrian National Socialists themselves.

[1] March 9th.

Government Statement

Matters appear to have come to a head on the morning of March 11, when Herr von Seyss-Inquart, who had been appointed Minister of the Interior as a result of the Berchtesgaden meeting, together with his colleague Dr. Glaise-Horstenau, presented an ultimatum to the Chancellor. They demanded the abandonment of the plebiscite and threatened that, if this was refused, the Nazis would abstain from voting and could not be restrained from causing serious disturbances during the poll. The two Ministers also demanded changes in the Provincial Governments and other bodies. They required, so I am informed, an answer from the Chancellor before one o'clock in the afternoon.

The Chancellor declined to accept this ultimatum, but he offered a compromise whereby a second plebiscite should be held later with regular voting lists. In the meantime he said that he would be prepared to make it clear that voters might vote for his policy but against him personally, in order to prove that the plebiscite was not a personal question of his remaining in office. Later that day, feeling himself to be under threat of civil war and of possible military invasion, the Chancellor gave way to the two Ministers and agreed to cancel the plebiscite on condition that the tranquillity of the country was not disturbed by the Nazis. There seems to be little doubt that this offer was referred by the two Ministers to Germany. In any event, the reply which they returned was that the offer was insufficient and that Herr Schuschnigg must resign in order to be replaced by Herr von Seyss-Inquart. It appears that the Austrian Chancellor was given until 4.30 p.m., Greenwich time, in which to reply, and was informed that, if his reply was not satisfactory, German troops would be ordered to move at 5 p.m. This fact seems to show that Germany was behind the ultimatum.

Later in the day a fresh ultimatum was delivered, which appears to have been brought from Germany by aeroplane. The demands made were the resignation of the Chancellor, his replacement by the Minister of the Interior, a new Cabinet of which two-thirds were to be National Socialists, the Austrian Legion to be re-admitted to the country and given the duty of keeping order in Vienna, and the total

Government Statement readmission of the Nazi Party. A reply was required before 6.30 p.m., Greenwich time. To these demands the Chancellor announced a little later, on the wireless, that, in view of the German threatened invasion, he had yielded in order to avoid the shedding of German blood. He said that he wished the world to know that the President and he had yielded to force, and that Austrian troops had been instructed to oppose no resistance to German troops if and when the latter crossed the frontier. The subsequent entry of German troops into Austria and the visit of the German Chancellor to Linz will be known to your Lordships.

His Majesty's Government have throughout been in the closest touch with the situation. I saw the German Foreign Minister on March 10 and addressed to him a grave warning upon the Austrian situation and upon what appeared to be the policy of the German Government in regard to it. In particular, I told him that His Majesty's Government attached the greatest importance to all measures being taken to ensure that the plebiscite was carried out without interference or intimidation. Later, on March 11, our Ambassador in Berlin registered a protest in strong terms with the German Government against such use of coercion backed by force against an independent State in order to create a situation incompatible with its national independence. Such action, Sir Nevile Henderson pointed out, was bound to produce the gravest reactions of which it would be impossible to foretell the issue. Earlier that day my right honourable friend the Prime Minister made earnest representations in the same sense to the German Minister of Foreign Affairs, with whom I also had two further interviews on that day. To these protests the German Government replied in a letter addressed to His Majesty's Ambassador in Berlin by Baron von Neurath.

I think I should read the terms of the communication in full. They are as follows:

'*Monsieur l'Ambassadeur,*

'In your letter of March 11th Your Excellency stated that news had reached the British Government that a German ultimatum had been delivered in Vienna demanding the resignation of the Austrian Chan-

Government Statement

cellor, his substitution by the Minister of the Interior, the formation of a new Cabinet with a two-thirds majority of National Socialist members, and the readmission of the Austrian Legion. Should this news be correct, the British Government protested against such coercion by force against an independent State in order to create a situation incompatible with its national independence.

'In the name of the German Government I must state in reply that the British Government is not within its right in claiming the role of a protector of the independence of Austria. In the course of the diplomatic conversations regarding the Austrian question the German Government have never left the British Government in doubt that the form of the relations between the Reich and Austria can only be regarded as an internal affair of the German people which is no concern of third Powers. It is superfluous to recapitulate the historical and political bases of this standpoint.

'For this reason the German Government must from the outset reject as inadmissible the protest lodged by the British Government, even though only conditional. At the same time, in view of the information quoted in your letter that the Reich Government had made demands of the character of an ultimatum in Vienna, the German Government does not desire to omit, in the interests of truth, to make the following statement respecting the events of the last few days.

'A few weeks ago the German Chancellor, recognizing the dangers resulting from the intolerable position which had arisen in Austria, initiated a conversation with the then Austrian Chancellor. The aim was to make yet another attempt to meet these dangers by agreement upon measures which should ensure a calm and peaceful development in consonance with the interests of both countries and with those of the whole German people. The Berchtesgaden agreement, had it been loyally carried out on the Austrian side in the spirit of the conversation of February 12th, would in fact have guaranteed such a development. Instead of this, the former Austrian Federal Chancellor, on the evening of March 9th, announced the surprising decision, taken on his own sole authority, to hold within a period of a few days a plebiscite, which, having regard to the surrounding circumstances and in particular the detailed plans for the carrying out of the plebiscite, was intended to have, as it could only have, as its purpose the political repression of the overwhelming majority of the population of Austria. This proceeding, standing as it did in flagrant contradiction to the Berchtesgaden agreement, led as might have been foreseen to an extremely critical development of the internal situation in Austria. It was only natural that those members of the Austrian Government who had taken no part in the decision to hold a plebiscite should raise the strongest protest against it. In consequence there ensued a Cabinet crisis in Vienna, which in the course of March 11th led to the resignation of the former Federal Chancellor and the formation of a new Government.

'It is not true that forcible pressure on the course of these developments

Government Statement

was exercised by the Reich. In particular the statement subsequently spread by the former Federal Chancellor—to the effect that the German Government had delivered an ultimatum with a time-limit to the Federal President, in accordance with which he was to appoint as Federal Chancellor one of certain proposed candidates and construct the Government in conformity with the proposals of the German Government, failing which the entry of German troops into Austria would have to be contemplated—is pure imagination. As a matter of fact the question of the despatch of military and police forces from the Reich was first raised by the fact that the newly-formed Austrian Government addressed to the Government of the Reich, in a telegram which has already been published in the Press, an urgent request that, for the re-establishment of peace and order and for the prevention of bloodshed, German troops should be despatched as soon as possible. Faced with the directly threatening danger of a bloody civil war in Austria, the Government of the Reich decided to meet the appeal then addressed to it.

'Such being the case, it is completely inconceivable that the conduct of the German Government, as is stated in your letter, could lead to unforeseeable consequences. A general review of the political situation is given in the Proclamation which the Chancellor of the German Reich addressed at noon to-day to the German people. In this situation dangerous consequences could only come into play if an attempt should be made by any third party, in contradiction to the peaceful intentions and legitimate aims of the Reich, to exercise on the development of the situation in Austria an influence inconsistent with the right of the German people to self-determination.'

Accept, etc.,
FREIHERR VON NEURATH.

I do not, my Lords, wish to enter into any long argument as regards the historical sequence of events described by Baron von Neurath, but I am bound at once to refute his statement to the effect that His Majesty's Government were not within their rights in interesting themselves in the independence of Austria, and that as, in the opinion of the German Government, relations between Austria and Germany are a purely internal affair, His Majesty's Government, as a third party, have no concern in them. The interest of His Majesty's Government in this question cannot, however, on any tenable ground be denied. In the first place, Great Britain and Austria are both Members of the League, and both were signatories, as was also the German Government, of treaties which provided that the independence of Austria was inalienable except with the consent of the Council of the

Government Statement

League of Nations. Quite apart from this, His Majesty's Government are, and must always be, interested in developments in Central Europe, particularly events such as those which have just taken place, if only for the reasons stated by the Prime Minister only a fortnight ago, that the object of all their policy has been to assist in the establishment of a sense of greater security and confidence in Europe, and that that object must inevitably be helped or hindered by events in any part of Europe.

Throughout these events His Majesty's Government have remained in the closest touch with the French Government, and the French Government have, I understand, also entered a strong protest in Berlin on similar lines to that lodged by His Majesty's Ambassador. In the judgement of His Majesty's Government the methods adopted throughout these events call for the severest condemnation, and have administered a profound shock to all who are interested in the preservation of European peace. It follows that what has passed cannot fail to have prejudiced the hope of His Majesty's Government of removing misunderstandings between nations and promoting international co-operation. It might seem unnecessary to refute rumours that His Majesty's Government had given consent, if not encouragement, to the idea of the absorption of Austria by Germany, were there not evidence that these are being sedulously put about in many quarters. There is, of course, no foundation whatever for these rumours. The statement which I have already made shows clearly that His Majesty's Government emphatically disapprove, as they have always disapproved, actions such as those of which Austria has been made the scene.

The attitude of Czechoslovakia to these events is a matter of general interest, and in this connexion I can give the House the following information:—The Czech Government have officially informed His Majesty's Government that, though it is their earnest desire to live on the best possible neighbourly relations with the German Reich, they have followed with the greatest attention the development of events in Austria between the date of the Austro-German Agreement of July, 1936, up to the present day. I am informed

Government Statement that Field-Marshal Goering on March 11 gave a general assurance to the Czech Minister in Berlin—an assurance which he expressly renewed later on behalf of Herr Hitler—that it would be the earnest endeavour of the German Government to improve German–Czech relations. In particular, on March 12 Field-Marshal Goering informed the Czech Minister that German troops marching into Austria had received the strictest orders to keep at least fifteen kilometres from the Czech frontier. On the same day the Czechoslovak Minister in Berlin was assured by Baron von Neurath that Germany considered herself bound by the German–Czechoslovak Arbitration Convention of October, 1925.

19

THE AUSTRIAN ANSCHLUSS. II

16 March 1938

[Two days later Lord Halifax made the following reply in a debate in the House of Lords on a motion of Lord Snell, who called attention to the situation created by the recent developments in Austria.]

MY LORDS, the problem of Austria has been with us always ever since the War ended with the break-up of the Austro-Hungarian monarchy, leaving a small German Austria stranded in the Danubian plains, with Hungary, Czechoslovakia, Rumania, and Yugoslavia around her as entirely independent countries. I do not dwell upon that problem here and now, but I assert that, faced with it, the attitude of successive British Governments has been quite consistent. They have never supposed that the *status quo* in Austria could necessarily be maintained for all time. They have been perfectly willing to recognize the special interest of the German Government in the relations between Germany and Austria. Therefore they have been perfectly willing to contemplate revision of the Peace Treaties. Whatever may have passed between General Goering and myself, or other German leaders and myself, in Germany—which was and must remain confidential—I have never in any conversation that I have had with German leaders taken any other line but this: that, while I did not suppose that anyone in this country was concerned to maintain the *status quo* in Europe for all time, what they were concerned to see was that no changes should be made in Europe by violence, or by something approaching violence, that might lead to incalculable consequences.

It is that against which we have always protested, because, whatever may be the merits or the demerits of the issues involved from the point of view of the German Government on the one hand or other Governments on the other hand, this at least was certain and quite incontrovertible: that any such action involving violent solution was bound, as has been repeatedly said during these last days, to administer a most rude and a most grave shock to European confidence. It was, indeed, the desire to avoid such sharp disturbance, I suppose, that in part moved the framers of the Treaties to do what they did. They recognized the special position of Austria and the peculiar problem that it represented owing to its purely German character. They foresaw, I imagine, that Austria might at some time wish to join Germany. But they also realized that such a union, involving, as it would, the transfer of something like 32,000 square miles of territory and something like 7,000,000 human beings from one sovereignty to another, would cause a serious and, in certain cases, a dangerous shifting of the balance of power in that part of Europe which had been the most unsettled by the War—namely, those territories which had previously constituted the old Austro-Hungarian Monarchy.

The framers of the Treaties accordingly stipulated, in effect, that the change, if desired, should only be brought about after the Council of the League had carefully considered the difficulties and the dangers that were involved, and had decided that those could be surmounted without endangering the paramount interest of European peace and European stability. Events have moved very differently.... Whether those events should be judged to have been inevitable or not, it is the ruthless application of power politics that has so profoundly shocked the world and is responsible for the grave apprehension that exists in so many quarters to-day.

I do not fancy that any British policy short of war could have checked the events of the last ten days. The world has been brought, therefore, face to face with the extremely ugly truth that neither treaty texts nor International Law have any influence when dealing with power politics, and that in that sphere, force, and force alone, decides. I say that quite objectively and, I hope, without passion, merely as a statement of a plain fact. It was suggested that the matter might usefully be referred to the League of Nations. I have, of course, had to give some thought before this debate to that suggestion. The juridical position of Austria as she existed up to a few days ago was that of an independent State which was bound by treaty not to alienate that independence without the consent of the Council of the League. That independence, in complete disregard of treaty provisions, has disappeared overnight, and the world, therefore, has been presented with a *fait accompli* in a fashion and in a setting of accompanying circumstance for which I can recall no parallel in history. But none the less, nothing that the League can do can undo what has been done, and I confess that I can see no good to be gained at this juncture for the League or for any of the great purposes the League represents, by bringing this matter before the League tribunal. Nothing short of war can put back the clock, and States Members of the League are not prepared to go to war on this issue.

Those facts, I suggest, must be perfectly squarely faced; and the conclusion that I reach is that the League, though it has a perfect legal right to interest itself in the question, cannot conceivably do anything at this moment which would compel Nazi Germany to turn back from the course on which she has now embarked. His Majesty's Government are therefore bound to recognize that the Austrian State has now been abolished as an international entity and is in process of being entirely absorbed into the German Reich, and that this is happening indeed without waiting for the plebiscite, the result of which, in view of the circumstances in which it is going to be held, is a foregone conclusion.

The noble Lord who spoke last addressed some remarks to the consequences of what has passed upon the lot of many in Austria who are held to be out of sympathy with the new régime. I think there was some report in the public Press this morning of what my honourable friend the Parliamentary Under-Secretary for Foreign Affairs had said in another place last night, which perhaps I may in substance repeat again to your Lordships. The representations on the subject of the need for moderation in the treatment of Jews and Socialists and of the supporters of Dr. Schuschnigg in Austria, which were referred to by my honourable friend, were made on the personal initiative, with the approval of His Majesty's Government, of our Ambassador in Berlin. I think that noble

Lords will agree with me that that was on the whole the wisest manner in which such representations could be made, and in view of their non-official character there was no question of an official assurance in reply being either expected or given. At the same time instructions were also sent to our Minister in Vienna to take any opportunity that he could to impress on those there in authority the desirability of exercising restraint in dealing with the persons to whom I have referred.

. . . . . .

I would like to say something about Czechoslovakia. No one who looks at a map can be blind to the new position that has been created for that country by what has passed, or to the significance that in certain circumstances these events might hold for that country and for Europe. It is true that certain assurances have been given to the Czechoslovak Government by the German Government. When I learned of those assurances I at once took steps to convey to the German Government that His Majesty's Government took note of them and would be glad of the German Government's permission to communicate them to Parliament. That permission having been accorded, I placed your Lordships, as my right honourable friend the Prime Minister placed another place, in possession of the actual terms of the assurances so given. By these assurances, solemnly given and more than once repeated, we naturally expect the German Government to abide. And if indeed they desire to see European peace maintained, as I earnestly hope they do, there is no quarter of Europe in which it is more vital that undertakings should be scrupulously respected.

Your Lordships will perhaps have noticed in the public Press the grave words uttered on these anxieties by Mr. Churchill and others. You will have heard the grave words uttered in this place this afternoon by Lord Cecil on the same subject. These words deserve the careful attention of His Majesty's Government, as also do the definite suggestions that have been made as to the methods by which we should deal with the situation with which we are faced. The House will not expect me to-day to say more in regard to these and other suggestions than that His Majesty's Government are giving, and will give, to them their most careful consideration; nor I fancy is it necessary to assure the House that we are in close consultation with the French Government on all these questions.

To appraise contemporary events is always difficult, for judgement is affected by many factors which are in their nature more transitory than the events themselves. And, as I have said, it is the method employed to effect these changes that has so deeply stirred public opinion in all countries outside Germany. However difficult it may be for German thought to understand it, it is the fact that the conscience of a great part of the civilized human race has been made suddenly aware of a naked contradiction between those things which they value and those things of which the methods of these last days seem to be the outward sign and substance. One thing stands out above all else for those who will try to view these events objectively. That is the damage that has been wrought to the stock of international confidence, which even before then was none too great. Many of your Lordships have laboured, as have His Majesty's Government and many in other countries, in the cause of the removal of international misunderstanding and the establishment of conditions in which co-operation and trust might, for the general good of men, replace disunity and that suspicion which is the natural child of fear. Yet there is not one of us who can deny how seriously our hopes have been belied and prejudiced by what has passed.

It is natural that, in these circumstances, there should be expression of opinion from different quarters as to what it is the duty of His Majesty's Government to do. The responsibility for decision in the light of all the facts, known and unknown, so far as they can be brought to judgement, rests, as it must, upon His Majesty's Government. But though there be diversity of counsel, as is inevitable, or even perhaps criticism as to the action taken, I do not believe, and I believe less than ever after this debate, that there is any shadow of disagreement, or any question at all, as to what must be the objectives of British policy; and I do not believe that anyone would differ from my statement of them. First, I would say that we must seek, in face of the present situation, so to conduct our foreign policy that it may deserve and command the support in this country of a united people and, in the Dominions, of a united Empire. Secondly, while relaxing no exertion in the pursuit of real peace wherever it may be found, it must be our purpose to reassert the claims of International Law as opposed to the exercise of force in the settlement of international disputes. To this end it behoves us to do all that lies in our power to strengthen the forces on the side of settling international differences by negotiation rather than by any other method.

Next, we must do everything to bring it about that means should be devised, whether through the machinery of the League or on lines in harmony with League principles, to direct the mind of the nations as much to the removal of injustice as to the maintenance of peace. Lastly, this country must, if our policy fulfils these purposes, show itself prepared not only by way of material and equipment, but in the spirit, determination, and discipline of its people. The Government can, and will, review the programmes for our material preparedness and the pace of the march towards their fulfilment. It is for the people to do their part, and I am satisfied that this general outline of the spirit which will, I hope, inspire the action of His Majesty's Government will command not only the assent of your Lordships' House, but also the approval and active support of the overwhelming majority of those whom Parliament represents.

20

CZECHOSLOVAKIA; BRITISH REARMAMENT

24 March 1938

[The first indication that German ambitions extended to Czechoslovakia was given in a speech made by Herr Hitler on February 12th, 1938, in which, with an obvious reference to the three and a half million Sudeten Germans, he claimed the right to exercise protection over ten million Germans living in territory adjacent to the Reich. Dr. Hodza, the Czechoslovak Premier, replied in the Chamber of Deputies that any claim by Germany to protect the Sudeten German minority was equivalent to interference in his country's internal affairs, and that Czechoslovakia, if attacked, would defend herself to the last. Nevertheless, the annexation of Austria left her southern frontier exposed and raised the question of what external support was available for the maintenance of Czechoslovak independence. Lord Halifax defined the British Government's attitude in the House of Lords, while Mr. Chamberlain made an identical statement in the House of Commons.

A White Paper on Defence, issued on March 2nd, disclosed the fact that the estimates for the three Defence Departments provided for expenditure of £343,250,000 in the coming year, an increase of £63,000,000 on the previous estimates. It surveyed the progress already made, particularly in the expansion of the Air Force, and it gave some account of the measures taken for the protection of civilians against air-raids. On March 23rd, the day before Lord Halifax made his speech, the Prime Minister met the General Council of the Trades Union Congress and appealed for their help in accelerating the defence programme.]

Government Statement

MY LORDS, His Majesty's Government have expressed the view that recent events in Austria have created a new situation, and think it right to state the conclusions to which consideration of those events has led them. They have already placed on record their judgement upon the action taken by the German Government, and to that they have nothing to add. The consequences of the action, however, remain. There has been a profound disturbance of international confidence. In these circumstances the problem before Europe to which, in the opinion of His Majesty's Government, it is their most urgent duty to direct their attention, is how best to restore this shaken confidence, to maintain the

Government Statement rule of law in international affairs, and to seek peaceful solutions to questions that continue to cause anxiety.

Of these, the one necessarily most present to many minds is that concerning the relations between the Government of Czechoslovakia and the German minority in that country; and it is probable that the solution of that question, if it could be achieved, would go far to re-establish a more normal situation over an area wider than that immediately concerned. His Majesty's Government have accordingly given especial attention to this matter, and in particular they have fully considered the question whether the United Kingdom, in addition to those obligations by which she is already bound by the Covenant of the League and the Treaty of Locarno, should, as a further contribution towards preserving peace in Europe, now undertake new and specific commitments in Europe, and in particular such a commitment in relation to Czechoslovakia.

It is right that I should here remind your Lordships what our existing commitments are which might lead to the use of our arms for purposes other than our own defence and the defence of territories of other parts of the British Commonwealth of Nations. They are, first of all, the defence of France and Belgium against unprovoked aggression in accordance with our existing obligations under the Treaty of Locarno, as reaffirmed in the arrangement drawn up in London on March 19, 1936. His Majesty's Government have also obligations by treaty to Portugal, Iraq, and Egypt. Those are our definite obligations in relation to particular countries.

There remains another case in which we may have to use our arms, a case which is of a more general character but which may have no less significance. This is the case arising under the Covenant of the League, which was accurately defined by the former Foreign Secretary when he said:

> 'In addition our armaments may be used in bringing help to a victim of aggression in any case where, in our judgement, it would be proper under the provisions of the Covenant to do so.'

Such a case might, for example, include Czechoslovakia, and the ex-Foreign Secretary went on to say:

Government Statement

'I use the word "may" deliberately, since in such an instance there is no automatic obligation to take military action. It is moreover right that this should be so, for nations cannot be expected to incur automatic military obligations save for areas where their vital interests are concerned.'

His Majesty's Government stand by these declarations. They have acknowledged that in present circumstances the ability of the League to fulfil all the functions originally contemplated for it is reduced. But this is not to be interpreted as meaning that His Majesty's Government would in no circumstances intervene as a Member of the League for the restoration of peace or the maintenance of international order if circumstances were such as to make it appropriate for them to do so. And His Majesty's Government cannot but feel that the course and development of any dispute, should such unhappily arise, would be greatly influenced by the knowledge that such action as it may be in the power of Great Britain to take will be determined by His Majesty's Government of the day in accordance with the principles laid down in the Covenant.

The question now arises whether we should go further. Should we forthwith give an assurance to France that in the event of her being called upon, by reason of German aggression on Czechoslovakia, to implement her obligations under the Franco-Czechoslovak Treaty, we would immediately employ our full military force on her behalf? Or, alternatively, should we at once declare our readiness to take immediate action in resistance to any forcible interference with the independence and integrity of Czechoslovakia, and invite any other nations, which might so desire, to associate themselves with us in such a declaration? From a consideration of these two alternatives it clearly emerges that under either of them the decision as to whether or not this country should find itself involved in war would be automatically removed from the discretion of His Majesty's Government, and the suggested guarantee would apply irrespective of the circumstances by which it was brought into operation, and over which His Majesty's Government might not have been able to exercise any control. The position is not one that

Government Statement His Majesty's Government could see their way to accept, in relation to an area where their vital interests are not concerned in the same degree as they are in the case of France and Belgium; and it is certainly not the position that results from the Covenant. For these reasons His Majesty's Government feel themselves unable to give the prior guarantee suggested.

But while plainly stating this decision I would add this. Where peace and war are concerned, legal obligations are not alone involved; and, if war broke out, it would be unlikely to be confined to those who have assumed such obligations. It would be quite impossible to say where it might end and what Governments might become involved. The inexorable pressure of facts might well prove more powerful than formal pronouncements, and in that event it would be well within the bounds of probability that other countries, besides those which were parties to the original dispute, would almost immediately be involved. This is especially true in the case of two countries like Great Britain and France, with long associations of friendship, with interests closely interwoven, devoted to the same ideals of democratic liberty, and determined to uphold them.

It remains for His Majesty's Government to state their attitude in regard to the proposal made by the Government of the U.S.S.R., that an early conference should be held for the purpose of discussion with certain other Powers of the practical measures which in their opinion the circumstances demand. His Majesty's Government would warmly welcome the assembly of any conference, at which it might be expected that all European nations would consent to be represented, and at which it might therefore be found possible to discuss matters in regard to which anxiety is at present felt. In present circumstances, however, they are obliged to recognize that no such expectation can be entertained, and the Soviet Government do not in fact appear to entertain it. Their proposal would appear to involve less a consultation with a view to settlement than a concerting of action against an eventuality that has not yet arisen. Its object would appear to be to negotiate such mutual undertakings in advance to

Government Statement

resist aggression as, for the reasons given, His Majesty's Government are unwilling to accept. Apart from this, His Majesty's Government are of opinion that the direct, but none the less inevitable, consequence of such action as is proposed by the Soviet Government, would be to aggravate the tendency towards the establishment of exclusive groups of nations, which must, in the view of His Majesty's Government, be inimical to the prospects of European peace.

Great Britain has repeatedly borne witness to the principles on which she considers the peace of the world depends. We do not believe that any stable order can be established unless, by one means or another, recognition can be secured for certain general principles. The first is that differences between nations should be resolved by peaceful settlement, and not by methods of force. The second, admittedly of no less importance, is that a peaceful settlement, to be enduring, must be based on justice. Holding these views, successive British Governments have accepted the full obligations of the Covenant of the League of Nations, and done their best to discharge them; they have acceded to special instruments designed to pledge the nations afresh to refrain from resort to aggressive war; and they have reinforced the general obligations thus undertaken by specific undertakings within the framework of the League towards countries with whom they enjoy special relations or in which they have special interest. On the other side they have constantly lent, and are prepared to continue to lend, their influence to the revision of relations between nations, established by treaty or otherwise, which appeared to demand review. They will continue, whether by way of action through the League or by direct diplomatic effort, to exert all their influence on the side of bringing to peaceful and orderly solutions any issues liable to interrupt friendly relations between nations.

So far as Czechoslovakia is concerned it seems to His Majesty's Government that now is the time when all the resources of diplomacy should be enlisted in the cause of peace. They have been glad to take note of, and in no way underrate, the definite assurances given by the German Government as to their attitude. On the other side they have

Government Statement

observed with satisfaction that the Government of Czechoslovakia are addressing themselves to the practical steps that can be taken within the framework of the Czechoslovak constitution to meet the reasonable wishes of the German minority. For their part, His Majesty's Government will at all times be ready to render any help in their power, by whatever means might seem most appropriate, towards the solution of questions likely to cause difficulty between the German and Czechoslovak Governments. In the meantime there is no need to assume the use of force or indeed to talk about it. Such talk is to be strongly deprecated. Not only can it do no good; it is bound to do harm. It must interfere with the progress of diplomacy and it must increase feelings of insecurity and uncertainty.

His Majesty's Government accept the obligations which rest upon them, and have made and are making strenuous efforts to place themselves in a position adequately to fulfil them. Nevertheless, in accordance with their expressed intention of reviewing their programme from time to time in the light of the circumstances of the time, they have considered the position afresh and have decided that still further efforts are now called for. These efforts must be devoted to increasing production and accelerating the completion of the rearmament programme. The details of that programme have been from time to time laid before Parliament. Recently in connexion with the Estimates for the Defence Departments, statements have been submitted in another place as to the steps to be taken in the next financial year. The existing programme, however, has been carried out with the intention of interfering as little as possible with normal trade. In practice, notwithstanding this limitation, an increasing degree of priority over civil work has been gradually accorded to rearmament orders, with the result that in some cases the execution of orders for home and export trade has been delayed. The additional skilled and semi-skilled labour required by the programme has occasionally had to be provided at the cost of withdrawing labour from other activities. Only by such means has it been possible to undertake the large-scale programme of production which, in spite of

Government Statement

some delays, is now continuously and rapidly increasing in volume.

His Majesty's Government had hoped that further acceleration, with its consequent interference with normal commercial work, might have been avoided; but it has been more than once made plain that the defence programme was flexible and was subject to review from time to time in the light of changes in the international situation. We have now come to the conclusion that in the present circumstances acceleration of existing plans has become essential, and moreover that there must be an increase in some parts of the programme, especially in that of the Royal Air Force and the anti-aircraft defences. In order to bring about the progress which we feel to be necessary, men and materials will be required, and rearmament work must have first priority in the nation's effort. The full and rapid equipment of the nation for self-defence must be its primary aim.

His Majesty's Government gratefully acknowledge the way in which workers and employers have co-operated in carrying out the programme hitherto. Such co-operation will be even more necessary for bringing to practical and early fruition the plans to which I have referred, and the Government are confident that they can rely on the continued help and goodwill of all concerned. In the view of the Government it is not for them to try to dictate to the great industries the detailed action which will be necessary for overcoming difficulties. It is in accordance with our traditions that these industries themselves, through their joint machinery, should work out the details in the manner which is most likely to be effective. Steps are already being taken to inform organized workers and organized employers of the nature of the demands which the accelerated plans will make upon their industries, and thus to place them in a position to devise practical methods for meeting those demands by mutual arrangements and with a minimum of Government interference. By such means it is expected that the volume of production, which in the new circumstances is not sufficient for our needs, will be substantially increased. The building operations necessary for the expansion of the three Services

Government Statement

will be expedited. This will facilitate the process of recruitment of naval, military, and Air Force personnel. The action already indicated will serve to accelerate the production of naval equipment. Similar measures will be taken for completing at the earliest date possible the erection of new factories. Further capacity with a view to advancing the output of anti-aircraft and other guns will be put in hand. This priority will also enable us to expedite the programme of air-raid precautions. The satisfactory response to the appeal for recruits in connexion with air-raid precautions is evidence of the widespread interest that is being taken throughout the country in this urgent question. By these and other measures within the Defence Departments themselves for the purpose of ensuring full and adequate co-operation with industry, His Majesty's Government are satisfied that they will be able to facilitate production and secure the necessary acceleration of the defence programme.

His Majesty's Government, however, do not differ from those who feel that the increase of armaments alone is no sure guarantee for peace. They earnestly hope that it may yet be possible to arrive at a reasonable balance of armaments by agreement rather than by free and unlimited competition. They have, on the other hand, felt it right to make their view known that, in the present state of the world, reliance upon the assertion of loyalty to the principles of the Covenant was not enough, in the absence of practical strength by which those professions might be supported. Accordingly the policy of His Majesty's Government recognizes, and is based upon, the necessity both of working untiringly to strengthen the cause of peace, and also of taking all steps requisite to make this country strong enough to meet whatever call may be made upon it. In their view the knowledge in all parts of the world that such steps are being taken with determination and dispatch will be a valuable contribution towards international reassurance.

21

THE PURPOSE OF BRITISH POLICY. I

29 March 1938

[The Government statement of March 24th, 1938, was debated in the House of Lords five days later. In the interval the National Council of Labour issued a manifesto calling for an immediate meeting of the Assembly of the League of Nations; an initiative by France, Great Britain, and Russia to bring about appeasement in Central Europe and Spain; and the raising of the embargo upon the supply of arms to the Spanish Government. After defending the maintenance of the policy of non-intervention in Spain, Lord Halifax replied as follows to the other two suggestions contained in the manifesto.]

MY LORDS, it has been suggested that His Majesty's Government should join with the French and Soviet Governments in holding an early conference for the discussion with other Powers of measures by which the European situation may be improved, and that they should bring the matter before the Assembly of the League of Nations. If I was convinced that any useful purpose would be served at the present moment by invoking the League of Nations, I can assure your Lordships that I would set the necessary machinery in motion to-morrow. It has been said that the Government were to be greatly blamed for not relying on the League at this juncture to keep the peace. We used to rely upon it; if we were once right, we are clearly wrong now. But does not that leave out of account that circumstances change, and that practical people must have regard to the changed facts?

I should like to ask what would in fact be secured by a reference to the League at this particular moment? Is it not true to say that the essential foundation of the League theory of international order was co-operation between all Powers of the world, great and small, and that it was on that basis that it was possible to contemplate coercion so unchallengeable of a would-be aggressor that he would certainly be deterred? The effectiveness of coercion depends on general consent to the rule of the Covenant. You cannot enforce that consent, and surely as practical people we have to recognize that to-day that general consent is lacking.

The first grave defection from the principles of the Covenant occurred more than six years ago in the Far East. That has been followed by events in Europe which have rudely shaken confidence, and indeed by a more recent development of the situation in the Far East, which only the niceties of judicial thought prevent from being characterized as war. But my main point is, I hope, plain, and I do not believe it is one from which any reasoning person can seriously differ. If some of the more powerful nations, for whatever reasons, are standing outside the League and are hostile to its operation, it is obvious that the League can only do one of two things. It can pass resolutions, which can only have the effect of exposing the League to failure and humiliation; or it can endeavour, with the limited resources arising from its restricted membership, to marshal the forces that are loyal to it in something very like a defensive alliance against those who stand outside. That may or may not be a good plan, but let us recognize that it is something essentially different from the Covenant, and do not let us ask support for it on the plea that it is the Covenant in another form. When that is translated into the proposal of the Labour manifesto for a joint conference of France, Russia, and ourselves, I must repeat that it does not seem to my mind that that would be a very helpful contribution to the adjustment of European difficulties, and I think that the only effect of such a policy as that would be still further to harden the lines of division which are the most dangerous impediment to better understanding.

It is surely significant of the unreal world in which the authors of that manifesto seem to live that not a word was said in it about rearmament. I accept that the Labour Party does not want war; but it is also true that they are constantly proclaiming a policy which must exert the maximum effect of provocation on other nations, and they are constantly urging us to accept what would be very like war commitments whenever any principles are infringed, and yet have nothing to say generally about the means by which such a policy as that might be adequately supported. I believe the ordinary man sees these things rather differently.

Whatever his attitude on international problems, he knows that he is looking out to-day on a very disordered world, and he is genuinely concerned, however anxious he is to reach conditions where he can see disarmament, to ensure that His Majesty's Government should push forward vigorously with measures, both to make this country secure in its own defence and also to assure it of its rightful influence in world affairs. Those efforts, as your Lordships know, His Majesty's Government are determined to make, and I believe that in them they will have the co-operation of the great bulk of the people in this country.

The British people are sometimes thought by those who do not know them to be cold and prudent and reserved. Yet I think that no people in the world is more generous, and at times impulsive, and no people would feel more uneasy if it were ever thought that they were pursuing a purely selfish policy. And, however much they want to keep out of war, they would not, I think, be well content if they thought that this country was not pulling its whole weight in getting the world straight. But the trouble is that some people think one way is the best, and other people think that another way is the best. The Labour Council would like to proceed by the way of what I may call, for brevity's sake, diplomacy by collective ultimatum. I do not think that that is a very good way. We believe in trying to make relations with individual nations better, because we think that, faced as we are with problems which interlock at all points, if you can relieve tension anywhere, you relieve it everywhere. And that is the justification of the policy of His Majesty's Government.

It is often a very good maxim to see one thing at a time, but it is essential in the affairs of to-day to see at least two things at a time. I go the whole way with those who feel that the world will never be at rest until it can turn back and found its life on the things through which alone real peace must come. I am not less anxious to see established the reign of law and to see justice enthroned above the nations. I believe in democracy, and all that democracy ought to mean, not less sincerely than many who speak so loudly in democracy's name. All these things are great causes, and they claim and command our loyalty irrespective of political parties. But, alongside these things, I cherish other ideals too—the ideal of seeing our people enjoying standards of life, and the opportunity that those standards may give to every citizen to win, in ordered freedom, the achievement of his or her personality. For these things we would spend ourselves, and all that we have, to save them for our successors. Accordingly, when I am invited in loyalty to high international causes to constitute this country the policeman of the world, I am surely bound—and everyone of you is bound—quite apart from any consideration of material capacity, to weigh the effect that such general readiness to risk war everywhere, in present circumstances and with a restricted League of Nations, must have upon the other purposes, not less honourable, that you and I are not less bound to try to serve. Therefore, if that argument is true, the decision is not so simple as some people would have us sometimes think.

After my right honourable friend's speech in another place, no one will suppose that this country rates its obligations lightly. Those to whom we have given our word know that if occasion arises we shall keep it faithfully. This country accepts all its Covenant obligations, but a distinction does undoubtedly exist between those obligations and the direct specific obligations to France and Belgium in cases of unprovoked aggression. There was no more significant passage in the statement made the other day than that wherein it was stated that 'the inexorable pressure of facts might well prove more powerful than formal pronouncements'. But, ready as this country will always be in letter and in spirit to meet the obligations that it has thought right to undertake, we shall not cease to try to point Europe to the more excellent way.

I do not believe there is any short cut, by threats or by exhortations or by resting on the theory of the balance of power or isolation or collective security or anything else which has been referred to in this debate, to reach the place where we seek to be. If we are to induce reason in others we must be reasonable ourselves. We maintain all our old friendships, which on every ground are precious to us and which in themselves constitute powerful guarantees for peace. If we can extend the circle of our friends through our present conversations with the Italian Government, by resuming old relations—unhappily but, as we hope, only temporarily interrupted—we shall render real service in my judgement to the common good.

It has been more than once said, and rightly said, that arms alone are never enough. I would say that arms and the man are both essential; and those who are asked to give their help in the matter of arms have a right to demand that policy should be based upon a moral principle that people can understand. The principle on which I would seek to see British policy based is twofold. At home we must preserve our own democracy, our institutions, our individual rights and liberties, through which alone the characteristics of our race are able to make their impact on the world. Abroad, we shall seek to uphold what we believe to be right, using all our influence to prevent the division of Europe into rival camps, and taking every opportunity to use our good offices to promote conciliation.

In looking over the field of foreign affairs I constantly find myself coming back to this country, to the home front. No Government can hope to formulate and to execute a foreign policy without the solid backing of the nation, and no policy is worth much unless the spirit of the nation is behind it, and unless the people of this country are inspired by a resolute determination to accept whatever sacrifice is necessary to make that policy succeed. We shall be judged abroad not by our policy or by our Government, but by ourselves. If we as a nation can convince others of our purpose, as of our moral and material strength, our policies will succeed. If we cannot do that, no policy, however skilfully devised, will bring salvation. I believe this nation is alive to its responsibilities. I believe that it has an instinctive insight into the things that really matter, and I believe also that once it understands how great a part in shaping the future of the world it may be this nation's destiny to play, it will respond to any effort that is demanded of it.

22

THE ANGLO-ITALIAN AGREEMENT

10 May 1938

[Proposals for the immediate opening of conversations between Britain and Italy, with a view to improving relations which had deteriorated with the continued presence of Italian troops in Spain, came before the British Cabinet on February 19th, 1938, and led to the resignation of Mr. Eden from the Foreign Office. Formal negotiations, commenced forthwith, ended in the signing of an agreement, on April 16th, for the settlement of all matters at issue between the two countries in the Mediterranean, North-East Africa, and the Middle East. Great Britain agreed that, at the forthcoming meeting of the Council of the League, she would raise the question of the recognition of the Italian Empire in Abyssinia. Italy, on her part, consented to the stipulation that the agreement should not come into force until a settlement of the Spanish question had been reached, and this was interpreted as implying the withdrawal of Italian troops from Spain. In pursuance of an undertaking by the British Government that the approval of the League of Nations would be sought for any agreement that might be arrived at, Lord Halifax formally brought the agreement to the notice of the League Council at Geneva.]

IT has always been, as is well known, in the mind of His Majesty's Government that, if and when they were able to reach an agreement with Italy, they would find a means of bringing that agreement to the notice of the League of Nations. Such an agreement has now been reached; and although its entry into force must await the fulfilment of certain conditions, I have nevertheless asked the indulgence of my colleagues for the purpose of making a statement to them on the subject, with the object of explaining to them the wider significance which may rightly attach to its conclusion. Copies of this agreement, which was signed at Rome on April 16, 1938, have been distributed to my colleagues for convenience of reference, but in any event its terms are probably already known to all present. There is, therefore, no need for me to embark on a detailed analysis of it, nor is there any need for me to expatiate on the history of Anglo-Italian relations during the few years following the Italian action in Ethiopia. The general result has been, as we know, to produce a regrettable state of tension between our two countries, the effect of which was felt not only upon our mutual relations but over a much wider field. Particularly was this so in the Mediterranean area, where it is true that, if relations between Italy and the United Kingdom are strained, the sense of security of many nations is impaired.

It has therefore been not only to their own specific interests, which run parallel in the Mediterranean and down the Red Sea to the Indian Ocean, but to the advantage also of many other countries that his Majesty's Government and the Italian Government have settled their outstanding differences and have laid down a basis which it is hoped will ensure good understanding between them in areas where their mutual interests are involved.

That is what the two Governments have sought to achieve by the conclusion of their recent agreement. Thus, although the agreement might be said to deal solely with Anglo-Italian affairs, I am convinced that the mere fact that the mutual interests of two great countries should be capable of reconciliation is significant. This fact might encourage all who wish to believe that, on a basis of reason and goodwill, international differences can be resolved. It must also react favourably upon the general sense of security not only in Europe but throughout the world. On these broad grounds, therefore, the agreement can in the view of His Majesty's Government be rightly regarded as a contribution to general peace.

Nor can His Majesty's Government fail to believe that it is the realization of this which has inspired the reception of the agreement in most countries, particularly in Europe. They have warmly appreciated the fact that the French Government have expressly welcomed it as a contribution to European peace, and that approval is also extended to it through the mouth of their chairman by the members of the Balkan Entente. The President of the United States, moreover, made a statement on the subject to the Press which was particularly gratifying to His Majesty's Government.

I should like to add a word regarding the value which His

Majesty's Government attaches to the agreement in its relation to the international situation as a whole. His Majesty's Government have close relations with many other Governments, especially the French Government, in Europe and elsewhere, but we do not regard these relations as by any means exclusive; and while strengthening existing friendships we seek always to increase their number and extend their scope. The newly signed agreement with Italy marks a further step in this direction, as well as towards the aim of the Covenant—namely, the maintenance of peace in this distracted world. For the same reason His Majesty's Government are following with interest and goodwill the progress made by the French Government in their efforts to reach a similar agreement with Italy.

The greatest purpose of the League of Nations is to promote peace in the world and to promote it by agreement. If there are differences between two countries, and these countries do not seek to solve them by agreement, the chances of their solution by war—the very alternative this great organization is designed to prevent—are brought sensibly nearer. The fact that His Majesty's Government and the Italian Government have been enabled to compose their differences by agreement entitles them to claim that they have contributed to the cause of international peace and thereby strengthened the purpose which this great Society exists to serve.

23

NON-INTERVENTION IN SPAIN

11 May 1938

[The Non-Intervention Agreement, which had been adopted in August 1936 as a means of isolating the Spanish Civil War, imposed an embargo upon supplies of war material to either of the two contending parties. This had as its consequence the withholding of belligerent rights from both, and, although the British Government put forward proposals on July 14th, 1937, for the granting of limited belligerent rights so soon as substantial progress had been made in the withdrawal of foreign nationals, the proposals remained abortive in default of the fulfilment of that condition. The continued presence of Italian contingents in General Franco's army provoked the British Labour Party to demand the raising of the embargo with the object of allowing arms to be purchased by the Spanish Republican Government. The demand became more insistent with the growing prospect of that Government's defeat. Speaking at Bristol on April 8th, 1938, Lord Halifax answered Opposition criticisms by maintaining that there were only two alternatives to non-intervention—an active support of the Spanish Government which would be countered by increased support for the other side, and a policy of strict neutrality from which the Spanish Government, having lost the command of the sea, would derive less benefit than its opponents. A month later he replied at Geneva to the Spanish Republican representative's appeal to the League Council for the re-establishment of normal international law.]

THE reference again to the Council of the Spanish question gives us an opportunity to consider once more the duties and obligations of members of the League towards these unhappy events.

One of the fundamental principles governing the relations of States to one another is that each independent State has the right to determine for itself its own form of government. How shall this principle be applied to Spain? In its origin the disturbance in Spain took the form of a military revolt against constituted authority, but within a comparatively short time it became clear that this military revolt had developed into a civil war. It follows from the right of self-determination that, when a dispute arises in one State as to how a people should be governed, other States should refrain from exercising any pressure upon the people of that State in one direction or another.

How does this apply to Spain? What are the obligations of Members of the League? We must recognize that the terms of the Covenant were not drawn up with an eye to civil war, and members therefore could not expect much guidance from its provisions. In this situation it was necessary to fall back upon general principles. It seemed to His Majesty's Government that there was incumbent on the members a paramount duty to recognize that this question was a matter wholly for the decision of the Spanish people and to refrain from assisting either side.

The position was rapidly reached where a state of belligerency existed in fact if not in name, and the normal procedure would have been for other States to assume the rights and obligations of neutrality, and for them to recognize that the two parties to the Spanish war were possessed of the rights and obligations of belligerents. If this had been done, it would have been for each State to decide either to allow munitions to be supplied from its territory to both belligerents, subject to the right of either belligerent to prevent, if possible, his opponent from receiving them, or to forbid such supplies to both belligerents.

In fact, as is known, a different policy was adopted by European countries. That policy is defined in the Non-Intervention Agreement by which participating Governments agreed to prohibit the dispatch of war material from, or its transit through, their countries to Spain. This undertaking was later extended with the object of preventing the nationals of participating countries from leaving their territory for the purpose of taking part in the conflict.

In both cases—neutrality and non-intervention—the principle of showing no favour to one side as against the other is upheld. His Majesty's Government claim that to supply arms to one side while refusing them to the other would contravene this principle.

There are two reasons why a policy of non-intervention, including a prohibition of the supply of arms, was preferred by His Majesty's Government to one of neutrality as hitherto understood. The first reason was the danger of the conflict developing into a general European war. The second was the presence of foreign participants on both sides in the Spanish conflict. This is the reason for the British plan presented to the Non-Intervention Committee last year, under which the grant of belligerent rights, albeit in a restricted form, was linked up with the question of the removal of the foreign participants from Spain.

Much criticism has been directed against the policy of non-intervention. We have never minimized the extent of the breaches that have taken place on both sides, but we claim that the policy has been at least partially successful. As Mr. Eden said when addressing the Assembly of the League last year, a leaky dam may yet serve its purpose. If in our second object—the leaving of the Spanish people to decide for themselves—we have only partially succeeded, our first and primary object—the maintenance of European peace—has been wholly successful.

We have been glad to note the encouragement given on two former occasions by the Council to the work of the Non-Intervention Committee. We shall continue our efforts, and we believe that the appeasement in the Mediterranean which will result from the Anglo-Italian Agreement and from the conversations which have been initiated between the French and Italian Governments will contribute to the eventual success of the Committee's plan for the withdrawal of the foreign participants.

For the reasons I have given, His Majesty's Government remain convinced that non-intervention is not only the best but the only practical policy, and they intend to persevere with that policy.

They deeply deplore the tragic loss of life which is inseparable from modern war, and their sympathy with the Spanish people is the more profound as the struggle which is raging in Spain has all the added bitterness of fratricidal strife. From the outbreak of this tragic struggle His Majesty's Government and, indeed, the British people have felt the necessity of doing whatever lay in their power to relieve the sufferings which have fallen upon the Spanish people. This necessity is no less imperious to-day, and we would urge that no effort should be spared to mitigate the disasters of this unhappy war to the wounded and the non-combatants.

His Majesty's Government appreciate the longing with which all patriotic sons of Spain must await the day when their country will no longer thus be desolated, and they would fain hope that some settlement based on reason and goodwill might soon be found to spare further agony to that unhappy country and to enable the whole Spanish people to play their full part in the community of nations with the vigour and courage which they have always shown.

The League of Nations may be held to have peculiar qualifications for acting as an organ of conciliation. If at any time there was anything which this institution could contribute towards bringing together the two contending parties in Spain, no one would be better pleased than His Majesty's Government. Moreover, I think all of us have the interests of the League and of Spain at heart, and hope that a time will come when the League may be able to play a part in the reconstruction of Spain once this unhappy strife is a thing of the past.

24

RECOGNITION OF THE ITALIAN EMPIRE. I

12 May 1938

[The decision taken by the Assembly of the League of Nations on July 4th, 1936, to abandon collective action in the Italian-Abyssinian conflict created an anomalous position. One Member State after another recognized the legality of the Italian conquest by accrediting diplomatic representatives to the King of Italy under the style of Emperor of Ethiopia. Other States still considered that recognition was the common concern of the League. In December 1937 the Netherlands Government suggested joint recognition of Italian sovereignty. The British attitude was one of suspense. Its Government resolved to consult other Members of the League before itself taking action, and undertook, under the terms of the Anglo-Italian Agreement, to clarify the situation at the forthcoming meeting of the League Council at Geneva. With this object Lord Halifax addressed the Council, inviting it to express the view that the question of the recognition of Italy's position in Abyssinia was one that each State should decide for itself.]

HIS Majesty's Government in the United Kingdom have taken the initiative in placing on the agenda of this meeting of the Council the consequences arising out of the existing situation in Ethiopia. In the letter which has been circulated to members of the Council they have drawn attention to the anomalous situation arising from the fact that certain Members of the League recognize that the Italian Government exercise sovereignty over Ethiopia, or have taken action which might be held to imply such recognition, while other States Members of the League have not done so.

His Majesty's Government in the United Kingdom have desired to take an opportunity for consultation between Members of the League before they, as an individual member, took a decision as to the question of the formal recognition of the Italian position. In taking up this attitude His Majesty's Government were influenced by the consideration that, while no express obligation had been assumed by Members of the League, yet, in view of the common action which Members of the League had agreed to take in the dispute between Italy and Ethiopia, the final recognition of

Italy's position in the latter country by one Member of the League was a matter of concern to other Members.

In raising the question in this manner His Majesty's Government do not wish to make any criticism, either express or implied, of those Members of the League who have already signified to the Italian Government their recognition that Italy is to-day exercising sovereignty in Ethiopia, whether by formal notification or by some action which might be held to amount to such recognition. His Majesty's Government appreciate that it was open to Members of the League to regard the Assembly resolution of July 4, 1936, as closing the question in so far as they were concerned; and, having regard to the action taken by so many States which are perfectly loyal to the League, His Majesty's Government do not think that the various steps which the League has taken in the course of the Italo-Ethiopian dispute can be held to constitute any binding obligation upon Member States to withhold recognition until a unanimous decision has been taken. Accordingly, I think it right plainly to state the view of His Majesty's Government that the situation is one in which Members of the League may, without disloyalty, take such action at such time as may seem to them appropriate.

In raising this question at this meeting His Majesty's Government have in view a strictly limited objective. It is far from their purpose to suggest that the Council, or any Member of the League, should condone the action by which the Italian Government have acquired their present position in Ethiopia and which the League, in corporate action, thought it right to condemn. Nor do they propose that any organ of the League should modify the resolutions and decisions which it took in the earlier stages of the dispute. On this issue we have declared our judgement in plain terms and we cannot go back upon it. His Majesty's Government hope, however, that other members of the Council will share their opinion that the question of the recognition of Italy's position in Ethiopia is one which every member of the League must be held entitled to decide for itself in the light of its own situation and obligations.

This would not by itself impose any obligation upon

Member States to take steps in the direction of recognition, and His Majesty's Government would in no way wish to interfere with the freedom of choice of States in this matter. The action of His Majesty's Government themselves will, as those who are here to-day are well aware, be dependent upon the progress made in the solution of another large and difficult question; and the acceptance of the opinion held by His Majesty's Government would, in fact, merely confirm the correctness of the attitude taken by a number of States, by no means unmindful of their obligations to the League, that with the adoption of the Assembly's resolution of July 4, 1936, their collective obligations in the matter of the Italo-Ethiopian conflict were discharged.

It follows that His Majesty's Government have no desire to embark on a discussion of legal points, such as a distinction between *de facto* and *de jure* recognition, and what action in a particular case can be held to amount to one or the other. There may be room for argument on these points, but His Majesty's Government would not regard such argument as relevant to the particular proposal which it desires to make; and, in any case, the importance of such matters clearly resides less in precise legal definitions than in the political significance which is attached to such action by the interested parties. In approaching this problem, His Majesty's Government are themselves influenced by considerations of a more general character. Nearly two years have now elapsed since the Assembly, in its resolution of July 4, 1936, took the decision which resulted in the discontinuance of the action taken by the Members of the League to apply Article 16 of the Covenant. The Assembly recognized on that occasion that various circumstances prevented the full application of the Covenant, and instituted an inquiry with the object of adapting the application of the principles of the Covenant to the results of experience. Since this resolution was passed the situation of fact with which Members of the League were then confronted has become more definitive and more stable.

I have compared the description of the situation contained in the communication from His Majesty Haile Selassie, circulated yesterday to members of the Council, with the information on the subject at the disposal of His Majesty's Government. This situation, according to our information, is that the Italian Government have obtained control of virtually all the former territory of Ethiopia, and, while resistance is still continuing in certain parts of the country, there is no organized native authority and no central native administration with the slightest prospect of reconquering the country.

The conclusion follows that the only means by which the Italian position could be challenged by League Members would be by concerted military action—in other words, by going to war. Such action is unthinkable, and would be proposed by no responsible person in any country. It was, indeed, by implication deliberately excluded by the Assembly resolution of July 4, 1936, and nowhere is there any desire on the part of any Member of the League to reverse the decision which the Assembly then took, and to revert to a policy of full sanctions against the Italian Government.

I do not overlook the fact that there are many in my own country, as, perhaps, in others, who feel none the less that any action designed to facilitate the recognition of the Italian conquest does impinge on principle, and who would, therefore, deplore the adoption of such a course. I regret that I cannot share their view.

Such anxiety arises in great part from the resolution adopted by the League in 1932, in the case of Manchukuo, upon the subject of non-recognition of the results of aggressive action. In that resolution it was agreed by all Members of the League that they would not recognize any situation, treaty, or agreement which was brought about by means contrary to the Covenant; and, if we desire to be honest with ourselves and with our fellow Members of the League, we must not be afraid squarely to face the facts in the light of that expression of opinion.

Those who seek to establish a better world upon the basis of universal acknowledgement of League principles are clearly right to feel reluctance to countenance action, however desirable on other grounds, by which they may appear to be infringed. But when, as here, two ideals are in conflict

—on the one hand the ideal of devotion, unflinching but unpractical, to some high purpose; on the other, the ideal of a practical victory for peace—I cannot doubt that the stronger claim is that of peace.

All life is indeed perpetually confronting us with difficulties not dissimilar. Whether in the affairs of nations or individuals, each one of us knows by painful experience how constantly it is necessary to reconcile that which may be ideally right with that which is practically possible. That is, in truth, one of the hardest laws which operate in a world so strangely composite of good and evil as that in which we live; and neither he who forgets ideals in the pursuit of practical achievement, nor he who, blinded by the bright light of the ideal, loses sight of the possible, will ever make his full contribution to the establishment of conditions on which alone progress can be made. Thus in an imperfect world the indefinite maintenance of a principle evolved to safeguard international order, without regard to the circumstances in which it has to be applied, may have the effect merely of increasing international discord and friction and of contributing to those very evils which it was designed to prevent. This is the position which His Majesty's Government feel bound to adopt in the case of Ethiopia.

It is the considered opinion of His Majesty's Government that for practical purposes Italian control over virtually the whole of Ethiopia has become an established fact, and that sooner or later, unless we are prepared by force to alter it or unless we are for ever to live in an unreal world, that fact, whatever be our judgement on it, will have to be acknowledged. If this is so—and I say this with every consideration for the feelings of those most closely affected by these events—it is plain that the issue between those who would be disposed to take action by way of recognition of facts earlier and those who would take the same action later is one of political judgement and not part of the eternal and immutable moralities.

In expressing their view His Majesty's Government in no way condone or approve the methods by which the Italian position in Ethiopia has been obtained, nor do they abandon in any respect the principles of the Covenant or their determination to do their utmost to secure that disputes arising between nations shall be resolved by peaceful methods and not by force. But no cause is served by vain lamentations over the past, when it is to the attempt to shape the future that the resources of constructive minds should be directed.

Meanwhile nothing is gained and much may be lost by refusal to face facts. Great as is the League of Nations, the ends that it exists to serve are greater than itself, and the greatest of those ends is peace. It has been truly said that peace is more than a mere negation of war, and that peace between nations, as between individuals, should truly be held to imply a state of complete freedom from all that might impair the perfection of harmony and understanding between them. Any such vision is, and always has been, far removed from the actual state of international relations at any time in human history. But time was when the peoples of Europe could look forward with reasonable assurance to immunity from war; and no special effort seemed necessary to secure peace in this restricted sense. How different is the state of the world to-day! Whether its anxieties be well or ill founded, we look out to-day over a world troubled and disturbed; and we realize as never before how vital it is to bend all the energy we possess to protect the world from a return of the dread scourge of war. His Majesty's Government believe that these great issues may be affected by the treatment of the subject which is at present before the Council; and, weighing all the considerations, political and moral, that arise, as fairly as I may, I cannot believe that it would be right to exclude the possibility of taking steps to secure the measure of good results for the world's peace that is within our power because it is not feasible to-day to secure full international acceptance of the high ideals for which the League stands and towards which its Members are pledged to work. It is for these reasons that His Majesty's Government have thought it right to bring this matter before the Council and to express their views upon it.

They do not ask for decisions on questions of principle, nor do they suggest that the Council should impose on any Member of the League a particular course of action. They hope, however, that Members of the Council will share their opinion that the question of the recognition of Italy's position in Ethiopia is one for each Member of the League to decide for itself in the light of its own situation and its own obligations.

25

RECOGNITION OF THE ITALIAN EMPIRE. II

18 May 1938

[A week later Lord Halifax elaborated in the House of Lords the arguments that he had used at Geneva. The occasion of his speech was a resolution by Lord Snell 'That in the opinion of this House the foreign policy of His Majesty's Government, which includes the acceptance of the sacrifice of Abyssinian independence, and is detrimental to the democratic Government of Spain, offers no certainty of any corresponding gain to the principles of peace and democracy'.]

MY LORDS, I doubt whether any of your Lordships has often assisted at a debate that has been maintained at a much higher level than that sustained to-day. It has been notable for the variety of approach made by all speakers to the great subjects that they have touched; for the force of argument with which the respective cases have been developed, and for the high quality of the contributions made from all parts of the House.

It may not be out of place if I remind your Lordships in a sentence or two what the actual position and history of this Abyssinian question has been, from an angle which I think has not been mentioned in the course of this debate. It is worth remembering that for this country the question has never been an individual question between ourselves and Italy. It has constantly been spoken of almost as if it were an Anglo-Italian dispute. It was never that. It was a dispute between the League of Nations—the collective assembly of nations—and Italy; and we on our side have always said—and we have never said more than this—that we were prepared to take our full part in collective action by all the nations who were willing to join with us in it. The League had taken that collective action which, as we all know, it had brought to an end in July, 1936; and, after that collective action had been brought to an end, something like twenty States had reached the conclusion that their collective obligation was at an end, and those States in one way or another expressed their recognition of the Italian conquest over Ethiopia at a time when it suited them to do so. There were other States which considered that the question of recognition was a matter of concern to the League as a whole.

I am not for the moment arguing which were right and which were wrong. All that I am concerned at this point to stress is that the result of that was a situation thoroughly discreditable to the League, about which there was nothing collective left, which was thoroughly anomalous, and which had in one way or the other to be cleared up. His Majesty's Government was one of the Governments who considered that, while no express obligation could perhaps be held to rest, yet the matter was one which concerned the League; and therefore we decided that at the appropriate time we ought and we would take the matter to Geneva. And at Geneva, as here, considerable thought was given to the actual question of the facts.

What are the facts with regard to the Italian occupation of Ethiopia to-day? No one as far as I know would deny that there is a degree of opposition, which I am not precisely able to estimate, in different parts of Abyssinia to the Italian conquest. I have no doubt that it is like a fire that flickers here and flames up there, and is making itself variously felt at different times. But while that is true, it is also true that as far as all our information goes there is no organized native authority at the present time, and there is no central administration with the slightest possible chance of reconquering the country and of disturbing the Italian occupation in its essentials. The noble Viscount, Lord Cecil, said that he would recognize if he was satisfied of the conquest, and he said that the ordinary tests of satisfaction of a conquest were the test of size and the test of duration of time. I think that the more true test is, What are in fact the effective chances of restoration of the sovereignty that has been dethroned? I say that for this reason, that I am quite convinced, at whatever level you put the weight of the opposition which the Italian Government is there encountering, this at least is quite certain, that the only way in which the Italian position can be challenged to-day in Abyssinia would be by concerted military action, that is, by war. That action was deliberately excluded by implication by the Assembly Resolution of 1936 taking off sanctions and, as I said at Geneva,[1] there would be no suggestion by any responsible person in any part of the world to revert to it.

All that, I think, rests upon a basis quite inexpugnable, and really I do not suppose greatly divides us. What does divide us is the question of principle on which I must say a word. I quite understand the feeling that a great many people have in regard to anything that may be called recognition of the action of the Italian Government in regard to Ethiopia. As I said the other day,[2] I do think that all life is continually presenting every one of us with the perpetual difficulty of trying to reconcile what is ideally right with what is practically possible. Every one of us knows that, and I also think that the full contribution to the establishment of practical conditions on which alone progress depends will often be out of the question if we allow ourselves to be so blinded by the ideals we are right to cherish and keep as to lose sight of what at any particular moment may be within our power.

I do think that in this matter it is true that two ideals—righteousness and peace—are in conflict, and you have to choose between the unpractical devotion to the high purpose that you know you cannot achieve except by a war you do not mean to have, and the practical victory for peace that you can achieve. I cannot hesitate between these two when both my conscience and my duty to my fellow men impel me directly in the direction of peace. It is for that reason I say that, faced by that sort of situation, the elements of which I do not think anybody denies, the difference between those who, like His Majesty's Government, would recognize sooner, and those who would recognize a little later, is really a question of political judgement, and is not a question of the eternal and immutable moralities. And as it is a question of political judgement, the task, as I conceive it, of the Foreign Secretary is so to endeavour to frame his policy that the fundamental ideals which are cherished by this country are not pushed to the extent that they outstrip and transcend the bounds of what it is practicable immediately to achieve.

Let me sum up this part of my argument as clearly and

[1] Page 154, above. [2] Page 155, above.

concisely as I can. I can understand perfectly well the position of people who say that we and others, or we alone, ought to have taken the strongest possible action at the beginning of all this business, and told the Italian Government it just was not going to happen, and we were going to block the Suez Canal, or do what you will, in order to prevent it. I can understand that. I can understand the position of people who would say that, even when the first efforts of the League had failed, the cause at stake was so great that no country ought to shrink even from the invocation of force to redress the wrong. I can understand either of those positions. But to admit, as we must, that the matter has in fact passed to a stage where only force could effect a change; to admit, as I think that we all do, that such use of force is unthinkable; and yet to say that you must go on for ever shutting your eyes to facts that you cannot alter, and thereby missing for no result whatever the chance of doing something practical for peace—I am bound to say all that seems to me simply not to make sense on any rules of this world or the next. Therefore, my Lords, my conclusion about that is a plea that we should not elevate matters on which, as I think, political judgement may legitimately vary, into high and venerable principles to which all men's allegiance must always stand pledged.

Having said that, may I make a few points clear regarding the action of His Majesty's Government. His Majesty's Government do not and never have and never will condone the Italian action, nor do they ask the League to condone the methods by which the Italian sovereignty was established. We have not asked and we do not ask the League to modify any decisions or resolutions previously taken in the matter. The League's judgement has been plainly expressed, and there is no question whatever of going back on it. We did not ask any State to violate its own principles. We did not abandon any principles of the Covenant, nor our determination to do our utmost to strive for the settlement of all disputes by peaceable means. Accordingly we thought it right to lay the whole matter in complete frankness before the Council of the League last week at Geneva.

Without any pressure but with much argument the large majority of the Council of the League of Nations expressed the definite and decided view that the question of the recognition of Italy's position in Ethiopia was one for each nation to decide for itself in the light of its own situation; and therefore to say that the attitude that we took was opposed to the majority of European nations is to assert what is flatly and demonstrably opposite to the facts. This does not mean that His Majesty's Government intend immediately to proceed to recognize the Italian conquest, for that step depends upon other circumstances on which I want to say a word in a moment.

But before I leave Abyssinia I ought perhaps to say a word or two about the suggestion that was made with regard to the possibility of the establishment of the Emperor of Ethiopia in an independent portion, or a quasi-independent portion, of his former territory under Italian suzerainty. That suggestion has been at varying times and by different persons brought to the notice of His Majesty's Government. I need hardly say that so far as His Majesty's Government are concerned there would be no objection of any kind to such an arrangement being made; but your Lordships will recognize, I think, that this is not a matter in which decision rests with His Majesty's Government, and it is clear to all of us that it is one which only the Italian Government and the Negus himself could decide in the light of their own interests and their own responsibilities.

I turn from Abyssinia to a rather wider field that is inevitably ploughed by this discussion. Reference has been made to the League of Nations and to the failure of the Powers, States Members of the League, to ensure respect for League principles. The noble Viscount, Lord Cecil, reminded us of the prodigious deterioration in the last five years in the international position, and was good enough to attribute the major share of the credit for that result to the National Government. I am not sure myself that the major part of it does not perhaps attach to the fact that in this country at least for many of those years we were placing what turned out to be an excessive trust in the issue of the

Disarmament Conference in which the noble Viscount, Lord Cecil, played so distinguished a part, and I am quite sure it has been the fact that this country was disarmed and weak that has been an unsteadying factor in European politics. However that may be, it is said that the passage of these events has involved humiliation for all concerned, not least for this country, and that such a state of affairs can be to-day redressed by a bold appeal to all League Members, or at least to all European Members of the League, to rally themselves once more beneath the banner of the Covenant.

It is not necessary for me to travel over the ground, which is all too familiar, of the weaknesses imposed upon the League by abstentions from it of powerful States. His Majesty's Government are not less concerned to-day than they have ever been to make the fullest use they can of the League. They are anxious and will be ready at the appropriate time to lend all their influence to do whatever can be done to strengthen the foundations and restore the authority of the League. But, my Lords, no good in this respect, or any other, is done by refusal to face the hard fact, that if some of the greatest Powers are in fact outside the League, and refuse to be bound by League rules, then the only way by which respect for League rules can be enforced is the way of war.

I think nothing would more effectively destroy the devotion of our people to the League as an instrument of peace than that they should once get the idea into their heads that it might be an instrument for involving them in war. I am quite certain of that. The noble Lord, Lord Allen, spoke of the weakness of the League, which he attributed in part to the Treaty of Versailles and to the failure of the League to deal with economic and kindred problems during these recent years. I have no doubt that is largely true. But another reason, I think, is that the League has never yet been able to find adequate machinery for the solution of the problems of revision. It has never, I think I am right in saying, invoked Article 19; and if it invoked Article 19 I believe that Article 19 would not be found to function satisfactorily for hypothetical problems, and that it might from time to time need revision by the Members of the League in Council.

Therefore, my Lords, my conclusion is that refusal to recognize a situation brought about in spite of the League may keep our principles intact on paper. If that were all that mattered, we might be well content with that satisfaction. But when we find that refusal to face facts does in fact keep resentments and antagonisms alive and threatens understanding, then we have to consider whether it is right to abandon the substance for the shadow. I well recognize that that may be held to be a cynical confession of failure. I think confession of failure is often the first step to better things. After all, most things produced by men throughout history have been evolved from a succession of failures—failures that have broken the hearts of men who have laboured in advance of their generation. But if the doctrine of non-recognition of failure had been adopted by our thinkers, or our inventors, or our reformers, or, I would add, by our statesmen and politicians, the advance of civilization would not have been made so smooth, and indeed I doubt whether it would in fact have been secured at all.

. . . . .

I would like to deal if I may on broad lines with some of the more general criticisms that have been made upon the general Anglo-Italian Agreement. The broad line of attack is that the Agreement is (*a*) wicked and immoral, for the reasons which we have been discussing—the question of principle—and (*b*) stupid. I perhaps may have been held to have dealt sufficiently with the question of principle, and I will deal with the stupidity, namely, that the Agreement will not itself be observed, and is only a cover for the sinister designs of the Italian Government. I must frankly admit that here the difference is one of outlook and one of judgement. Lord Snell is not disposed to believe the Italian assurances, and therefore quite naturally sees no merit whatever in the Agreement. We, however, do accept these assurances and believe that they will be honourably carried out. Therefore, accepting those assurances, we think it is worth while to re-establish good relations between two great Powers, with all that follows in the direction of relief of world anxiety and in the diminishing of real dangers to world peace.

That is not to say that we approve of Italian intervention in Spain, any more than we approve of Italian action in Ethiopia. We have always made it our purpose to get rid of all foreigners from Spain; but I must make it plain that we have never asked or expected that the Italians should withdraw unilaterally; and provided that we are satisfied, as we are, that the Italian Government do not mean to use Spain for the alteration of the Mediterranean *status quo* when the Spanish trouble is over, we do not see why the fact that the Italian Government takes a strong view on one side, as against a strong view taken by large sections of opinion in this country on the other side, should preclude us from an attempt to improve our relations with them over the wider international field. Everybody must want to see conditions existing in the world that might with reasonable security promise peace.

We believe that by our Italian Agreement we have made a beginning, and we are resolved to seek every possibility of continuing and developing that action. And highly as we value our existing friendships, and intimate as we happily are with France, we do not regard those friendships as by any means exclusive; and, whilst strengthening them, we seek always to increase their number and to extend their scope. We should, for example, like to see removed all causes of mistrust and suspicion that may be held to stand in the way of complete understanding between ourselves and Germany. That desire is shared, I believe, by the mass of the peoples in both countries, who have such close affinities of language and origin. . . .

Many people think and speak to-day of the inevitability of war. I believe such talk to be both dangerous and essentially untrue, and that for this reason: I would far rather think that there are enough sensible people in all countries who realize that war is the only alternative to an understanding, and that, as war cannot be regarded as other than the supreme disaster for civilization, the true conclusion is that it is peace through understanding, rather than war, which is inevitable. And those are the terms in which, I should hope, we should think and speak and act. But if we want that sort of end it will not come of itself, and we have to take positive steps to try to secure it. . . .

It has been significant to me to note the degree of support that has, in fact, been given to this Anglo-Italian Agreement. I found the other day, at the Council of the League of Nations, representatives speaking in the name of the French Government, the Powers of the Little Entente, the Balkan Entente, the Belgian Government, and the Polish Government, all testifying in warm terms to the significance of what we have done.

When I outlined what I conceived to be the advantages to be drawn from it, no voice at all was raised in criticism or in the sense that the Agreement was not a gain to the principles of peace and democracy that the Resolution of the noble Lord, Lord Snell, is designed to serve. The only breath of doubt came—and perhaps we might have expected it—from the representative of the Soviet Union, who welcomed the Agreement, however, as he said his Government would welcome any agreement reached between various Governments removing misunderstandings and disputes, and it is worth while to quote his words:

> 'My Government, which takes particularly to heart everything which relates to international peace, quite naturally welcomes any agreement reached between various countries removing the misunderstandings and disputes existing between them. From this point of view, one cannot but welcome the British-Italian Agreement.
>
> 'But in dealing with bilateral pacts, we have to take into consideration not only their effect upon the relationship between the two parties concerned but also upon the relations between those parties and the rest of the world. We have also to take into consideration the effect which such agreements may have on those problems which are still before the League of Nations and which still remain to be dealt with. We, therefore, reserve our final judgement upon the importance of this Agreement from this point of view. We may still express the hope that these problems will certainly not suffer from that Agreement.'

I do not think that is too bad a judgement from the representative of the Soviet Union, and it is noteworthy that His Majesty's Opposition are in the whole of Europe almost alone in condemnation and dislike of what we have tried to do.

May I make one very pedestrian observation? I think we do well to remember that friendship is really very like health.

As long as you have got it you take it for granted, and you do not realize how much it means to live with it until you have to live without it. That is as true of friendship as it is of health, and therefore we have thought it worth while to do everything in our power to restore those feelings of mutual trust which are the foundation of international friendship. As I said just now, the estimate of Europe is on the whole worth more to me than the estimate of His Majesty's Opposition.

May I turn for a few moments to what is the other great subject that is in the minds of noble Lords, and that is the threat, as they see it, in all these doings to the democratic Government of Spain. Let me say quite clearly that I understand perfectly well the deep feeling of all who feel quite sincerely that the cause of democracy in Spain, and perhaps the cause of democracy generally, is threatened and endangered by foreign action. I understand that perfectly well. It rests upon the feeling that non-intervention is a sham and that non-intervention works to the detriment of the Spanish Government. The real point at issue is the feeling that in refusing to supply arms to what they hold to be the legitimate Government of Spain we are denying that Government its legitimate rights. All that depends upon what view you take about the unhappy war that is going on in Spain.

We have taken the view that from fairly early on it assumed in fact the character of a civil war, and I do not think that you can deny that. That being so, two alternative courses presented themselves as possible. One was to recognize a state of belligerency in fact if not in name, and then the normal procedure would have been for States to be neutral and for them to recognize that the two parties to the civil war had the rights of belligerents. If that had been done each State would have been able to decide whether to allow munitions to go to both belligerents, subject to the right of either belligerent to prevent, if possible, such supply to the other. The other policy, which we have seen adopted, was the non-intervention plan on which general agreement was early secured, in which the participating Governments agreed to place themselves under a self-denying ordinance.

That was the position as regards the thing viewed from

Spain. As regards the thing viewed from the wider angle of Europe, it was held to be a source of great potential danger. Supposing you had never had non-intervention, or supposing that you now denounced it, so that we supplied arms freely to the Spanish Government, would not the inevitable result have been that others would have sent still more arms to the other side, whatever might be the side of their choice? And other people probably would have had more arms to send than we had. Supposing that to have been the consequence, as I think it certainly would have been, would it not then have been proposed that we should stop by force, alone or with others, the supply of arms to Franco? That indeed was the proposal that was made to the Council of the League last week by Señor del Vayo.

In the end either of these things would clearly, I think, have meant war. Therefore either of those courses that might be proposed would have meant a much larger degree of foreign intervention all round, or a European war between supporters of the respective sides. I am told that in the great demonstration in Hyde Park on May 1 one of the most distinctive of the banners had this strange device: 'Arms for Spain are arms for peace.' I am bound to say, making all allowance for the broad character of truth as portrayed on banners, that that demonstrably failed to fulfil the test.

Therefore His Majesty's Government were driven to support non-intervention, not because they thought it perfect, not because they did not think it open to objection, but because of all courses it seemed to them much the least dangerous, and therefore they do not believe that it has broken down. They will do their best to continue to work it and will continue to press all the Powers to try to work together to make it work better. They are not without hope of effecting progress in that direction. I agree, however, with those who have said that the only right solution of the Spanish trouble is to stop it; and if any opportunity of action in that direction by way of mediation were ever to be offered by the willingness of both sides in Spain to try it, I can assure your Lordships that His Majesty's Government would not be slow to render any help they could in that direction.

May I in a few words in conclusion say one or two things of rather wider import? I am anxious that in all these matters on which we obviously feel deeply and must feel deeply, we should not, if we can avoid it, exaggerate our divisions. The Opposition, if I may with respect say so, is perfectly right to attack the Government for what they do if they think we are doing things in the wrong way or at the wrong time. Criticism is good for us all and I have no doubt is best for our characters when we deserve it least. I recognize that many people feel that over Abyssinia we were wrong to make a move now, but I also think, as I said just now, that no one who is not prepared to restore the Emperor by force can possibly say that he would not at some date have been prepared to recognize facts, as we have now placed ourselves in a position to do. I recognize that you may not think British policy in Spain or in regard to the Italian Agreement is well judged to secure the ends that we seek. We disagree; and on us rests the responsibility for decision, which we are perfectly prepared to assume, though we may feel reasonably sure that were noble Lords opposite in our place they would be following a policy that would not greatly differ from our own.

But whatever may be our disagreement upon the actual policy of day to day, I do not believe that there is any deep difference in the foundations of our common thought. There are two things on which the great mass of English public opinion is solidly united. One is democracy, with all that it means to us, and the other, which is consequential, is the protection of those things on which democracy depends against external interference. The Socialist Party are most rightly resentful of any suggestion that they are, or would be if in office, less careful of national and Imperial interests than my noble friends behind me on this side of the House. It fell to me to serve as Viceroy of India under a Socialist Government when India passed through very disturbed times, and no Government could have given any Viceroy more loyal and wholehearted support than I received from the Labour Government. Therefore it is both from that personal experience and from my general observation that I have never been tempted to think that the Socialist Party with responsibility of office would fail in their duty as custodians of the wider interests of the British Commonwealth.

Indeed, part of their concern over Spain I know is based on their anxiety about the effect that may be exerted by what is going on in Spain upon the vital interests of this country in the Mediterranean. All that I feel. If therefore it is wrong for my friends, as I think it would be, to impute carelessness to our Socialist opponents in this matter, I would ask our opponents to believe that it would be no less wrong for them to impute to us any lesser loyalty than their own to the cause of democracy and to all that that cause means. We, not less than they, recognize that democracy is the foundation on which nearly everything else in this country is built; so that, if anyone here ever sought to be disloyal to democracy, he would himself be surprised to find how much of the structure of English life would go down with it. By it, indeed, we live; for the spirit of democracy is far too deeply set in British nature to be overthrown either by pressure from without or by indifference from within. It is part of that strange blend of thought, of instinct, and of tradition which we call British character, and which none of us can any more shed than we can shed our own skin. Therefore, I would repeat that when we agree upon so much and upon what is so vital, do not, please, let us exaggerate our differences. This country needs all the unity that it can find, and I would say that in all our judgements the recognition of that necessity must constantly find place. That unity is essential to our influence abroad; it is not less essential to the accomplishment of those tasks that we have to accomplish at home. Therefore I would hope that, while we must expect to differ upon times and methods, with regard to which the responsibility for final decision must rest upon the executive Government, we might all be able to feel such confidence in one another as regards the broad basis of national policy as may enable this country to play the part which only a united country can play in whatever circumstances the uncharted future may hold in store.

26

CZECHOSLOVAKIA: THE MAY CRISIS

23 May 1938

[The annexation of Austria by the German Reich encouraged the Sudeten Germans to press their claims for autonomy upon the Government of Czechoslovakia. Unsatisfied by a political amnesty and by the introduction of a new Nationalities Statute, their leader, Herr Henlein, announced at Karlsbad on April 24th, 1938, the minimum demands of his party. These included not merely complete autonomy for Sudeten Germans, but a demand that Czechoslovakia should abandon her alliances with France and Russia and subordinate her foreign policy to that of Germany. Three days later the French and British Governments engaged in conversations on the subject of Czechoslovakia and undertook to use their joint influence for securing fair treatment for the Sudeten Germans. A new crisis developed in Czechoslovakia on the eve of municipal elections which had been fixed for May 22nd. It was credibly reported that Germany was concentrating several divisions on the frontier. The story of the crisis, which ended in a temporary relaxation of tension, was told in identical terms by Mr. Chamberlain to the House of Commons and by Lord Halifax to the House of Lords.]

Government Statement

MY LORDS, I would propose first to give a very brief summary of events of the past few days that have tended to show that the situation in regard to the German minority in Czechoslovakia might be entering on a dangerous phase, and then to indicate the action taken by His Majesty's Government. On May 19 rumours began to gain currency of German troop movements in the direction of the Czechoslovak frontier. The German Government informed His Majesty's Ambassador on the following day that there was no foundation for these rumours, and they gave a similar assurance to the Czechoslovak Government. On May 20 a number of serious incidents occurred in Czechoslovakia.

On the morning of May 21 the Czechoslovak Government intimated that they were calling up one class for training and for the purpose of maintaining order in the frontier areas. On the same day, an unfortunate incident took place in which two Sudeten Germans lost their lives in an incident near the frontier, the full facts of which are not yet entirely

Government Statement

clear. The Czechoslovak Minister for Foreign Affairs informed the German Minister of this incident and told him that disciplinary measures would be taken against those responsible. On the same day—May 21—His Majesty's Ambassador in Berlin received further assurances from the German Government that stories of German troop movements were completely unfounded. The Czechoslovak Minister for Foreign Affairs informed His Majesty's Minister in Prague on May 21 that a formal invitation had been sent to Herr Henlein to negotiate on the Nationalities Statute, which had been approved on the 19th by the Czechoslovak Government. But on the same day—May 21—it was announced in the Sudeten Press that the Political Committee of the Sudeten German Party had decided to inform the Prime Minister that the Party were not in a position to discuss the Nationalities Statute so long as peace and order in the Sudeten districts and, above all, the constitutional rights of freedom of opinion, of the Press and of assembly, were not guaranteed. I now learn, however, that it has been arranged for Herr Henlein to see the Czechoslovak Prime Minister either to-night or to-morrow morning.

In face of this situation, the principal concern of His Majesty's Government has been to use all their influence, wherever it could be effective, on the side of restraint in word and deed, while keeping open the way to peaceful negotiation of a satisfactory settlement. With that object, they have represented to the Czechoslovak Government the need of taking every precaution for avoidance of incidents and of making every possible effort to reach a comprehensive and lasting settlement by negotiation with the representatives of the Sudeten Party. In this, His Majesty's Government have enjoyed the full co-operation of the French Government. The Czechoslovak Government have responded to this representation with an assurance that they appreciate the interest which His Majesty's Government have manifested in this question, and are fully resolved to seek an early and complete solution. His Majesty's Government have represented to the German Government the urgent importance of reaching a settlement if European peace is to be preserved, and have expressed their earnest desire that the German Government would co-operate with them in facilitating agreement. His Majesty's Government have at the same time informed the German Government of the advice tendered in Prague and of the assurances received from the Czechoslovak Government. The German Minister for Foreign Affairs stated that he welcomed the efforts being made by His Majesty's Government and that the German Government fully shared their desire to see negotiations succeed. At the moment the situation appears to have somewhat eased, and I understand that the elections passed off quietly yesterday without untoward incident.

Government Statement

27
THE PURPOSE OF BRITISH POLICY. II

21 June 1938

[The following speech was made by Lord Halifax at the eighth annual dinner of the Royal Institute of International Affairs.]

WE are only now appreciating the cataclysmic effect of war, and learning that it unsettles at least as much as it settles; and therefore that its influence on human affairs is often rather disruptive than decisive. For this reason all nations to-day are interested, in varying degree, but to a far greater extent than formerly, in foreign policy. The common folk of every nation want peace. They realize that, if peace is to be secured, relations of contentment must be established between nations, and that the foreign policy of all nations is the instrument through which these efforts will either succeed or fail. Incidentally, they realize that, whereas war used to be able to find some sort of rough solution for practical differences between nations, in these days, when the disturbing factors are intangible ideas running through the world like a prairie fire and respecting no international boundaries, war is a very uncertain remedy.

This interest in foreign policy leads the British nation to desire to make the most effective contribution that it can to the treatment of present world anxieties. It is sometimes exhorted, in face of all its imperial obligations, to keep itself to itself and avoid gratuitous incursion on to dangerous ground outside. But in spite of all its attractions I doubt whether the gospel of isolation is winning many converts, partly because our people would feel instinctively that to try to cut clear of lending a hand when things are difficult was an unworthy attitude for a great nation, and was not pulling the weight in the world that might rightly be expected of it, and, partly, because in their hearts the British people do not believe that isolation is likely to prove practicable.

They see the world every day becoming more and more interlocked. They think Mr. Cordell Hull spoke words of profound truth the other day when he said that 'it was his firm conviction that national isolation was not a means to security, but rather a fruitful source of insecurity'. And if this is true of the United States of America, how much more is it likely to be true of Great Britain, the centre of a great world Commonwealth? This does not mean that we, any more than the United States of America, want to see our country involved in quarrels that do not concern us, but it does mean that we realize that facts may be more powerful than the wills of men and that, once war starts, it is impossible to predict where it may not end. In 1914 no one would have expected the great American nation to be involved in war because an Austrian Archduke had been murdered in a small town of which few people had ever heard the name.

If therefore we assume that no nation can feel assured of the prudence or even the possibility of isolation, it is our plain duty to bend all our efforts to the avoidance of the catastrophe, against which even isolation may not suffice to give protection. And for such a task our country seems by history, geography, and character to have certain qualifications, though these are not unaccompanied by some disqualifications on the other side.

Let me take these last first.

(1) Our position as an island (though we are beginning to understand that with the development of the air an island may have as many disadvantages as advantages) makes it difficult for us to understand the attitude of mind of Continental Powers. Our own immunity from invasion against our will since 1066 makes such realities appear very differently to us from the guise in which they appear to those who are constantly set, as they think, in the midst of so many and great dangers.

(2) Our own history, rich in experiment and experience as it has been, has for so long given us geographical and racial unity that it is difficult for us sometimes to appreciate the outlook of other nations whose experience has been less fortunate, and whose achievement of national unity is more recent.

(3) We are as a nation sadly lacking in imagination, and therefore often fail to understand the thought and actions of other nations, or to realize that in their position and with their history we might ourselves not think or act very differently.

But while these things are true, I think we may claim the possession of certain positive qualities—the mechanical result of history rather than of original virtue—to right the scales. First I would place the British respect for law, founded as it is upon the conviction that no social life is tolerable, or indeed possible, on any other terms. This is, we believe, as true of nations as it is of individuals; and the first necessity of ordered life, whether national or personal, is that settlement of differences by force should be abjured and be replaced by settlement through some process akin to law. Second, through experience we have learnt that law, to be acceptable, must not only be just, but must also be generally *thought* just. In other words, that no law can effectively claim obedience unless it is broad-based upon the assent of those affected by it. Many law-givers have been in trouble for the neglect of this truth, and both the municipal and international spheres have furnished and still furnish many examples for our guidance. And, thirdly, but by no means least, is the fact that by its development of democracy the British people has trained itself insensibly in the practice and atmosphere of toleration. This, indeed, is of the very essence of the democratic faith, with its emphasis on the value of personality; and, so taught, it is no temptation for us to interfere with other forms of government, provided they do not wish to interfere with us.

These three qualities, if such they may be called—respect for law, recognition that law must rest upon consent, toleration—are quite indispensable to any sound or constructive approach to the international problems of to-day. And their possession of these in a particular degree does seem to call the British people to play a very distinctive part in the guidance of world movements. I noticed the other day that Count Ciano, the Italian Foreign Minister, said this: 'At the bottom of many international situations there is a problem of mutual knowledge, and no lasting and fruitful work can be accomplished unless it is based upon the consciousness of the new realities which history necessarily creates in its course.' That is well said. Most true it is that the solutions which we seek can only be found through appreciation by nations and peoples of one another's aspirations and difficulties; and the law that we would enthrone for the protection of peace must be closely related to the realities of life. Never must we forget that all the problems we deal with in our offices are, in some way or other, human problems, due to some maladjustment of human life, which it is our duty to correct. For all life means change; and any attempt to cast world affairs into an eternal mould, hard and unchangeable, is foredoomed to tragic failure. 'All life means change'; but there are various kinds of change, from the convulsion of the earthquake to the slow development of the forest tree. What we have to seek is the way of orderly progressive change, and the problem is an easier one to state than it is to solve. It will never be solved except by mutual confidence in good intentions. For ourselves, we are ready to play our part to the utmost. But, unless through general restraint this confidence can be created and maintained, public opinion, in this country at least, will never be brought to have great faith in the successful issue of any efforts that its Government may make.

But if we have to take account of new realities that history makes, we also have to take account not less carefully of old realities, of principles and practice, through which the life of peoples is ultimately nurtured and maintained. The wise householder is he who mingles in his treasure the just proportion of things new and old. Our own generation is called upon to play a part of great responsibility in this world, transforming itself so rapidly before our eyes. Any foreign policy must combine two things, if it is to yield the kind of result we want. There must, of course, be flexibility in adaptation to changing circumstances, but there must also be steadiness in pursuit of the main purpose. The just combination of these two are the foundation of most political wisdom.

I can perhaps best illustrate what I mean by reference to the League of Nations. The League was not an artificial product of any single brain. The ideas from which it grew had indeed been shaping themselves in men's minds long before the War, though it was through the War that the opportunity came to give them concrete expression in a written document.

The motive force in the Covenant was not to find means of furthering the interests of some countries as against those of others, but rather to serve the real interest of all through general co-operation. The last twenty years have seen many failures and disappointments, but a great deal of human history is the record of perseverance through failure to new effort and ultimate success. And in spite of all setbacks and hopes destroyed, the fact remains that if the world is to survive it must find some reasonable basis for international relations, whether it does it through the Covenant or by some other road.

Events have made the full application of the Covenant impracticable to-day, and it is of no service to refuse to acknowledge facts. But that is no reason why a country like ours, which believes the spirit of the Covenant to be the right spirit in international affairs, should not continue to practice that spirit in our dealings with other nations. And that is what we are trying to do. My own reading of British foreign policy is that, however intimate our relations may be with any other Power, as they happily are with France to-day, we are always trying to feel our way towards a wider sense of unity in international relations. Sometimes we succeed, sometimes we fail, for success does not lie in our hands alone. But the purpose remains the same.

You will, therefore, find British policy repeatedly emphasizing what unites nations, instead of what divides them; and for the same reason we are not interested to secure so-called diplomatic successes, and win the plaudits of the crowd, if by so doing we prejudice the attainment of our principal objective.

No one with knowledge would pretend that the role of peacemaker was an easy one. That role is one that demands great patience and fairness, and at the same time firmness and strength. Motives are frequently misunderstood; restraint and cool heads are liable to be mistaken for weakness. Moreover he who seeks peace cannot succeed unless others are animated by the same spirit, for no peace can endure which is not built upon respect for law and justice. Nor will such a policy ever appeal to the mind which hankers after short cuts, and feels that, if only we had Lord Palmerston still with us, we could rapidly and decisively impose British solutions on an acquiescent world. We unhappily have to work under different conditions and with different instruments, but there is one great reinforcement of our influence which is always within our power, if we will, to use.

If our voice is to carry conviction abroad, it must be the voice of a united nation. It is no doubt inevitable that in troubled times, especially when the issues involved stir deep passions, sharp differences of opinion should emerge as to what is the path of prudent and enlightened statesmanship. Frequent discussions arise in Parliament and, in the thrust and parry of debate, sharp words are used, which do not further the cause of peace, and which are not well calculated to facilitate the task of the Foreign Secretary. On the other hand, it is plainly right that Parliament, if it is truly representative, should interest itself in these things; and whatever may be the party differences as to particular actions of Governments, there is, I venture to assert, no real divergence of view in any quarter upon what ought to be the purpose of British policy.

I would indeed go so far as to say (though not without expecting to be contradicted) that no body of men with the actual responsibility and the full knowledge of the Government would in present circumstances take any very different action from our own. But however this may be, it is quite certain that whatever Government may be in office it will have the same ends in view. None of us has any desire to do anything to embarrass any other country; we have no wish to cramp legitimate development, or to encircle any nation with a ring of potential enemies. Still less do we wish to interfere with a system of government with which we may not happen to agree. We are none of us out for sinister motives to improve political relations with Governments of a different political complexion from our own in order to influence the course of political development at home. Every sensible Englishman (and luckily they are the vast majority) knows that kind of suggestion to be wholly untrue. But we are all alike determined to throw all our weight on the side of securing world peace through respect for law based on just settlements; we have no use for a world society in which law would be expected to be the obedient handmaid of lawless force; and we are all resolved to preserve British rights and liberties against attack, from whatever quarter, within or without the State, these may come.

Two things follow from this essential unity of thought. The first is that anyone who has the honour to occupy my position must remember that to foreign countries he represents the whole British nation, and not a party. No British Government could hope with any success to conduct a foreign policy which was not broadly acceptable to the whole nation, and this is a fact which both here and elsewhere should always be borne in mind. The second is that a great mistake would be made abroad if it was ever thought that our domestic controversies upon the day-to-day conduct of foreign policy, inseparable as these are from our democratic system, under which we all think and speak freely, would in the least degree affect the primary instinct of our people to stand solidly together in any real emergency. They have always done so, and would do so again. Both their history, with its long experience of self-government, and their character formed by it, have given them a sense of continuity which, while enabling them to face facts and make peaceful changes, protects them from being revolutionary in regard either to their own affairs or to the affairs of other people.

They have developed this gift largely because they have insisted on forming their own judgements on the facts of whatever might be the problems in hand. For this reason they do not take kindly to propaganda, and the best propaganda you can do for the British people here and throughout the Empire is to give them facts, as objectively as you can. I am not afraid, if they have these, of their conclusions.

And that is the particular value of an institution like Chatham House. In communities like ours what Government can do is closely determined by public opinion; and though Government can and should influence and seek to guide opinion, its force and direction must in the main be determined by the people themselves. Chatham House is restrained by the terms of a charter it framed for itself from expressing any opinion on foreign policy. Your primary function is to give the public the material for forming theirs.

28

CZECHOSLOVAKIA: THE RUNCIMAN MISSION

27 July 1938

[With the passing of the crisis of May 1938, German pressure upon Czechoslovakia slackened for a space, but no progress was made in reaching a settlement of the Sudeten German question, for Herr Henlein refused even to consider the Czech Government's proposals for a Nationalities Statute. By way of bridging a gap between the two parties and finding a solution, Lord Runciman was sent out to Czechoslovakia at the instance of the British Government to attempt mediation. In the course of a general review of foreign affairs given to the House of Lords before rising for the summer recess, Lord Halifax surveyed the situation in Czechoslovakia.]

MY LORDS, through all the developments of recent weeks and months in Czechoslovakia the single purpose of His Majesty's Government has been to impress in all quarters the necessity and urgency of reaching an agreed solution of an issue that might gravely menace the preservation of European peace. The problem is not a new one, for the historic provinces of Bohemia and Moravia have long been one of the great nerve centres of Europe. It is in these provinces that contact between Slav and German have been most intimate and where the problem of their relationship has been most acute. There was indeed a time in the Middle Ages when, under the King of Bohemia who became the Emperor Charles IV, a harmonious blending of German and Slav culture and tradition appeared capable of realization. But that promise was unfulfilled, and to-day the racial self-consciousness, and the rise of fierce national ideals that our own day has seen, reinforced by the violent clash of philosophies that perplexes the modern world, have now, within the old political frontier of Bohemia, bred the antagonism, still sharper, which we know.

The problem there is, within that political frontier and without destroying the integrity of the Czechoslovak State, to find, by peaceful means, a way to confer substantial rights of self-administration upon the German-speaking population, and with them upon the other populations, such as the Polish and Hungarian, who live within the Czechoslovak borders and possess Czechoslovak citizenship. The problem is a very real one, and of a kind in regard to which we ourselves are not without experience. Accordingly His Majesty's Government, in close accord with the French Government, agreed, in response to a request made by the Czechoslovak Government, to take the action that was detailed by my right honourable friend the Prime Minister yesterday; and His Majesty's Government have been fortunate in enlisting the assistance of Lord Runciman. I have been asked whether I had information as to the acceptance by the Sudeten leaders of the services of Lord Runciman. I am in a position to state that they received the idea favourably, and I hope, therefore, so far as we can at present judge, that the way seems to be clear for Lord Runciman to proceed upon his most public-spirited and patriotic mission. We feel that Lord Runciman does indeed bring to his task of independent investigation and mediation many qualities which those who have had the opportunity of working most closely with him are in the best position to appraise.

Several of your Lordships have asked what precisely is his status when he goes to Czechoslovakia. His status is one of complete independence of His Majesty's Government, and I think that that is not a very difficult status for either him or us to maintain. I have made it quite plain to him, and quite plain also to all those concerned, that he is in no way acting as a representative of or on behalf of His Majesty's Government, nor do we take any responsibility for the suggestions that he may make. His achievement, as I see it, will be to inform public opinion not only in this country but in a great many other countries; and, more important than that, he can as mediator bring the two sides together and explain perhaps where there is misconstruction and conceivably make new suggestions. Perhaps I might, without breach of confidence with Lord Runciman, tell your Lordships what Lord Runciman said after I had so lucidly explained to him what his functions were to be. He said: 'I quite understand; you are setting me adrift in a small boat in mid-Atlantic.' I said, 'That is exactly the position'.

There is one other thing that I must say before I leave Lord Runciman, and it is this. We cannot but feel that any public man of British race and steeped in British experience and thought may have it in his power for this reason to make a contribution of peculiar value. The British people, both at home and in the Dominions, have repeatedly found themselves confronted with the problem of reconciling the unity of the State with the position of men of a different race included within the body politic. The British Commonwealth itself is the outstanding example of the attainment of single unity through great diversity. It may be that the particular problem that faces the Czechoslovak Government is not strictly analogous to those with which the British Government have had to deal, but it is of the same order of difficulty, and requires the same kind of genius for its solution. It therefore naturally occurs to British thought that the solution of the problem created by the position of different nationalities within a single State is most likely to be found through the application, in some form appropriate to local conditions, of the principle of partnership in self-administration, by which our own problems, not totally dissimilar, have been so happily resolved, and that in a form which has, through the contentment so brought to many different races, been the seed of greater strength to the whole community of which they form part.

It is the earnest hope of His Majesty's Government that, through the application of some such principles as these, the way may be found at once to strengthen the foundations of contentment within the Czechoslovak State and to relieve Europe of a great anxiety. For reasons with which we are all conversant, upon the handling of this problem depend the interests not merely of Czechoslovakia herself but those of peace, and it is this fact which both entitles and compels this country, with others, to be interested in the treatment of it. We recognize the justice and the necessity of change, but it is none the less our desire to see it effected by peaceful means. The lesson of history must surely be that such an achievement would have greater chances of survival than any settlement imposed by force, which must inevitably create more problems than it solves.

Your Lordships will no doubt have seen the recent speech of M. Daladier in which he defined the position of his country in relation to these questions, and repeated the obligation that in certain events would rest upon it to fulfil its undertakings. Of that obligation the French Government can alone be the interpreter and judge, but your Lordships will have noticed with no less interest that M. Daladier asserted in clear terms his refusal to believe in the inevitability of war. By that opinion I would wish definitely to range my own. During the last few days, as your Lordships are aware, there have been certain contacts between His Majesty's Government and the German Government, which His Majesty's Government have warmly welcomed and which lead them to hope that peaceful means will be found to an agreed solution.

The noble Lord who opened the debate asked me whether I thought that I could properly tell him the matters that were discussed between Captain Wiedemann and myself last Monday week. I do not know that I can go quite so far as that, because those discussions were necessarily confidential; but I can tell him that it was an opportunity that I think we both welcomed of exchanging views on matters of common interest to both our Governments, and that the effect of our conversation was to show that, however much we differed on some matters of internal interest to both countries, it was evident that both nations were anxious to lose no opportunity of establishing the better relations between the two countries of which the noble Lord opposite spoke.

I do not believe that those responsible for the Government of any country in Europe to-day want war. Every Government must know the great desire for peace among the people of every nation, and every Government must reflect upon what would be the consequences of war to all the fairest hopes they cherish for the future of the millions that are entrusted to their charge. His Majesty's Government believe that a just and reasonable settlement is capable of attainment if the problem is handled prudently, with a spirit of restraint and a spirit of accommodation on all sides. Here I should like to express a hope. I think that everyone will agree that it is only reasonable that Lord Runciman should be enabled to carry out his delicate mission in an atmosphere of calm and of confidence. I trust, therefore, that all those concerned, both within and without the frontiers of Czechoslovakia, will do all they can to help to create this atmosphere and thus assist Lord Runciman in the difficult task that he is willing to undertake. Above all, if this work of mediation is to proceed smoothly and successfully, it is clear that the less there can be of recrimination or threats in the Press or elsewhere, the better. Since we are pressing the Czechoslovak Government to be generous and conciliatory, we confidently count on Germany to give similar advice where she may, with a view to avoiding a deadlock the consequences of which might be incalculable.

A problem which in one form or another has challenged solution for five hundred years cannot be suddenly resolved; and provided always that those who are seeking for a settlement are animated by sincere intentions, it cannot fairly be made a cause of reproach that matters so closely affecting the structure of the State should be handled with due precaution and, as far as may be, with the assent of all concerned. Given such sincere and honest intentions, His Majesty's Government are anxious, as we have tried to prove, to lend any help within our power; and I feel bound to say plainly that public opinion in this country would quickly declare itself against any action which, whether by obstructing reasonable compromise or by rendering impossible its fair consideration, might imperil the settlement and jeopardize the cause of European peace.

29

CZECHOSLOVAKIA: THE SEPTEMBER CRISIS

3 October 1938

[Lord Runciman reached Prague on August 3rd, 1938. The draft Nationalities Statute had been published a few days earlier, but, a fortnight after Lord Runciman's arrival, the Sudeten leaders rejected the proposals contained in the Statute as a basis on which negotiations could proceed. On August 24th Lord Runciman reported to London and obtained the approval of Lord Halifax for new proposals under which the Sudeten Germans were to be granted cantonal self-government. The gravity of the situation was increased by the issue of a proclamation by Herr Henlein to his followers ordering them to resort to self-defence, and by the subsequent breaking off of negotiations over the cantonal proposals. On September 12th Herr Hitler made a speech in the Nazi Party Conference at Nuremberg promising German armed support to the Sudeten Germans in their claim for self-determination. The speech produced an outbreak of revolt in Sudeten territory and a declaration by Herr Henlein that the demands made in the Nuremberg speech superseded those of the Karlsbad Programme. In this critical position of affairs Mr. Chamberlain sent to Herr Hitler, on September 14th, a message stating that he proposed to come over to Germany at once and see him with the object of finding a peaceful solution. The two statesmen met at Berchtesgaden on the following day. Returning to London, Mr. Chamberlain invited the French Prime Minister and the French Foreign Minister to meet him and his colleagues on September 18th. The representatives of the two Governments were acquainted with Herr Hitler's intentions and had before them at their meeting a report from Lord Runciman advocating that those portions of Czechoslovakia having a predominant German-speaking population should be given the full right of self-determination at once. This proposal was put to the Czech Government, who very reluctantly accepted it in the night of September 21st–22nd, as providing the only hope of averting a general disaster and saving Czechoslovakia from invasion. Within a few hours the Czech Government fell, and Mr. Chamberlain set out on a second visit to Herr Hitler.

On this occasion Mr. Chamberlain met Herr Hitler at Godesberg, only to be confronted with additional demands which he undertook to transmit, but not to recommend, to the Czech Government. That Government found the Godesberg terms wholly unacceptable, and ordered general mobilization. On September 25th British and French Ministers met and resolved to support the Czechs if they were attacked. Mr. Chamberlain continued to work for peace, and sent a personal appeal to Herr Hitler on September 26th and again on the following day, when he also sent a personal message to Signor Mussolini. On September 28th, when war seemed inevitable, a message arrived from Herr Hitler, accepting Mr. Chamberlain's proposal and inviting him, along with M. Daladier and Signor Mussolini, to meet him on the following morning at Munich. The terms arrived at in the Munich Conference were accepted on September 30th by all parties—by the Czechs under protest. They were considerably more onerous than the proposals of Berchtesgaden, less so than those of Godesberg. On October 1st Mr. Chamberlain returned to London, bringing with him a declaration signed by Herr Hitler and himself. In it the signatories referred to the Anglo-German Naval Agreement as symbolic of the desire of the two nations never to go to war with one another again, and recorded their determination that the method of consultation should be the method adopted with any other questions that might concern their two countries. Two days later Mr. Chamberlain in the House of Commons, and Lord Halifax in the House of Lords, delivered, in substantially identical terms, a defence of the Munich Agreement, comparing the Godesberg and Munich proposals, and announcing the grant of a credit to the Czech Government.]

Government Statement MY LORDS, by reason of events which are now part of world history your Lordships had no opportunity of debate last week, and you will perhaps therefore forgive me if I am obliged this afternoon to make a somewhat longer draft upon your patience than in other circumstances I should have done. So quickly have events moved that the situation to-day is so transformed that much that might have fallen to be said last week is now inappropriate. The story of the last days and weeks and months is familiar enough, and there is no need to recapitulate it in any but the briefest form.

It is just eight weeks since my noble friend Lord Runciman, with such great public spirit, went out in the hope, if not in the expectation, of finding some way of accommodation in Czechoslovakia. His Majesty's Government and the world owe to him and his staff a great debt; and certainly it was through no lack of effort on their part that his mission failed. Lord Runciman himself has given a Report, in terms objective and impartial, of the main conclusions at which he arrived, and that Report is published in the White Paper laid before Parliament last week. While there recording the impression left on his mind of what might not unfairly be said of Czechoslovak rule in Sudeten areas for the last twenty years, he had no hesitation in placing the responsibility for

Government Statement

the final break in negotiations upon the shoulders of the Sudeten leaders and those of their supporters, inside and outside Czechoslovakia, who were urging extreme action. The broad conclusion that he reached was that matters had gone so far that it was necessary to recognize, in his own words, 'the full right of self-determination' over a given area; that there should be immediate cession of those frontier districts where the Sudeten Deutsch population was in an important majority; and that in other districts where the Sudeten Deutsch numbers were not so large, arrangements for wide autonomy on the basis of the final Czechoslovak plan should be made.

For some days before Lord Runciman made this report, on September 21, things had, however, been moving with startling speed. On September 12 Herr Hitler had made his speech at Nuremberg, and two days later the Prime Minister had made his proposal to have personal discussion with him on a situation that was rapidly becoming one of open and immediate danger to the peace of Europe. At that meeting the German Chancellor had pressed strongly for the recognition of that principle of self-determination which Lord Runciman himself had judged inevitable; and in doing so had implied that, once the principle was recognized, discussion as to method might be expected not to be too difficult. It was accordingly on that basis that was held the first meeting with the French Ministers on September 18, which resulted in the presentation of the Anglo-French proposals of the following day, which are printed as document No. 2 in last week's White Paper. These proposals were accepted by the Czechoslovak Government under strong pressure by the French and British Governments, and the Prime Minister accordingly returned to Godesberg for his second consultation with Herr Hitler on September 22.

From that visit emerged, on September 23, the document known generally as the German Memorandum, which is printed as document No. 6 in last week's White Paper. That document went a very great deal farther than we had been led to expect at Berchtesgaden, but the Prime Minister, while indicating that in his view the Czechs would be obliged

Government Statement

to resist the demands, undertook in his capacity of intermediary to transmit it to the Czechoslovak Government. Two days later, on September 25, we were officially informed by the Czechoslovak Government that 'in their present form' the demands of the German Government were 'unconditionally unacceptable', and on that day further conversations were held with the French Ministers in view of the increasing gravity of the situation. The following day, September 26, the Prime Minister sent Sir Horace Wilson to see the German Chancellor with Letter No. 9 in the White Paper, which, however, produced no relief in the extreme tension. On the morning of the 28th, when hope was almost dead, the Prime Minister sent his final message to Herr Hitler in which he asked for an International Conference and simultaneously urged Signor Mussolini to support this request for a conference at Berlin. And then the miracle—for such it must have seemed—happened which led to the assembly at Munich, less than twenty-four hours later, of the representatives of the four great Western Powers. The results of their meeting are before us, and on them I want to make a few observations.

From the first, two principles, I think, have been in conflict in the British mind. The first has been the necessity, in the light of what has been the liberal inspiration of every political experiment our own people have made, of somehow meeting the claim preferred on behalf of the German population; and secondly, there has been the feeling that, whatever might be said about this abstract claim, its determination by force was in the long run destructive of European order and of those relationships between nations on which alone security can rest. It has accordingly been the purpose of His Majesty's Government to do their best to distinguish where they must be distinguished, to reconcile where they might be reconciled, these two conflicting claims. We were accordingly prepared to go to unusual lengths in placing pressure upon a friendly and independent Government to accept the Anglo-French proposals for full cession of Czech territory down to the majority German population line. These proposals, as your Lordships will remember, had been based

Government Statement

on the execution of their detail—the adjustment of frontiers, the questions arising out of the exchange of population on the basis of the right to opt—by an international body, including a Czech representative; and it was partly because the Godesberg Memorandum contained no equivalent provisions for these vital purposes that we felt it was impossible to press its acceptance upon the Czech Government.

The Godesberg Memorandum was in fact, though not in form, an ultimatum with a time limit expiring on October 1, and it is important to realize the distinction between it and the plan agreed upon at Munich. The Munich Agreement reverts, though not in express terms, to the Anglo-French plan referred to in its preamble, and charges an international body on which, along with the four great Powers, the Czechoslovak Government is represented, with the execution of its provisions. Under the Godesberg Memorandum the German occupation was to be effected in such fashion as the German Government alone might decide, to be completed in one operation by October 1. Under the Munich arrangement the occupation by German forces is to be carried out in five clearly defined stages between October 1 and October 10. Moreover, the line up to which the German troops will enter into occupation is no longer the line as laid down in the map attached to the Godesberg Memorandum but is a line to be fixed by an International Commission of the five Powers, including Czechoslovakia. Under the Godesberg Memorandum the areas on the Czech side of the German line which were to be submitted to plebiscite were laid down by Germany in the map, while those on the German side of the line were left undefined. Under the Munich Agreement all plebiscite areas will be defined by the International Commission.

The criterion of the line of occupation by German troops by October 10 is, under Munich, to be the 'preponderantly German character' of the areas concerned, the interpretation of which is left to the Commission. The German line, on the other hand, took in some areas which were certainly not of a preponderantly German character. The Godesberg Memorandum provided for the occupation of plebiscite areas by

Government Statement

German and Czech forces, as the case might be, up to the plebiscite, and their evacuation by those forces during the plebiscite. Under the Munich Agreement the plebiscite areas are to be occupied at once by an international force. The Godesberg Memorandum did not indicate on what kind of areas the vote would be based, and gave rise to fears on the Czech side that large areas might be selected which would operate to the disadvantage of Czechoslovakia. The Munich arrangement, by stating that the plebiscite is to be based on the conditions of the Saar plebiscite, indicates that the vote is to be taken by small administrative areas. The Czech Government, while bound under the Munich arrangement to carry out the evacuation of the territories without damaging existing installations, is not placed under the objectionable conditions of the Appendix to the Godesberg Memorandum, which provided that no foodstuffs, goods, cattle, or raw materials were to be removed. Under the existing Godesberg Memorandum the detailed arrangements for the evacuation were to be settled between Germans and Czechs alone. Under the Munich Agreement the conditions of evacuation are to be laid down in detail by the International Commission.

Unlike the Godesberg Memorandum, the Munich Agreement has provisions as regards the right of option, facilities for the transfer of population, and other questions arising out of the transfer of the territory, and gives the Czechs a period of four weeks for the release of Sudeten Germans from the Army and police, and for the release of Sudeten German political prisoners. The Annex to the Munich Agreement also gives to the Czechoslovak State an assurance of the joint guarantee by the United Kingdom and France of their new boundary against unprovoked aggression. It thus gives the Czechs an essential counterpart which was lacking in the Godesberg Memorandum. Your Lordships will have observed that Germany and Italy also undertook to give a guarantee when the question of Polish and Hungarian minorities has been settled. And, finally, there is a declaration by the Four Powers that, if the problems of the Polish and Hungarian minorities in Czechoslovakia are not settled within three months by agreement between the respective

Governments, another Four-Power meeting will be specially convened to deal with them.

There are two other aspects of what has passed to which your Lordships will rightly expect me to make some reference. I shall be asked by noble Lords opposite why we consented to the omission of Russia—so closely connected with Czechoslovakia—from these discussions. I would venture, with your Lordships' permission, to repeat here what I said to the Soviet Ambassador a day or two ago. Five days ago it seemed to us vital, if war was to be avoided, somehow or other to get matters on to a basis of negotiation; but if we were to face the facts—and nothing was to be gained but rather everything was to be lost by not facing them—we were obliged to recognize that in the present circumstances the heads of the German and Italian Governments would almost certainly—at least without much preliminary discussion for which there was no time—be reluctant to sit in conference with a Soviet representative. Accordingly, if our principal purpose was to ensure negotiation, we were bound to have regard to the practical conditions within which alone this purpose could be secured. But the fact that it was impossible, if we were to talk to the German and Italian Governments in those days at all, to include the Soviet Government directly in those conversations, in no way signified any weakening of the desire on our part—any more no doubt than on that of the French Government—to preserve our understanding and relations with the Soviet Government.

The other matter on which I must say something is the guarantee which is referred to in the Annex to the Munich Agreement and which first found place in the Anglo-French proposals of September 19. There we said that:

'His Majesty's Government in the United Kingdom would be prepared, as a contribution to the pacification of Europe, to join in an international guarantee of the new boundaries of the Czechoslovak State against unprovoked aggression. One of the principal conditions of such a guarantee would be the safeguarding of the independence of Czechoslovakia by the substitution of a general guarantee against unprovoked aggression in place of existing treaties which involve reciprocal obligations of a military character.'

Government Statement

By that offer they stand under the terms of the Annex to the Munich Agreement which also, as I mentioned just now, includes an assurance that

'when the question of the Polish and Hungarian minorities has been settled, Germany and Italy for their part will give a guarantee to Czechoslovakia.'

I understand, and largely share, what will be the feeling of many of your Lordships as to the assumption by this country of a new and difficult commitment, concerned, as it might be held, with something that was not a direct or vital interest of this country. I can anticipate from another quarter the criticism that a guarantee, given at the very moment that existing treaty and covenant obligations had failed to prevent the quasi-forcible disruption of the Czechoslovak State, proclaimed by inference its own futility. Both these criticisms are weighty and must be met. As to the first, we felt that if we were, in conjunction with the French Government, to press the Czechoslovak Government to accept proposals so drastic as those which we thought it right to lay before them in the Anglo-French plan, in order to preserve Europe as a whole from war, we were bound ourselves to make a counter-contribution to balance the reduction of Czechoslovakia's defensive strength. In no other circumstances, I think, should we have felt morally justified in pressing her Government to go so far.

As to the second, I would say three things. The first is this. Nothing has been more persistently pressed upon me during the last two or three anxious months than this. If only Great Britain would say clearly and unmistakably for all to hear that she would resist any unprovoked aggression on Czechoslovakia, no such unprovoked aggression would be made. We never felt able to use that language; but so far as there was force in the argument—and I do not underrate it—the deterrent value of such a statement will be in full force under such a guarantee as we have expressed our willingness to give. The second thing I would say is this. To guarantee a Czechoslovakia including within her borders restless and dissatisfied minorities was one thing: to guarantee Czechoslovakia when these explosive minority questions have been adjusted is quite another. And lastly, the guarantee itself is reinforced and buttressed by two other vital elements. First, Germany and Italy have expressed their readiness to guarantee Czechoslovakia when the other minority questions have been settled; and secondly, Great Britain and Germany have mutually expressed their desire to resolve any differences arising between them through consultation. In these circumstances I hope that your Lordships will be prepared to take the view that we were right to feel the moral obligation to play our part in stabilizing the new situation more weighty than our natural objection to undertake on behalf of this country a new liability. There are, of course, a great many questions connected with this guarantee that will require more careful consideration than it has yet been possible to give to them. Such will be whether its form should be joint or several, what States should be invited to assume its obligations, and in what circumstances these obligations should be held to arise. These matters, and possibly others, will of necessity be matters for early exchange of view between the several Governments concerned.

No one will deny—even as presented in the Munich Agreement—how bitter has been the sacrifice demanded of the Czechoslovak Government, affecting so vitally the social, political, and economic structure of the State. Nor has it been made less bitter by the presentation, on the morrow of these demands, of further demands from the Polish Government backed by ultimatum, to which the Czechoslovak Government have felt obliged in all the circumstances to accede. There is no one of your Lordships who would not wish at this time to pay his tribute and extend his sympathy to President Beneš and his people. No head of a State could have been faced with a more cruel and merciless dilemma. The choice lay between accepting the reduction—some would say the mutilation—of his State and, on the other hand, exposing it to certain conquest and devastation, with the added horror of plunging the whole of Europe, and more than Europe, into war as well. Faced by that grim dilemma, President Beneš chose the path of peace, and I cannot believe but that the judgement of history will accord to him a special

Government Statement

place for the wisdom of his choice. So far as we ourselves are concerned, let us make no mistake; without his help, it would have been impossible to avoid a European war. Therefore it behoves us all to be grateful to him, and to do what we can to assist the Czechs, once more as they have done through history, to rise superior to the sacrifice that these hours have demanded.

Yesterday His Majesty's Government received a communication from the Czechoslovak Minister in London pointing out that the new Czechoslovakia expects to have to make provision very promptly for assistance to a large total of citizens moving from the ceded territory, and that the loss of these Sudeten areas inevitably calls for heavy outlay in readjusting the economic life of the nation. Accordingly, the Czechoslovak Government put forward a request for a guaranteed loan of £30,000,000. So far as we have been able to ascertain, the Czechoslovak Government have not as yet addressed any similar request to any other Government, and it is evident that the terms and conditions of a guaranteed loan, and the question of what Governments would participate in it, may raise matters which could not be decided immediately. But this is manifestly a case where the old proverb applies that assistance which is given quickly is of double value. His Majesty's Government are therefore informing the Czechoslovak Government that they are prepared immediately to arrange for an advance of £10,000,000 which will be at that Government's disposal for their urgent needs.

How this advance will be related to the final figure which may be decided upon hereafter is for the future. All this manifestly depends on many factors, some of which cannot be instantly determined. The precise character of the problem will require expert examination in which His Majesty's Government would be willing to be associated, and during these coming weeks the needs of the resultant situation can be more fully explored. But what we feel to be required and justified now is that the action I have mentioned should be taken without any delay so as to assist the Czechoslovak State in what must be the crisis of its difficulty. The

Government Statement

Chancellor of the Exchequer accordingly has addressed, on behalf of the Government, a letter to the Bank of England, requesting the Bank to provide the necessary credit of £10,000,000, and this will be done. When the House resumes in November, Parliament will be asked to pass the necessary legislation to reimburse the Bank from the Exchequer.

So much for what has been done, and some of its immediate consequences. In the doing of it, Dr. Beneš, like ourselves, had to face very hard realities. Let us not forget that in the event of war, whatever force the French, the Russians, and we had been willing to employ, nothing could have saved Czechoslovakia from destruction or protected countless of her sons and daughters from sudden death. We could no doubt have engaged in a war of indefinite duration with all its consequences, knowing before we ever embarked upon it that, after we had won, no body of statesmen drawing the boundaries of a new Czechoslovakia would have redrawn them as they were left by the Treaty of Versailles. And that, my Lords, brings me to say one word about the question of Treaty revision, for which Article 19 of the Covenant purports to make provision. I remember saying to your Lordships—and others of your Lordships have said the same—that unless we could regard the world as set in a mould, rigid and unalterable, we were bound to expect change, change that would often be right, if justice as well as peace is what we seek. Yet if we are to be honest with ourselves we must acknowledge that there are only three ways in which Treaty revision can be secured. One is by consent, the second way is by force, and the third way is by the threat of force. However strongly, therefore, we may condemn resort to the only other methods, we must in fairness admit that the way of consent, laid down in Article 19, has not hitherto in vital matters been made effective. Europe is not free, and the League of Nations is not free, of responsibility in this matter.

I do not underestimate the gravity of the events which in such swift passage have crowded one upon the other during the last three weeks. I am very conscious of all that has to be entered upon the debit side, but if the whole matter is

Government Statement

fairly weighed, I cannot doubt in my own mind, for Czechoslovakia herself as for the world, where the balance rests. And, apart from the sheer avoidance of the catastrophe of war, with all that that would have meant for the men, women, and children of every nation that would sooner or later have been dragged to take part in that dance of death, there seem to me certain things of which we should be utterly wrong to underestimate the significance. The mutual confidence between the French Government and ourselves, strong as it was before, emerges stronger from this searching test. Beyond this we have surely witnessed the emergence of strong forces, more powerful than we had suspected, to condemn resort to war. From every part of the world, led by the President of the great Republic of the United States of America, and given constructive form through the support extended to the Prime Minister's last request by Signor Mussolini, the pressure of moral opinion on that point was clear. May it not be a great thing for the future of the world that, when brought to the very edge of disaster, the feeling of all nations—not only of our own—should have drawn back from force and expressed itself so powerfully, as I believe, in favour of negotiation? Is it a small thing that the representatives of the British and German Governments should have publicly proclaimed the desire of their peoples never to permit war between one another, and their own determination to employ the method of consultation in any differences that might arise between them?

No man can predict the future, and no declaration can absolve a nation like ours from doing whatever is necessary to secure itself against all eventualities. Indeed, one of the principal lessons of these events is that the diplomacy of any nation can only be commensurate with its strength, and that if we desire this country to exercise its full influence in world affairs, the first thing that we have to do is to ensure that it is in all ways fully and rapidly equipped to do so. I have no doubt that at the appropriate time your Lordships will wish to give fuller consideration to the issues involved in the statement of that principle.

I am well aware that there will not be wanting those who

Government Statement

will maintain that immediately to attach weight to such declarations as that to which the German Chancellor and the Prime Minister have set their names is merely to lay up for ourselves certain and disastrous disappointment. Time alone will show. I have never felt able to take the view of the inevitability of war, which is perhaps more easily taken by those who are fortunate enough to have no final responsibility; and he is a rash man who would attempt to write history before the time. The rejoicings in all countries have shown how the peoples have acclaimed the success of this method of conference which has brought them all back from the very brink of ruin. There has been in Germany a spontaneous outburst of public feeling. Herr Hitler has had a great triumph, and I for one would grudge him nothing of a triumph which he knows to be accorded, not only for what he has gained, but also for the contribution which he made to settlement through agreement in preference to the arbitrament of catastrophic war. I see in Munich not only a conference at which hard terms were imposed on Czechoslovakia, but also an occasion on which it was found possible by discussion to effect real abatement in claims made, and at which all the nations taking part contributed to win a real victory for reason and understanding over the forces of unreason, hatred, and mistrust. There is not one of your Lordships who will not hope with me that what has been done may prove only a beginning of more promising approach to other problems that may yet stand in the way of friendly and fruitful co-operation.

I am not greatly moved, therefore, for myself or for His Majesty's Government, by the reproaches that may be levelled against us for the action to which your Lordships' attention is now directed. The only reproaches that can wound are the reproaches of a man's own conscience, and he alone can know in what language conscience speaks. As I look back on these anxious weeks, I readily confess that I may have had my share in decisions that can be held by some to be ill judged. In a time of crisis, with grave questions demanding urgent answer at every moment, no body of men would dare claim to be judged infallible. There was

Government Statement

indeed no clear way, but almost always a hideous choice of evils. I can only know, for myself, that my mind will be at rest for having taken no decision inconsistent with what on all the facts I felt right.

Would your Lordships allow me, before I close, to say something of the part that it has fallen to the Prime Minister to play in these events? His courage in taking every political risk, his perseverance and faith in refusing to admit failure, his resource in the invention of new means to snatch success when all seemed to have failed—these are things that the world has understood. They were, indeed, the qualities by which the nations were led back from the great darkness that seemed to be finally descending on them. But what the world can never measure was the almost unbearable weight that rested personally, and alone, upon his shoulders. This no colleagues could share, and for the manner in which he bore it no thanks of his fellow men can be too great. He was engaged all these days in a race against time, the stakes the lives of millions, and I shall always be grateful for the privilege of having been allowed to work so closely with him.

In one of the country churches of England is set an inscription to its builder, who had had the faith to build it nearly three hundred years ago, during the Civil War. It is, I think, in spirit, not inapt to express some of the deeper thought on what it has been, under God, permitted to the Prime Minister to do. It runs thus:

> 'In the year 1653, when all things sacred were either demolished or profaned, this church was built by one, whose singular praise it is to have done the best things in the worst times, and to have hoped them in the most calamitous.'[1]

[1] The inscription is at Staunton Harold in Leicestershire. The exact wording is: 'In the yeare 1653 when all thinges Sacred were throughout ye nation either demollisht or profaned Sr Robert Shirley, Barronet, founded this church; whose singular praise it is, to have done the best things in ye worst times, and hoped them in the most callamitous.'

30

AFTER MUNICH

24 October 1938

[The Munich settlement produced the disintegration of Czechoslovakia. President Beneš resigned. Slovakia and Ruthenia asserted their autonomy. Hungary claimed for the Magyar minority in Slovakia the same privileges that had been conceded to the Sudeten Germans and commenced negotiations with the Slovaks for the restoration of Magyar districts to Hungary. Meanwhile in this country British Ministers admitted the inadequacy of national defence. A new race in armaments began.

The following speech, made by Lord Halifax at Edinburgh, is printed from a text supplied by him.]

THIS is the first occasion which I have had for addressing a public audience since the great events of three weeks ago, and I am glad to have this opportunity of making some comment upon them while they are fresh in our minds.

What first of all were the facts? The problem itself—centuries old—raised in an acute form difficult questions of race, made more difficult by the impulse given to all these racial factors by the philosophy inspiring the German Government.

The claim to choice of their own political destiny by a fairly homogeneous German population in Czechoslovakia was one side of the case. And this claim was difficult for British people—who have stood for it in one form or another in most parts of the world—to reject. The other side of the case was that this claim, whatever may be said to justify German action, was in fact advanced and pressed under an overwhelming show of force, which was impossible to reconcile with the spirit of what we believe must be the basis of international relations.

The question the Government had to decide was whether it was right or wrong to allow Europe and countries far beyond Europe to drift into war, meeting force by force; or whether it was right, with the French Government, who were bound by direct treaty obligations to Czechoslovakia of which we were free, to use all our influence to secure the best settlement possible by other means.

Do not underestimate the price of settlement that Czechoslovakia has had to pay, or the hardships, social, economic, political, that it has imposed upon her. I recognize all the cruel human problems of refugees of all kinds, which these events have created. And it is to no purpose now to discuss the question of whether or not the damage could have been avoided, if the rulers of Czechoslovakia had pursued a policy of greater foresight and imagination. It may be so, but the principal feeling in all our minds is one of sympathy in a disaster that has generally only befallen States after being vanquished in open war.

But I must ask in all sincerity those who would criticize the choice we made to avert general war, what in fact was the alternative? It was the plain fact, which no one has ever denied, that no war—no combination of effort by France, Russia, and ourselves, rallying to our cause any others who would have joined—could have protected Czechoslovakia herself from destruction far more sweeping and complete than those sacrifices, great as they are, that have been demanded of her. We could have embarked upon a general war, in which Czechoslovakia would have endured—as would all taking part in what would have become a general holocaust of human life—cruel losses of her manhood and of her resources, and at the end no one would have redrawn her frontiers in the form which they had ostensibly gone to war to protect.

There was indeed no perfect course, but only and always a hard choice between alternatives, one of which meant war and for Czechoslovakia destruction, and the other of which means the terms for Czechoslovakia that we know. Deeply, therefore, as we must feel the misfortunes of a small country, with brave rulers and stout-hearted people, I cannot doubt that the decision to secure a settlement by which war might be averted from half the world was right. In this respect I am glad to find myself in agreement with Lord Cranborne, who has not always seen eye to eye with His Majesty's Government in recent months, and who, speaking at Weymouth, said that it was a complete misconception of his position that he would have preferred England to go to war rather than accept the terms of the Munich Agreement. He added that he could not conceive of anybody who would embark upon a war if there was any practicable alternative.

Day and night—for weeks—the dread burden of responsibility lay upon the shoulders of His Majesty's Government. In that burden every member of Government to greater or less degree was obliged to share. But no one of his colleagues could share the load that rested personally and individually on the Prime Minister. Over and over again during those last days in September, it seemed as if nothing could prevent the final plunge over the precipice; and of all human agency it is to the Prime Minister, on whom lay the deadweight of ultimate decision, to his unflinching perseverance in the cause of peace and to his refusal to accept defeat, that the world owes an incalculable debt of gratitude.

I have seen it suggested that there are people in England who want war. If anyone in other countries really thinks that—and I find it hard to believe that such an opinion could be seriously held—let me assure them that I have never met any responsible person so insane. People in England want war no more than people in Germany or any other country want war. Perhaps the most remarkable thing that emerged from recent events was the unanimous revolt of simple folk in all countries at the idea that their leaders might in fact be leading them up a road, of which the end was the abyss.

Under this impulse the four Powers took common action to avoid war, and laid, as we may surely hope, a foundation on which we may build better things. The Prime Minister and Herr Hitler signed a declaration which included three points: (1) they recognized that the question of Anglo-German relations was of the first importance for the two countries and for Europe; (2) they recognized the desire of their two peoples never to go to war with one another again; (3) they recorded their joint resolution that the method of consultation should be the method adopted to deal with any other questions that might concern their two countries, and their joint determination to continue their efforts to remove possible sources of difference and thus to contribute to assure the peace of Europe.

There may be some who will be disposed to underrate the value of that statement, but if its spirit can be kept alive and sincerely made the basis by both sides of mutual approach, may it not turn out to be a larger thing for the world than many doubters are to-day prepared to think? General Smuts, speaking ten days ago, said: 'We hope the favourable opportunity now existing will not be allowed to pass without another resolute and determined effort to secure such a settlement. Lost opportunities have been largely responsible for the worsening of European conditions in recent years. The mistake should not be repeated.' Those are wise and weighty words from a man, than whom no one has a greater right to be heard throughout the British Empire. We talk much to-day of guarantees: I do not hesitate to say that, if the German and the British nations could really succeed in reaching understanding, it would be the strongest guarantee that could be devised against the dangers to which the world has been brought so close.

I hope indeed that the rectification of frontiers according to the racial distribution of population which is now taking place in Central and South-Eastern Europe may contribute to stability and peace. What we are now witnessing is the revision of the Treaty of Versailles, for which provision was made in the Covenant of the League, but which has never till now been made effective. The Hungarian Government are now in negotiation with the Czechoslovak Government, and we hope that they may reach an equitable solution which will remove or lessen racial grievances. We recognize that Hungary has had legitimate claims, and we trust that means may be found to meet them. There is no ideal solution of such problems, and there must always be minorities left on one side of the line or the other. But if the two parties can negotiate in a spirit of goodwill, and in the desire to find a remedy for clear grievances, we hope it may be possible for them to agree also on safeguards for minorities that will minimize injustice, and make more easy in future friendly co-operation between them.

But if this country is to play its full part with others in securing peace, it must be able to speak with equal weight. One-sided armament and one-sided disarmament are both impossible and give no help to peace. And therefore we must take all measures—already taken months ago by continental countries—that are essential to our strength and safety. We have no reason to apprehend attack, but if other nations have found it wise to take such measures, it is not for them to reproach us when we follow their example. We have obligations in all parts of the world—which certainly do not diminish—and those obligations we have to meet.

It is sometimes argued by our critics that the policy of His Majesty's Government to work for peace, and the faith in the possibility of their efforts being successful, is inconsistent with the determination to build up the defensive armaments of the country. If you preach peace, it is said, and if you are prepared to rest your efforts upon the belief that others are as sincere as yourselves, what is the sense of spending all these millions in a competitive race of arms? Such an argument rests upon a complete misconception both of Government policy and of what I believe to be the common sense of the matter. No one would pretend that any declaration between statesmen can of itself bring a remedy to all our ills. Nor can anyone say for certain—because it is given to no man to foretell the future—whether or not our hopes of peace can be fulfilled, for this depends on many things which are not within our own control. But that it is right to make the attempt, I can have no kind of doubt.

To refuse to make it is indeed in effect to accept the position that war is inevitable, and that therefore it is futile to waste your time and energy on what is foredoomed to failure. I could never take that view. It seems to me a gospel of pure fatalism, and must impel you to strengthen yourself against the certain war by defensive alliances of the old pattern, call them by what name you will. That in present circumstances must in turn lead straight to the division of Europe into antagonistic blocs, and bring more close the catastrophe against which it professes to prepare.

Rather do I hold that there is a growing sense everywhere that war, quite apart from its horror and damage, unsettles more than it settles, and that accordingly there are strong forces at work which will make any country think once and twice before resorting to it. There are then in my view many influences, and I think they may be the most powerful, working for peace. There are others that pull in a different and more dangerous direction; and the right conclusion to my mind in this matter of armament for national defence is that there is a good deal of sense in the old-fashioned idea that an umbrella often helps to keep the rain away.

It is the recognition of these facts that has inspired in all classes and quarters a desire to see the State make greater call upon the service of individuals than it has yet felt it necessary to do. No one can move about this country without realizing the wave of feeling in this direction, that is so powerfully affecting the minds of our people. Everybody is anxious to see the nation resume its ancient strength, and everybody is anxious to lend what help he may. The Government on their part will certainly wish to make the fullest use of this spirit of co-operation.

About this there are two things that may usefully be said. The first is that if we are to make more swift progress with the re-equipment of all branches of our defensive power, it is certain that this can only be achieved by the readiness of all people and interests to make great sacrifices to the common end. It is not for me to say what form those sacrifices may need to take. That is a matter which will obviously require most careful and skilled examination. For some, the sacrifice will be of money, in order to provide financial resources for what we need to do; of others it may be necessary to demand sacrifice in other forms.

But none of these things, if they are necessary, as I believe them to be, can be accomplished unless there is a real unity of spirit right through the nation. And that unity will depend on the conviction, everywhere felt, that, in spite of our own domestic political differences, we all value the same things, and are determined to preserve them. The world that we desire to see is a world in which all nations may exist side by side, their just rights respected by all, and differences resolved by free discussion; a world in which the men and women and children can live decent lives, no longer haunted by the dread spectre of war that stalked the world a month ago.

Yet, if we are to succeed in bringing the world into smoother waters, we must face frankly the three possibilities that the future seems to hold. The first is war. The second is an armed peace. The third is a peace of understanding. We wish to escape the first, and we wish to achieve the third; but it may be that, just as Dante made the entry into Paradise through the way of Purgatory, so we, if we are to reach the true peace, have to pass through the stage of armed peace to get there. For let us remember peace will not come, like Christmas, just by waiting for it. Peace is not a passive thing: just as good is all the time an active struggle against wrong, so peace must be an active struggle against the things that make for war.

But if we are to succeed, it is vital that all nations should so far as possible concentrate upon the things on which they are able to agree, rather than block their own progress towards the main purpose by interferences in one another's internal affairs. It is not our custom, and it is certainly not our desire, to interfere in other people's business so long as they do not interfere with ours; and the world would be an easier place if some of those who comment on foreign affairs both here and abroad were able to exercise a greater measure of restraint.

Our own course is clear. We must lose no opportunity of helping forward, so that they may take substantial shape, the results of the personal contacts established between Germany, Italy, France, and ourselves at Munich. In doing so, we shall not abandon old friends in the search for new. But we do intend if we can to improve our own relations with all who are willing to improve their own relations with us, and if we can to work for a general understanding in which all can meet on common ground of mutual tolerance and respect.

That surely must be the goal for which everybody, who has imagination to realize the price of failure, has to work. The world, as General Smuts reminded us, has missed opportunities enough since 1918 and we cannot afford to miss more. But while we try to grasp with both hands at any chance of building the foundations of real peace, do not let any of us be afraid to acknowledge the difficulties that have to be overcome and face them squarely. There are profound differences of thought upon many fundamental things which to-day replace what used to be a common background, shared by all Christian nations. There are those in all countries who, sometimes from genuine conviction, sometimes from motives much less worthy, are unable to rid themselves of deep suspicion, which destroys before it is born the faith that can alone be the parent of better things. For reasons which it is not hard to understand, the gospel of force has gained a hold in many quarters, and it is this which is the real enemy to the free growth of confidence between nations, without which they can only move uneasily from one dangerous crisis to another. But we shall not substitute for this gospel of force what we think a better creed, merely by catching the infection ourselves, by resigning ourselves for all time to nothing better than the necessary attempt to meet force by force, and letting go all hope of exorcizing the evil spirits that torment and oppress the souls of men.

And just because we have the conviction that we have something of priceless value to give the world, we need the whole strength, moral and material, of the nation to enable us to maintain and discharge the responsibilities that seem to have been providentially entrusted to our keeping. If I were asked to state what was the most marked characteristic of the British people, I think I should reply that it was a quality of balance and judgement. And I believe that it is because of this characteristic that we have worked out our own system of democracy, which is an even balance between rights and responsibilities. We assert our rights when things go smoothly; we assume our responsibilities when the times are troubled. We are living to-day in a time when, besides claiming rights, we must assume our full responsibilities. In this task, I do not doubt that we shall enlist the goodwill and active support of all who love their country, and who wish to see their country make its full contribution to the creation of a better and a happier world.

31
ADDRESS TO AMERICA

27 October 1938

[At the height of the September Crisis President Roosevelt had appealed to Herr Hitler and to Signor Mussolini to use their influence for the maintenance of peace. On this, as on other occasions, American popular opinion was extremely critical of British policy. Lord Halifax's broadcast address to the United States was given in explanation of the line pursued by his Government.]

I AM happy to have been given the opportunity to address a few words to what I know must be a large and thoroughly representative American audience. I am the more happy to do so as this is the first occasion since the crisis that a member of the British Government has been able to speak direct to the American public, and I should like to preface my remarks by saying how immensely helpful was the contribution that your President made in those dark days. It was as valuable as it was welcome. Most deeply do we appreciate what the President and Mr. Cordell Hull have done and will, I am sure, continue to do in the cause of peace.

At the outset of my talk I would say that I consider it just as important for us in England to understand your position as it is for you to understand ours. There is, I believe, a very real understanding among us here of the American attitude towards world affairs. You have your responsibilities and we have ours. We fully accept your desire not to be caught up in disputes and controversies which are far from your shores and which do not seem to touch you directly. We do not question the motives which have inspired your Neutrality Legislation. And no one on this side expects you to do anything which we have the sense to know to be impossible.

But at the same time it has not been lost on us that you have been following with acute interest and anxiety the passage of events in Europe. We know that with your own deep-rooted belief in liberty you must have watched with concern, not less than our own, the influence that these events might exercise upon the rights of men, which you and we both base upon the ultimate and eternal value of individual lives.

On all these matters I am sure that I can associate the American and British people. And I say this with all the greater confidence because I have seen sharp criticisms in your Press on the action taken by the British Government from time to time during recent weeks. Those criticisms are the best proof that you feel as strongly as we do about the things which it is vital for the world to hold on to, if international relations are to be at all securely founded. Your criticisms therefore bring you nearer to us than would an attitude of indifference on your part. But when you feel impelled to criticize, may I remind you of something which I have no doubt is true.

There is, I fancy, little, if any, real difference between the attitude of the average man and woman here and in your country in their general outlook on the turbulent currents which are to-day sweeping across Europe. Such differences as there may be spring from the map and not from psychology. We who are, so to speak, on the spot and have a direct part to play, must needs exercise restraint in speech and action which is less incumbent on your people, widely removed as you are from the first impact of these events.

Twenty years ago we fought in the same cause. Twenty years ago we were confident that war had saved and preserved the cause for which we fought together. We convinced ourselves that war would prove a solvent, and thought that the spectre of war might be exorcized for all time and not only for our generation. There we were wrong. But were we not also wrong in believing that war was a sure solvent? We have learnt by bitter experience that, however righteous the cause, war is likely to leave a legacy of greater difficulties than it can resolve, for the heat of conflict is fatally apt to blur the issues, and the evils of war drag on into the peace that follows.

There will perhaps, until human nature is transformed, be cases in which war will be unavoidable and right; but there will be few to say that the great catastrophe that war is should not if at all possible be averted. My own conscience is clear that the Government to which I belong, and the Prime Minister on whom so direct a burden lay, acted rightly in the endeavours that were made to prevent war in the recent crisis. In no way would I minimize the sufferings inflicted on a small nation, to the rulers and people of which the world owes a deep debt of gratitude. But through all the days and nights of difficult decision, we could not forget that the sufferings of Czechoslovakia would have been far greater, had we and they acted otherwise.

There were before us all the time two points which were unescapable. The first was that, if Germany had carried out her intention of invading Czechoslovakia, there was nothing which France, or Russia, or we, or any others, could together have done which would have saved Czechoslovakia from being overrun. The second was that, even if war had come, we should have embarked upon it knowing that no body of statesmen when the war was over would ever have been able, as in the case of Belgium after the Great War, to redraw the boundaries of Czechoslovakia as they had been drawn by the Treaty of Versailles.

You will say to me, 'Yes, but where is all this to end?' To that I would say this: We are not less alive than you to the fact that no true peace can exist until the nations are agreed that law and not force shall rule the world. We know well enough that peace will not come just by waiting for it, for peace is something more than the mere absence of destructive war. The only foundation for such a peace is understanding, and the first stage on that road is that nations who share the same ideals should be prepared to think together.

It may be that the peace we all desire will only come through sacrifices, freely flowing from a spirit of determination and from a quality of national resolution not less strong than those by which a nation is inspired in war. For we are living in one of the great periods of human history, of which we have read but of which few foresaw that we were destined to experience the repetition. There have been times when it almost seemed that there was a restless spirit in mankind forbidding him to tread steadily the straight path of progress.

Some strange and sinister spirit of this sort surely roams

the world to-day. When man's creative powers are at their height he is driven, as if possessed, to imperil all that through the centuries he has created. Yet every people knows that it would be the greatest tragedy in all human history if, at a moment when man's knowledge has reached the highest point yet known, that knowledge were to be employed to destroy the hope and opportunity of its own perfection.

For countries like yours and mine which have been so favoured in the past by history and circumstance there is a heavy responsibility to use all our energy to guide our fellow men towards a future which may serve us all. If, recognizing the high stakes for which we play, we may all win such a peace of understanding between nations, we shall indeed have set a crown on man's achievement. But let the nations make no miscalculation; if, in the alternative, they fail, they will assuredly all sink together into the same abyss, which knows no distinction of geography, philosophy, or race.

32

SI VIS PACEM

3 February 1939

[During the winter of 1938–9 British rearmament gained momentum. Special attention was given to the protection of the nation from air attack. A Minister was appointed to deal with the problem of Civilian Defence, and a National Voluntary Register was set up. Fear of future war was not confined to Europe. On January 4th, 1939, President Roosevelt, in a message to the American Congress, spoke of the threat to religion, democracy, and international good faith, with obvious reference to the Totalitarian States.

The fall of Barcelona on January 26th decided the issue of the long Spanish conflict, but did not at once improve the relations between France and Italy, in the deterioration of which it had been a major factor. A friendly reception was, on the other hand, accorded to Mr. Chamberlain and Lord Halifax during their visit to Rome on January 11th–14th.

In a speech in the Reichstag on January 30th Herr Hitler, while declaring his belief in a 'long peace', announced that Germany would stand by her friend Italy were she attacked. Germany, who, he insisted, had been attacked in the last war to eliminate her from world trade, must to-day export or die. Speaking the next day in the House of Commons Mr. Chamberlain once again asserted that, in his view, all questions at issue could be settled by negotiation, although there must first be concrete evidence of willingness to enter into arrangements for the limitation of armaments.

The general situation was surveyed by Lord Halifax on February 3rd in a speech delivered at Hull, here printed from a text supplied by him.]

THERE has, I suppose, never been a time when it was more important that the country should understand the issues before us and appreciate the attitude of those who are charged with the responsibilities of Government. That responsibility to-day is not light, and no body of men can discharge it rightly unless they can feel that they are supported by the great majority of their fellow countrymen. Time was when the attention of the country could be almost exclusively directed to domestic issues touching the daily life of our people. And indeed these have lost none of their importance. But they can no longer be considered in separation from foreign affairs, for at every point domestic and foreign problems react on one another. Problems of defence, for example, are not, and cannot be, limited to the problems of the three Service Departments, for our strength in defence, as also any foreign policy, is dependent on the general strength and soundness of the nation over the whole field.

. . . . . .

Industry and agriculture are both vital to national defence, and it is no exaggeration to say that under modern conditions the problem of defence covers such wide ground that it involves a complete reorientation of outlook for all countries and most of all perhaps for our own. We no longer live in days when we could look merely to our navy and our army to protect this country and the Empire. Air warfare has not only introduced a new arm into the fighting services; it has brought the front line into the heart of every country. We have to think of this country as a whole in terms of the home front. In such circumstances, when something like a revolution of method is involved, there are bound to be differences about practical questions of administration. How far ought we, in order to concentrate upon rearmament, to sacrifice the claims of our export trade, which affects so closely the life and cost of living of our people? How best can we deal with the great expenditure we have to face, without impairing our financial strength? We have to defend the country not only by armaments, not only by developing our defences against possible attack from the air, but also by maintaining our exports and our vital services. A just balance has somewhere and somehow to be struck between all these manifold requirements. A serious error might easily upset the whole structure on which the equilibrium of the State depends, and we do not want our rearmament to be a Colossus with feet of clay.

There has been, and is, anxiety in the country in regard to our preparations against any possible trouble. I certainly would not maintain that these preparations were complete. It is impossible that they should be. Factories had to be built, machinery laid down, new workers trained. We, longer than other nations, persisted in the hope that others would follow our example in holding off this race of armaments in which the whole world is now engaged. And for that all sections of opinion are alike responsible. But just as it would be quite indefensible for anyone to pretend that our defensive schemes were complete, it is in the highest degree wrong and dangerous to depreciate the enormous efforts that the country is making, and the immense results that these efforts have brought. On the sea, on land, and in the air, as a result of the last two or three years' intensive drive, this country is a long way on the road to resuming its ancient strength; and if trouble came, and there was a temptation in any quarter to think that this country would not give a good account of itself, those holding that opinion would make a very bad mistake. We should suffer, of course, for modern war is a cruel thing and it is right to do everything in our power to avoid it. But, while the last thing the British people want to do is to pick quarrels with anybody, they are nevertheless so made that if a quarrel was ever forced upon them, I should have no shadow of doubt either as to what their answer, or what the ultimate outcome, would be.

On my shoulders rests the responsibility for Foreign Affairs, and I often think it is a misleading phrase. Although there is no subject that occupies so large a place in public thought, the phrase gives the impression that these things are not directly the concern of the ordinary man and woman in the street. If we think about it, we quickly see how far divorced any such idea is from reality. One of the outstanding achievements of modern science has been to narrow—or even abolish—distance. You listen at will to foreign stations on the wireless; you fly in hours what a comparatively short time ago took days, or a little earlier took months; and all the time the telegraph and the Press are making the whole world aware of what is going on in every part of it. That is one side. The other is that while this destruction of separating distance is going on, a sharper division of thought is taking shape upon many of the things that go right down to the roots of our individual and national life. The relations between the State and the individual, which for us have been as I believe firmly established on the basis of liberty and respect for human personality, are elsewhere replaced by philosophies which are opposed to many things that we regard as fundamental. And it is this clash of philosophies which, in addition to all the legacy of feeling and disturbance left by the Great War, is to-day responsible for the present atmosphere in which intolerance is often regarded as a sign of strength, and tolerance as a sign of weakness. And it is in this atmosphere that we in this country, Government and people, are called upon to try to build real peace.

I can understand the temptation sometimes to throw up the sponge and abandon efforts that seem to bring no reward. It would have been very easy for Mr. Chamberlain to have stopped trying to restore confidence in Europe—many would. He has been violently assailed for his perseverance. But no man that I know is less tempted than Mr. Chamberlain to cherish unreal illusions—it is after all by deeds, not words, that history is made, and all men must be judged—and neither he nor any member of His Majesty's Government is the least likely to under-estimate the difficulties or the dangers of the present international situation. And I do not hesitate to say that it has been the great merit of the Prime Minister that he has not yielded under criticism in this country—you see very little of it abroad—to the temptation to give up his efforts for real peace. And even if all our efforts were to fail, and this country found itself obliged to face war, I should have no sort of doubt that we had been 100 per cent. right to make the efforts we have made, and are making, to show Europe the more excellent way. For in such event the whole British people, irrespective of party and everything else, would be united as one man; their honest desire for peace would have been shown beyond any possibility of doubt; they themselves would have an invincible spiritual conviction of right; and the effect on the moral opinion of the world, with all that that would mean, would be incalculable.

I am not one of those who regard war as inevitable, and those who speak and act as if it was, do no service to the cause of peace. But it is no good merely wanting peace; you have got to take active steps to secure it. And it was in that spirit that the Prime Minister was glad the other day to accept Signor Mussolini's invitation to Rome. With no country have our differences been sharper in the recent past than with Italy. The Fascist régime is totally different from ours, and Italy forms part of the Berlin–Rome Axis, which is an essential point in Italian policy, just as the Anglo-French Entente is in our own. Yet the impressions which remain uppermost in my mind after the visit are the cordiality with which we were received by Signor Mussolini and the Italian Government; the absolutely spontaneous character of the enthusiasm with which the Prime Minister was greeted by the people wherever he went; and the very definite assurance which we received from Signor Mussolini that the policy of Italy was one of peace. Speaking of the Mediterranean in particular, Signor Mussolini assured us that he was well satisfied with the Anglo-Italian Agreement, by which both parties undertook to respect the existing *status quo* in the Mediterranean. He also emphatically declared that, once the Spanish conflict was over, all Italian military support would be withdrawn, and he would have nothing to ask from Spain by way of territorial concessions.

For more than two years, Spain has been the disturbing element in European politics. It has aroused emotions, deep, passionate, intense on all sides, for the causes that were involved. It has excited anxieties both here and in France as to possible threats to vital interests of both countries, and for that reason we attach the greatest importance to the assurances that Signor Mussolini has given to us. And all the time we have been perpetually reminded of the profound human tragedy of which Spain is the scene, translated into terms of human life and suffering. Not the least unfortunate reaction from the Spanish war has been its effect upon the relations between Italy and France. While we welcome the improvement in our own relations with Italy, those between Italy and France have become more difficult. So long as those relations are what they are, it is bound to cause concern to ourselves, for whom close contact and co-operation with France, based upon identity of interest, are fundamental to our foreign policy, and who wish also to have relations of cordial confidence with Italy. Therefore, while that state of things continues, it is not possible for international tension to be reduced, as we should wish, in an area where, as I have said, British interests are directly and vitally concerned.

Whatever difficulties may exist between France and Italy, they have been greatly aggravated by events in Spain. It has excited deep and most natural resentment in the minds of all those, whether in France or here, who sympathize with the Spanish Government, to have watched General Franco achieving success, as they think, with the help of foreign support. And consequently we have been sharply blamed for adhering strictly to the policy of Non-Intervention. But the criticism is not only from one side, for in other quarters it is alleged with equal force that, by denial of belligerent rights to General Franco, we have made it impossible for him to take advantage of his superiority at sea. Whether departure from Non-Intervention in one direction or the other would have had or have all the advantages for Republican Spain or for General Franco that some people think, I greatly doubt. But of one thing I have no doubt at all. And that is that if the policy of Non-Intervention *were* generally abandoned, it would immediately and dangerously increase the risks of the Spanish struggle becoming a general European war. Standing, therefore, as we have always stood, for strict and impartial Non-Intervention, we have deplored all breaches of it—from whatever side. We neither sympathize with, nor defend, such action. We have regarded it as at once one of the causes and symptoms of distrust in Europe, and we have made repeated efforts to bring it to an end. But whatever we may feel about these breaches, we all have to ask ourselves whether things are going to be better for European peace by deliberately extending the area of intervention, and how long is it going to be, if that were done, before the respective supporters of the two sides engaged in this bloody struggle were themselves fighting one another.

Nor is it so certain that any nation which has actively intervened in the strife will in the long run benefit from it. Those who take part in other people's quarrels not infrequently find themselves in the end less popular with either side than they would wish. Our only wish is that Spain should settle her own troubles by herself in her own way. Our policy will continue to be what it has always been—to mitigate, so far as we may, the horrors and limit the scope of this fratricidal conflict; to do everything that we can do to succour those who are its innocent victims; and if we ever see the opportunity, to do anything in our power to bring it to an end.

What the Spanish Civil War is in the West the conflict in China is in the Far East—a stumbling-block to any real improvement of international relations there. It is inevitable that so many problems in all parts of the world should give rise to honest difference of opinion, and in these days I am as much impressed as anybody can be by the need for national unity. And if I am impressed by the need for unity, I am as much alive as anybody else to the doubts and divergences of opinion that stand in the way of full agreement on policy to-day. I make no complaint of honest criticism, based upon sound argument and genuine regard for national interest. The fact that criticism exists shows that people realize how vital these things are; and no body of men composing His Majesty's Government, doing their best in the face of immense difficulties, would claim to be infallible. But here as always the future is more important than the past. We are living in days when the usual machinery of international contacts is largely out of gear, and when in consequence the air has become so thick with rumours that it has almost seemed as if there must be some central factory working overtime for their output and dissemination. But much as I deplore unnecessary alarms, the only effect which I have observed is to increase the national solidarity and the calm determination of all our people. Well over a million volunteers have already been enrolled in connexion with the various air-raid precautions services. What is more, the people now have it in their power, by their response to the call of the National Service Register made at the end of January, to show the world by what spirit they are moved. And I have no doubt that here, as in every other part of the United Kingdom, that response will be made in no uncertain fashion. There could, I am convinced, be no stronger reinforcement to the cause of peace than would be found in the spectacle of the free citizens of a free nation thus enrolling themselves for voluntary national service. I do not indeed believe that there is any fundamental difference in the purposes that all sections of thought among British people set before them.

You sometimes hear people reproaching one another, or the Government, with being *pro* one side or the other in the several conflicts that are taking place. It is inevitable when deep feeling is aroused that partisans on different sides will exaggerate mutual differences. But one thing I know very well. At bottom all our people are solidly only *pro-British*, and are prepared for whatever is necessary to secure interests they adjudge vital. However much British people may want peace, they feel instinctively that there are things without which life as they know it would not be worth living. They would not be slow if need arose to make up their minds what these things are, remembering that for them the life of the nation consists not only in material possessions, but in the assurance of independence and freedom to live that life according to the fashion they desire.

A few weeks ago we heard striking expression given to these ideas by President Roosevelt. It was the voice of a people which owes its independent existence as a nation to its love of liberty. Throughout American history the rights of the individual have been regarded as the most treasured heritage of the nation. Individual initiative brought prosperity to a whole continent, and it required unbounded individual initiative to overcome the dangers and difficulties of America's pioneering period. That same spirit remains as strong to-day as it always has been, and it is not less the spirit which inspired the men of this country who built the British Commonwealth.

It may well be that in revolutionary times—and we live in revolutionary times to-day—things will be done elsewhere, as they have been done, which shock the moral sense of our people, and which are directly opposed to the Christian doctrine on which European civilization has been built.

But whatever we may feel about those things, and however difficult the task may be made, no one who has a share in the direction of a country's international policy ought to forget that the end of all his efforts is to resist the forces that would destroy peace; and I am certain that the peoples of all nations recognize that peace—a peace based upon justice, right, and upon equality—is their great and abiding interest. But peace has also its responsibilities. Peoples must live. Herr Hitler declared the other day that the German nation must live—that is, he said they must export or die. No doubt this is true of Germany: it is certainly true of the United Kingdom. But what is quite untrue is his statement that the War was waged to exclude Germany from world trade. Germany was England's best foreign customer before the War. Her trade had flourished when ours had flourished; it had declined when ours declined. No two countries were more closely bound together by commercial and financial partnership. Why should we, then or now, wish to exclude Germany from world trade? We have never believed in England that competition is exclusive. We believe that, in days of development and prosperity and peace, it promotes trade all round. But what destroys trade is partly the waste of effort, expressed in both capital and labour, on unproductive purposes such as armaments; and, above all, lack of confidence and the fear of war.

Herr Hitler has predicted a long period of peace. No one hopes more devoutly than I do that this prediction will be fulfilled. Give the world real assurance of peace, trade will revive, and an economic development will be possible, by which all will benefit and which will leave the achievements of the last century far behind. It is not my business to discuss the extent to which the difficulties of Germany, or of any other country, might be reduced by action that it is within the power of a single country to take. But I know that so long as the world remains an armed camp, the present difficulties will in greater or less degree persist for all. And if we do, in fact, desire to see the world become once more a place where man strives with man in friendly rivalry to harness the forces of nature to his service, then we must learn the lesson of the past that peace, assured and maintained, is the only basis for national recovery and improved standards of life. If there is any one thing certain it is that these basic economic standards—which in simple terms mean the amount and quality and price of food that people have to eat, the rent at which they are able to live in their houses, the taxes they have to pay—cannot be improved unless all nations work together for the common good. This we are at all times prepared to do, if others will join hands with us in genuine determination to win this advance for all our peoples. The last thing we desire is to obstruct the natural expansion of trade, from which others will reap direct benefit, for we know well enough that such trade development is for the good of all.

As a matter of fact, within the last few days, we have reached a very satisfactory agreement with Germany, whom we have been charged with wishing to exclude from world trade. The agreement was one freely negotiated between the German coal industry and the British coal industry to regulate competition and prevent undercutting in third markets. I welcome this agreement as a very practical contribution to co-operation between the two countries and a hopeful sign for the future. For I believe that collaboration between the two countries is not only desirable, but necessary. Further, there are shortly to take place in Germany a series of negotiations between other British and German industries, with the same object—to limit competition and to avoid price-cutting in third markets. These negotiations will take place between the industries, but it is the earnest wish of the Government that they should succeed and that they will facilitate a fair and friendly understanding as to competition in the world markets which we want to see. The needs of the world give sufficient scope for the industries of both countries, and the prospects for each lie, not in attempting to cut the other out, but in working to enlarge the volume of trade in which both share.

There were passages in his speech in which the German Chancellor dealt in more specific terms with particular questions affecting German relations with ourselves and other

Powers. On these I cannot add anything to what the Prime Minister said in the House of Commons on Tuesday night, to the effect that there were no questions arising between nations, however serious, that could not be settled by conversations and discussions round the table. That is an opinion which His Majesty's Government have consistently held and which I myself have more than once expressed. But, as the Prime Minister reminded us, it is no use to embark upon discussions with a view to the general settlement of differences, the satisfaction of aspirations, and the removal of grievances, unless the atmosphere is favourable, in the sense that all those taking part in such discussions must be convinced of their own desire to pursue a common end and to reach a peaceable settlement of the points at issue. No useful result could be secured by such methods, unless there were to prevail in Europe a far greater measure of confidence and collaboration in both political and economic spheres than exists to-day. It is the object of all our policy to bring about that confidence and collaboration, and we are ready now and always to work with any who, with goodwill, will join with us in the formulation of concrete and practical measures to that end. That we have many and great difficulties—and it may be dangers—to meet I have no doubt. But I am satisfied that we can render no better service at this time than that we should equip ourselves with the material strength that comes from sure defence, and with the moral strength that may enable this nation to play its full part in bringing a measure of reassurance to an uneasy and disordered world.

33

DEMOCRACY AND FOREIGN POLICY

13 March 1939

[On February 27th, 1939, following upon General Franco's conquest of Catalonia, the dispersal of the Spanish Republican Government, and the resignation of the President, France and Great Britain simultaneously recognized General Franco's Government as the Government of Spain.

A speech made by Lord Halifax at Sunderland is here printed from a text supplied by him.]

ONE of the commonplaces in public speeches and writings of to-day is that democracy in this country is on trial. If that is true, it is certainly true in this country above all, for nowhere is the Constitution more democratic and the democratic tradition more firmly established by long practice and historical experience. Since the War the democratic development has been carried to its logical extreme. All men and women over twenty-one are now in a position to vote and share direct responsibility for the government of the country. At no time, therefore, was it more necessary for the electorate to be in a position to form sound opinions upon the problems which the country has to face. As a result, I suppose, of history, experience, and character, the British people have acquired a shrewd instinct in arriving at political judgements. Taking them as a whole and over a period of years, they can be shown to have had generally a very clear idea of what is right. This does not mean that they always think along the same lines, or that they rally easily to ready-made ideas drummed into their ears by politicians or the Press. But it does mean that at really crucial moments their fundamental instinct for what is possible and what is not possible, finds expression, with the result that the nation has again and again followed a just policy when essential principles were at stake, and in instances where a certain doubt was permissible has avoided extremes which have proved disastrous to other countries.

Twenty years ago the great question was whether democracy, even at that day, could run an empire. In other words: 'Would the people of this country have sufficient imagination to appreciate that the daughter lands had grown up and were rightly conscious of the fact and so jealous of their independence?' That question has been decisively and wisely answered. Against this country at least no one can bring the charge that we denied the principle of self-determination. Wherever we have been in the world, we have left a trail of freedom and self-government; and in the result the influence of liberty in making for unity has been immense, and beneficial not only to the peoples of the Empire, but, I think we may justly claim, to the world at large.

The question we now hear most frequently is, 'Can democracy, having vindicated its imperial policy, run a foreign policy?' To that I will answer that so far as the British people is concerned I have no manner of doubt. My doubts —very considerable doubts—only begin to arise when I consider the Official Opposition.... Perhaps the fundamental fact is that the present Labour leaders do not grasp the difference between home politics and foreign politics. In home politics we reach results by all manner of means—argument, vigorous debate, even some abuse which does no permanent harm; we have the machinery of voting and we abide by the results of elections. But in foreign politics we have no such wide choice of means: we can reach results only by agreement or by war, and the more the technique of domestic politics—public arguments, abuse, questioning of opponents' motives and the rest—is used, the more difficult it is to reach agreement and the more likely you make the only other alternative, which is war. . . .

In no field of national policy is it more important if we can to maintain national unity than in Foreign Policy, and I know only too well that sharp differences exist to-day in regard not so much perhaps to a particular policy pursued, as to what some people conceive to be the general background of thought from which the policy proceeds. What is responsible for this? In part, I think, it is due to bewilderment, which is not indeed surprising, about the passage of events during the last twenty years. After the War, we made up our minds that the world had learnt the lesson of what war meant well enough to leave it in no danger of any repetition of the experience, that was still so fresh in all men's minds. Our own nation, more perhaps than any other, accepted, believed in, and worked for the realization of those international ideals, of which the League of Nations was the outward symbol and expression. And when we saw those ideals blurred, as great nations have withdrawn from the League, and the world seems to have returned to the doctrines of power politics, we have all been sharply disappointed and disillusioned. But because the world has failed to make the ideals we tried to set before it real, that is no reason for us to let them go. We all know that in the case of individuals, though performance often lags behind, the essential thing is to keep an ideal. Without it, the standards of conduct and performance will gradually fall. So it is with nations; and all nations, who are to be true to themselves, must perpetually seek to renew their faith.

What does that mean for us? We are, as I have said, as close an approach to a democracy as the complex conditions of the modern industrial State allow. The first duty of such a State, the first thing its citizens will demand of its Government, is that they shall be assured a healthy life in mind and body, and that such conditions shall be created as will enable them to build up their personality, which is the foundation and justification for any true democracy. And it is for that reason that our people, and successive Governments throughout the last half-century, have attached increasing importance to what we term the social services: education, housing, slum clearance, health provision in all its aspects; provision for unemployment, sickness, old age; increased facilities for physical training and the like.

. . . . . .

The essence of democracy is liberty. We do not seek to interfere with other nations. But we do ask for the same respect in return, and our strength is the only solid guarantee that we shall receive it. Therefore we couple rights with duties, which are indeed always inseparable, but which we are accustomed to secure by different means. A man's rights may be secured to him in the main by law; but under our system of voluntary service in all fields of citizenship it is left largely to each one of us how we interpret duty to the State. It is not enough for either States or individuals to insist on rights alone; the individual who thinks only of rights is a bad citizen, and the State which thinks of nothing but rights is an unpopular member of the human family. Within the nation the same must at present be said of the man who makes difficulties about A.R.P., who is not prepared in an emergency to give all he can to the common cause, and be ready for any kind of national service for which he is best fitted. If it is the Government's duty to call on citizens for such service in a purely defensive enterprise, it is not less certainly the duty of citizens to respond to the full measure of their capacity.

In these days the British Commonwealth—the family of nations and States of which this country is the origin and centre—has a tremendous responsibility. I do not forget that, as was once finely said, patriotism is not enough; and I would have little use for the British Empire if I could not honestly feel that in its present form it did minister directly to the happiness of one-quarter of the human race, and was able by its influence to affect for good the whole. That would be my answer to those who sometimes speak as if there was some conflict between British interests and what ought to be British ideals of international relations. That feeling I suppose arises in part from the thought that the League of Nations was the beginning of a process by which all national rights and interests would gradually be merged into universal, equal brotherhood. I yield to no one in my attachment to the ideals of the League Covenant, and in my admiration of the spirit which actuated its creators. But the closest students of history, and still more of human nature, never expected the League to establish the Kingdom of Heaven on earth. No Government or association of Governments can undertake that, for the simple reason that the Kingdom of Heaven is not—and cannot be—a kingdom of this world. It is something for which we must untiringly strive, but which must be founded in the hearts and sustained by the personal lives of individuals.

It was impossible for the League, founded as it was for the purpose of promoting international collaboration, to escape the limitations which its members, or certain of them, placed upon it; and it was this which defeated the long attempt of His Majesty's Government, often at no small risk, and certainly with damage to ancient and well-tried friendships, to make it an instrument not merely for checking the aggressor, but for getting at the root of grievances and international distrust. The League's failure to do all that was hoped of it was the result of many large countries being outside it, and of the consequent unwillingness of certain of its members to take vital risks for their people in causes which did not appear to a large proportion of their populations to be causes in which they were immediately concerned. That is the simple truth, and in admitting it His Majesty's Government are not more to be charged with disloyalty to the League than, for example, the pacifist is disloyal to his principles because he recognizes the necessity in present circumstances of this country being rearmed.

There are people who take the view that this country should have made itself, alone, the universal policeman of the world. They proclaim that this or that action by a foreign Government is immoral or criminal, and demand that His Majesty's Government should intervene to put a stop to it. But the responsible father of a family, even if moved by the highest humanitarian feeling, would not so act. He might well be stirred to indignation at reading of some brutal assault in a distant part of the country. But no one would taunt him with cowardice if he refused to take train and, either alone or with some of his enthusiastic neighbours, go off to knock the distant aggressor on the head. Only if such an action came home to his family, came directly into the sphere of his duty and interests, would his intervention be approved by the bulk of sane opinion. And if as individuals we thus have higher and lower calls of duty, how much more must Governments, with the lives of millions, it may be, hanging on their decisions, give the most anxious thought to this question of intervention. They must risk charges of timidity, if not worse, but they alone have to bear the final responsibility, and they alone can have full knowledge of all the factors of the case.

In my considered opinion, there was no occasion during the past few years when British policy on a major international issue could have followed a different line than it did, without the grave risk of that policy leading to a major European war. And, as the world learned twenty years ago, it is a good deal easier to start a war than to stop one when it has started. Therefore, while I am not more afraid of war for this country than for any other, I do know what war would mean for the world, and what a deadly wound it would inflict on the civilization which is the life-blood of us all. . . .

A Government, like an individual, may be rightly moved by indignation, but it has, more than the individual, the imperative duty of weighing the consequences of its actions, for its own country and the world; and I am absolutely certain that His Majesty's Government has been right to follow the policy of non-intervention in Spain, in spite of everything that might be said—and there is much that can be said—against it. It is not only that they have kept this country from the horrors of war, though that surely is nothing for which we need apologize; it is rather that with no Spanish blood on our hands we might be better able to lend special help in allaying some of the bitterness and repairing some of the damage of that most unhappy conflict. . . .

I may be asked how the Government can defend the recognition of General Franco. Here, some people say, is the last of the immoral actions committed by the Government. But, though there are of course moral considerations which no Governments can ignore, in recognizing an obvious state of fact, and giving diplomatic expression to it, there is neither morality nor immorality. For recognition does not mean approval of the form of the Government recognized, or of the means by which it obtained power. Apply such a principle and you would reduce international relations to indescribable confusion. It means simply drawing the conclusion that a certain Government commands the allegiance of the great majority of the inhabitants of the country, and is thus the authority with which other Governments must have official contacts. That is all, and, in according recognition to General Franco, His Majesty's Government merely recognized an obvious fact, and proceeded in accordance with regular English practice and tradition.

The task of those who have to guide the international policy of the country to-day is not an easy one, and if that policy is to be successful, it must enjoy the convinced support of the great majority of British people. I make no complaint of honest criticism, for these are times when people are driven to think and feel deeply upon many very fundamental things. But just as I can respect the attitude of those who differ from myself, I would ask them to believe that the motives by which His Majesty's Government are moved are not less honourable, and based perhaps upon greater knowledge and a more personal sense of responsibility, than their own. It is not surprising in these times that many nerves are taut and overstrained; and strained nerves and calm judgement go ill together. Almost every week events occur in some part of Europe which are represented as a crisis. Regardless of whether these events directly concern them or not, this prevents people feeling carefree, and keeps everybody's minds on the stretch. Quite apart from what is happening, the air is constantly filled with sensational rumours of what is going to happen, and some of us, I am afraid, take little trouble to distinguish between fact and fiction. Still more have not time to do so, and by far the greater number really have not the means of obtaining an all-round objective view of foreign situations.

It may be that it suits some people, for whatever reasons, to propagate rumours or spread distorted views. This means that the responsibility laid on the Press is a heavy one; it is perhaps heavier in this country than in others because of our complete freedom, and I would appeal both to those who write and those who read the newspapers to weigh carefully all reports of foreign Governments' alleged intentions. Distorted or sensational presentation of foreign news is not only dangerous in itself, but tends to defeat the purposes which, almost without distinction of party, we all have at heart. So far as His Majesty's Government are concerned, their action will be deflected in neither one direction nor the other by those unsupported speculations, but we shall, while working steadfastly for peace, continue to take whatever steps are necessary to give the country the strength and self-confidence that its position and circumstances demand.

We shall do that partly because we are just as resolved as any other Great Power to maintain our independence on terms of equality with all others, and partly because we believe that we can make at least as great a contribution as any other Power to the building of a better world. While thus discharging as faithfully as we may our first duty to our own people, we shall neglect no opportunity of friendly and sincere approach to or by the Governments of other countries which may hold real promise of removing misunderstandings or suspicion, and so strengthening the forces that make for peace. The great French thinker, Pascal, once said: 'Justice without power is unavailing, power without justice is tyrannical. We must therefore combine justice and power, making what is just strong, and what is strong, just.' No higher ideal could be set before the world, and His Majesty's Government will do their best to further the conditions in which it may be realized.

34

THE GERMAN OCCUPATION OF CZECHOSLOVAKIA. I

15 March 1939

[After the Munich Agreement the Czechoslovak Government granted autonomy to Slovakia, which was embodied in a law of November 22nd, 1938. On March 9th, 1939, the Government at Prague received information that Slovak separatists were plotting to overthrow the Republic. The rapid succession of events in the following week was recounted by Lord Halifax in the House of Lords. An identical statement was simultaneously made by Mr. Chamberlain in the House of Commons.]

Government Statement

MY LORDS, on March 10 last the President of the Czechoslovak Republic dismissed certain members of the Slovak Government, including the Prime Minister, Dr. Tiso, on the ground that certain factors in the Slovak Government had not been showing sufficient resistance to subversive activity and that the federal interests of the State were thereby threatened. On March 11 a new Slovak Government was appointed under the Presidency of M. Sidor, the former Slovak representative in the Central Government at Prague. Dr. Tiso appealed to Herr Hitler and received an official invitation to go to Berlin. He had an interview with Herr Hitler on March 13, after which he returned to Bratislava to attend a special session of the Slovak Diet which had been called for the morning of March 14. At the conclusion of this session the independence of Slovakia was proclaimed with the approval of the Diet. A new Slovak Government was constituted under Dr. Tiso, including M. Sidor.

Yesterday afternoon the President of the Czechoslovak Republic and the Foreign Minister left for Berlin. They had an interview with Herr Hitler and Herr von Ribbentrop, at the conclusion of which a signed communiqué was issued. This communiqué stated that the serious situation which had arisen as a result of the events of the past week on what was hitherto Czechoslovak territory had been closely and frankly examined. Both sides gave expression to their mutual conviction that

Government Statement

the aim of all efforts in this part of Central Europe should be the safeguarding of calm, order, and peace. The Czechoslovakian President declared that in order to serve this purpose and in order to secure final pacification, he placed the destiny of the Czech people and country with confidence in the hands of the German Reich. Herr Hitler accepted this declaration and expressed his determination to take the Czech people under the protection of the German Reich, and to guarantee to it an autonomous development of its national life in accordance with its peculiar characteristics.

The occupation of Bohemia by German military forces began at 6 a.m. this morning. The Czech people have been ordered by their Government not to offer resistance. The President of the Czechoslovak Republic is returning to Prague. Herr Hitler issued an order to the German armed forces this morning to the effect that German military detachments would cross the frontier of the Czech territory in order to assume impartial control of the safety of the lives and property of all inhabitants of the country. Every German soldier was to regard himself not as a foe but as a representative of the German Government, to restore a tolerable order. Where opposition was offered to the march, it was to be broken down at once by all available methods. The armed forces were to bear in mind that they were treading on Czech soil as the representatives of Great Germany. Meanwhile on March 14, as a result of incidents on the frontier between Ruthenia and Hungary, Hungarian troops crossed the border and occupied a Czech village. Thereafter the Hungarian Government sent an ultimatum to Prague demanding among other things the withdrawal of Czech troops from Ruthenia, the release of Hungarian prisoners, and freedom for persons of Hungarian nationality and race in Ruthenia to arm and to organize. This ultimatum expired this morning, but I have not yet received official reports of the way in which the situation is developing.

It will no doubt be asked how these events affect the guarantee which was described by Sir Thomas Inskip in the following words on October 4 last:

'The question has been raised whether our guarantee to Czecho-

Government Statement

slovakia is already in operation. The House will realize that the formal treaty of guarantee has yet to be drawn up and completed in the normal way, and, as the Foreign Secretary has stated in another place, there are some matters which must await settlement between the Governments concerned. Until that has been done, technically the guarantee cannot be said to be in force. His Majesty's Government, however, feel under a moral obligation to Czechoslovakia to treat the guarantee as being now in force. In the event, therefore, of an act of unprovoked aggression against Czechoslovakia, His Majesty's Government would certainly feel bound to take all steps in their power to see that the integrity of Czechoslovakia is preserved.'

Only recently His Majesty's Government endeavoured to achieve an agreement with the other Governments represented at Munich upon the scope and terms of such a guarantee, but up to the present they have been unable to reach any such agreement.

In our opinion the situation was radically altered as soon as the Slovak Diet declared the independence of Slovakia. The effect of this declaration was to put an end by internal disruption to the State whose frontiers we had proposed to guarantee, and accordingly the condition of affairs described by Sir Thomas Inskip, which was always regarded by us as being only of a transitory nature, has now ceased to exist and His Majesty's Government cannot accordingly hold themselves any longer bound by this obligation.

As regards the financial assistance to the former Government of Czechoslovakia, which was authorized by the Act of Parliament passed last month, the position, so far as I have been able to ascertain, is as follows: Section 1 of the Act provided that the Treasury should repay to the Bank of England the £10,000,000 which had been placed at the disposal of the National Bank of Czechoslovakia, and that has been done. The amount that has been withdrawn by Czechoslovakia since this advance was first made available—last October—is £3,250,000. The balance of £6,750,000 has not been drawn upon but remains with the Bank of England. The scheme as originally devised between ourselves, the French Government, and the former Czechoslovak Government included the issue by the last-named Government of a loan on the London market by means of which the assistance

Government Statement

given to that Government, so far as it took the form of loan, would be repaid. In the new circumstances, when it would appear that the Government of Czechoslovakia has ceased to exist and the territory for which that Government was formerly responsible has been divided, it would seem impossible that the scheme can be carried through, and steps have been taken to request the Bank of England to make no further payments out of the balance of the £10,000,000 until the situation has been cleared up and definite conclusions reached. I may say that I have no reason to suppose that the £3,250,000 already drawn has not been applied in accordance with the provisions which were set out in the recent White Paper, and a substantial portion of the sum has been directly devoted to the assistance of refugees.

In the meantime, having regard to the effect on general conditions in Europe that these events are bound to exert, His Majesty's Government feel the present moment to be inappropriate for the proposed visit of the President of the Board of Trade and Secretary of the Department of Overseas Trade, which has accordingly been postponed. The German Government have been so informed.

To a large extent the information I have given the House is based on Press reports and, while there is little reason to think that the general effect is not as I have described it to be, final judgement on all the circumstances should await further confirmation. I do not want to make any specific charges as to breach of faith, but I cannot admit that anything of the kind that has now taken place was in our minds at the time of Munich or was in any way contemplated. The Munich Agreement constituted a settlement, accepted by the Four Powers and Czechoslovakia, of the Czechoslovak question. It provided for the fixation of the future frontiers of Czechoslovakia (which has been effected) and laid down the limits of the German occupation which the German Government accepted. They have now, without, so far as I know, any communication with the other three signatories of the Munich Agreement, sent their troops beyond the frontier there laid down. Even though it may now be claimed that what has taken place has occurred with the acquiescence of

Government Statement

the Czech Government, I cannot but regard it as inconsistent with the spirit of the Munich Agreement.

There is a further point which I cannot omit to mention. Hitherto the Reich Government, in extending the area of their military control, have defended their action by the contention that they were only incorporating in the Reich neighbouring masses of people of German race. Now for the first time they are effecting a military occupation of territory inhabited by people with whom they have no racial connexion. These events cannot fail to be a cause of disturbance to the international situation. They are bound to administer a shock to confidence, all the more regrettable since confidence was beginning to revive and to offer the prospect of concrete measures which would be of a general benefit. Unless there is some material change in the situation as it now appears, there must inevitably be a postponement of these measures.

35

THE GERMAN OCCUPATION OF CZECHOSLOVAKIA. II

20 March 1939

[At 9 a.m. on March 15th, 1939, German troops entered Prague. On the following day Herr Hitler issued a proclamation declaring Bohemia and Moravia a Protectorate within the German Reich and simultaneously accepted the protection of the Slovak State. Hungary had invaded Ruthenian territory on March 14th, and on the 16th its Prime Minister announced the incorporation of Ruthenia in Hungary. On March 20th Lord Halifax replied in the House of Lords to a motion asking for a statement of Government policy in regard to Czechoslovakia.]

MY LORDS, it is quite true that recent events have been a profound shock to all thinking people in this country and very far outside it. It may perhaps be of use if with all brevity I give the House a short narrative in order to make sure we have the setting correct of what has actually passed during the last few days. The German military occupation of Bohemia and Moravia began on the morning of March 15, and was completed, as we know, without serious incident. It is to be observed—and the fact is surely not without significance—that the towns of Mährisch-Ostrau and Vitkovice were actually occupied by German S.S. detachments on the evening of March 14, while the President and the Foreign Minister of Czechoslovakia were still on their way to Berlin and before any discussion had taken place. On March 16 Herr Hitler issued a decree proclaiming that the former Czechoslovak territory occupied by German troops belonged henceforth to the German Reich and came under its protection under the title of 'The Protectorate of Bohemia and Moravia'.

It is not necessary to recapitulate the terms of that decree—it has been published—but it should be noted that, while the head of the administration now to be set up is said to hold the rank of Head of State, and while the Protectorate is said to be autonomous and self-administering, a Reich protector is resident in Prague with full powers of veto on legislation.

Foreign affairs and the protection of nationals abroad devolve on the German Government, which will also maintain military garrisons and establishments in the Protectorate. The Protectorate is, further, in the German Customs Union, and finally the German Government can issue decrees valid in the Protectorate and take any measures for the preservation of security and order. Perhaps I might quote one short article which seems to me to sum up the situation. It says:

> 'The Protectorate of Bohemia and Moravia shall exercise its sovereign rights in consonance with the political, military, and economic importance of the Reich.'

As to Slovakia, the independence of Slovakia was proclaimed on March 14, but at the request of Dr. Tiso, the head of the Slovak State, Herr Hitler has undertaken to place Slovakia under German protection and the military occupation of the territory by German troops is now proceeding. As regards Ruthenia, the occupation of Ruthenia by Hungary, which began on March 14, has also proceeded. By March 16 the Hungarian troops had reached the Polish frontier and had virtually completed the occupation of the province. Therefore, as a result of these several actions, the dismemberment of Czechoslovakia may be said now to be complete.

I would like to say something as to the grounds on which the German Government seek to justify the action that they have taken. The immediate cause of the present crisis in Central Europe originated in Slovakia, and it is claimed that the German Government was entitled to intervene on receiving the request for assistance of the dismissed Slovak Prime Minister. As your Lordships are well aware, there has always been a party in Slovakia which advocated autonomy. That autonomy was in fact achieved after Munich in agreement between the various Slovak parties and the Central Government in Prague. The extremist elements in Slovakia, however, were not satisfied with these arrangements, but on all the evidence that is available to me I find it impossible to believe that the sudden decision of certain Slovak leaders to break off from Prague, which was followed so closely by their appeal for protection to the German Reich, was reached independently of outside influence.

It is said that German intervention in Czechoslovakia was justified owing to the oppression of the German minority by the Czechs. But, as a matter of fact again, it was only very shortly before Herr Hitler's ultimatum to the Czech President that the German Press began to renew its campaign of last summer about the alleged Czech brutalities against German citizens. Actually the position of the German minority, which is about 250,000, would appear, since the Munich Agreement, to have been one of what might be termed exceptional privilege. Notwithstanding the right of option which had been accorded by Article 7 of that Agreement, the members of the German minority were encouraged to remain in Czechoslovakia in order that they might form useful centres of German activity and propaganda; and advice to that effect was given to the minority by its leader.

It was as a result of the German-Czechoslovak Agreement for the mutual protection of minorities that the German Government obtained the legal right to take a direct interest in the treatment of their minority in Czechoslovakia. That minority at once obtained the right to set up separate organizations, and the Czechoslovak Government subsequently agreed that the German National Socialist Party in Czechoslovakia should be given full liberty to pursue its activities in Bohemia and Moravia. It is difficult to avoid the conclusion that the bulk of the incidents which occurred before the German invasion were deliberately provoked and that the effects were greatly magnified. It must be added in fairness that the Czechoslovak authorities received orders to act, and did act, with great restraint, in the face of that provocation. It is not necessary, I think, to say much upon the assertion that the Czechoslovak President really assented to the subjugation of his people. In view of the circumstances in which he came to Berlin, and of the occupation of Czech territory which had already taken place, I think most sensible people must conclude that there was little pretence of negotiation, and that it is more probable that the Czech representatives were presented with an ultimatum under the threat of violence, and that they capitulated in order to save their people from the horrors of a swift and destructive aerial bombardment.

Finally, it is said that Germany was in some danger from Czechoslovakia. But surely the German Government itself can hardly have expected that that contention could be seriously entertained in any quarter. Indeed, if I may sum up my own thought on these various explanations, I could wish that instead of the communications and explanations which have been issued and which carry scant conviction, German superior force had been frankly acknowledged as the supreme arbiter that in fact it was.

In these circumstances, as you are aware, His Majesty's Government thought fit at once to take certain action. They immediately suspended the visit of the President of the Board of Tràde and the Secretary of the Department of Overseas Trade to Berlin, by means of which it had been hoped that His Majesty's Government could directly intervene in those unofficial contacts of industrial representatives which were at that very moment taking place. We felt, as I think I said in my statement a few days ago, that in the circumstances which have arisen any development of our efforts in that direction was frankly out of the question, and that that and many other things must remain indefinitely postponed. His Majesty's Government, as your Lordships also know, have recalled to report His Majesty's Ambassador in Berlin, and he reached this country yesterday.

Further than those two practical steps, we have lodged a formal protest with the German Government in the sense of informing them that we cannot but regard the events of the last few days as a complete repudiation of the Munich Agreement and a denial of the spirit in which the negotiators of that Agreement bound themselves to co-operate for a peaceful settlement. We have also taken occasion to protest against the changes effected in Czechoslovakia by German military action, and have said that in our view those changes are devoid of any basis of legality. I think, therefore, that we may claim to have left the German Government in no doubt of the attitude of His Majesty's Government; and although I do not cherish any exaggerated hopes of what may be the effect of protests, I think your Lordships will feel it abundantly right that such protests should be registered.

I have from time to time seen efforts made by German apologists to justify the action of their Government by some reference to the past history of the British Empire. It is not necessary to remind you that the principle on which the British Empire is conducted is education in self-government. Wherever we have been in the world, we have left a trail of freedom and of self-government, and our record has nothing in common with the suppression of liberty and independence of people whose political developments had already brought them to the point of enjoyment of those opportunities for self-expression. It has also been objected that what has happened in Czechoslovakia is of no interest or concern to this country. It is quite true that we have always recognized that, for reasons of geography if for no other, Germany must from some points of view be more interested in Czechoslovakia or South-Eastern Europe than we are ourselves. It was the natural field for the expansion of German trade. But apart from the fact that changes in any part of Europe produce profound effects elsewhere, the position is entirely changed when we are confronted with the arbitrary suppression of an independent sovereign State by force, and by the violation of what I must regard as the elementary rules of international conduct.

It is natural enough that in the light of these events His Majesty's Government should be told that the policy of Munich was a tragic mistake. The policy pursued by the Prime Minister has been referred to as a personal policy. If by that is meant that it was a policy to which the Prime Minister had given every ounce of energy, imagination, and resolution that he possessed, I should not disagree; but if it is suggested that it was a policy that was pursued without the fullest co-operation of myself as Foreign Secretary, and of every member of His Majesty's Government, then I must take leave to oppose the most emphatic contradiction.

The Munich settlement, which was approved by this House and in another place, was accepted by His Majesty's Government for two purposes, quite distinct. The first purpose was to effect a settlement, as fair as might be in all the extremely difficult circumstances of that time, of a problem which was a real one, and of which the treatment was an urgent necessity if the peace of Europe was to be preserved. As to that, I would say, as I have said before in this House, that I have no doubt whatever that His Majesty's Government were right, in the light of all the information available to them, to take the course they did. The second purpose of Munich was to build a Europe more secure, upon the basis of freely accepted consultation as the means by which all future differences might be adjusted; and that long-term purpose, my Lords, has been, as we have come to observe, disastrously belied by events. We are charged with having too readily believed the assurances which were given by Herr Hitler—that after Munich he had no further territorial ambitions, and no desire to incorporate non-German elements in the Reich. I can assure your Lordships that neither the Prime Minister, nor I myself, nor any member of His Majesty's Government, has failed at any moment to be acutely conscious of the difference between beliefs and hope. It was surely legitimate and right to have hopes. But we have always acted in the knowledge that only with time can hope be converted into sure beliefs.

It is no doubt the case that previous assurances had been broken, whatever justification might have been advanced by Herr Hitler, on the grounds of his mission, as he conceives it, to incorporate ex-German territory and predominantly German areas in the Reich. But in his actions until after Munich a case could be made that Herr Hitler had been true to his own principles—the union of Germans in, and the exclusion of non-Germans from, the Reich. Those principles he has now overthrown, and in including 8,000,000 Czechs under German rule he has surely been untrue to his own philosophy. The world will not forget that in September last Herr Hitler appealed to the principle of self-determination in the interests of 2,000,000 Sudeten Germans. That principle is one on which the British Empire itself has been erected, and one to which accordingly, as your Lordships will recollect, we felt obliged to give weight in considering Herr Hitler's claim. That principle has now been rudely contradicted by a sequence of acts which denies the very right on which the German attitude of six months ago was based; and whatever may have been the truth about the treatment of 250,000 Germans, it is impossible for me to believe that it could only be remedied by the subjugation of 8,000,000 Czechs.

What conclusions are we to draw from this conquest of Czechoslovakia? Are we to believe that German policy has thus entered upon a new phase? Is German policy any longer to be limited to the consolidation of territory predominantly inhabited by persons of German race? Or is German policy now to be directed towards domination over non-German peoples? These are very grave questions which are being asked in all parts of the world to-day. The German action in Czechoslovakia has been furthered by new methods, and the world has lately seen more than one new departure in the field of international technique. Wars without declarations of war. Pressure exercised under threat of immediate employment of force. Intervention in the internal struggles of other States. Countries are now faced with the encouragement of separatism, not in the interest of separatist or minority elements but in the imperial interests of Germany. The alleged ill-treatment of German minorities in foreign countries which, it is true, may sometimes, perhaps often, arise from natural causes, but which may also be the subject and result of provocation from outside, is used as a pretext for intervention.

These methods are simple and, with growing experience, quite unmistakable. Have we any assurance that they will not be employed elsewhere? Every country which is Germany's neighbour is now uncertain of the morrow, and every country which values its national identity and sovereignty stands warned against the danger from within, inspired from without. During the last few days there have been rumours that the German Government were adopting a harsh attitude in their negotiations with the Rumanian Government on economic matters. I am glad to say that the Rumanian Government have themselves denied a report that went so far as to speak of an 'ultimatum'; but even if there is no menace to Rumania to-day, or even if that menace has not to-day developed, and even though it may not develop on these lines, it is not surprising if the Government of Bucharest, like other Governments, should view with the gravest misgivings the happenings of these last few days.

I think I must, before I leave the category of the results of the happenings of the last few days, say something about a subject which I have no doubt will be very much in the minds of every one of your Lordships who has considered these things. That is the fate of those persons who had taken refuge in Czechoslovakia. It is well known that the Czech Government gave the most generous asylum to refugees who had left their country on political, religious, or racial grounds, and their difficulties were further increased by an influx of such persons after the Munich Agreement. During recent weeks the arrangements for the emigration of Sudeten German and many other classes of refugees have been on the whole proceeding smoothly, with the co-operation of the British private organizations concerned, the Refugee Institute in Prague, and the British liaison officer in Prague, Mr. Stopford. I think that by the middle of last month something over 5,000 refugees had already emigrated, and others have since come out.

The conclusion of the arrangements for giving financial assistance to Czechoslovakia enabled further plans to be discussed for further emigration, and some of these arrangements were in an advanced stage at the time of the German occupation. In particular, some hundreds of refugees had received permission to enter the United Kingdom, or were actually waiting for such permission to be granted. When these events happened we at once sent urgent instructions to His Majesty's Minister in Prague to do his best to expedite the issue of permits, and to do everything that he could to accelerate the departure of persons on the British lists. At the same time we instructed His Majesty's Ambassador in Berlin to make urgent representations direct to the German Government on this matter, and to ask them to put no obstacles in the way of the departure of refugees on the British lists.

Moreover, as your Lordships know, in the arrangements

for financial assistance to Czechoslovakia a sum of £4,000,000 had been set aside to be employed for this purpose, and we take the view that, if proper safeguards can be established, this money should, if possible, still be available for the purpose for which it was intended. But I am not in a position at the present moment to tell your Lordships how, or indeed whether, with due safeguards that end can in fact be achieved. We are placing ourselves in consultation with other Governments also as to what further action is possible to alleviate the hardships of those unhappy individuals. To these refugees will now be added the Czech refugees who wish to leave their country. At the moment the position is that no person can leave Czechoslovakia without a visa given by the German authorities. His Majesty's Government, I need hardly say, are doing and will continue to do whatever they can to mitigate the consequences of recent events, operating as they do in this particularly personal and unhappy fashion upon these unfortunate individuals. But it is quite plain that the success of anything that we may attempt depends in present circumstances upon the attitude of the German Government.

And that leads me to say this. For years past the British people have steadily desired to be on friendly terms with the German people. There is no stronger national instinct among our people than the instinct that leads them, when they have a fight, to shake hands and try to make it up. Our people were not backward in recognizing some of the mistakes of the Versailles Treaty that required remedying, but each time during these last years that there has seemed a chance of making progress in understanding, the German Government has taken action which has made that progress impossible. More especially has that been the case in recent months. Very shortly after Munich certain measures were taken by the German Government that gave a profound shock to world opinion. Quite recently it was to be hoped, although there were many clouds still over and below the horizon, that we could look forward to closer economic collaboration, and it was in the hope of developing that economic collaboration into something wider that, as your

Lordships know, we had decided on those visits to which I referred a moment ago. All that initiative has been frustrated by the action of the German Government last week, and it is difficult to see when it can be easily resumed.

These affairs have raised wide issues, and the events in Czechoslovakia require His Majesty's Government and require every free people to rethink their attitude towards them. Broadly speaking there have been, at all events since the War, two conflicting theses as to the best method of avoiding conflicts and creating security for the nations of the world. The first thesis is that which supports machinery for consolidation, conciliation, and arbitration with, if possible, the sanction of collective force, and involves an invitation to all States, willing to accept a wide degree of obligation to one another, to agree that an attack on one should be treated as an attack on all. That, your Lordships know well enough, has been the thesis expressed in the Covenant of the League of Nations. Perhaps it is true to say that more precise effect was sought to be given to it in the Geneva Protocol, and it has itself given rise to a number of regional agreements for mutual assistance between the several Powers concerned. That is the first thesis.

The second conflicting thesis has been upheld by those who consider that systems seeking to provide collective security, as it has been termed, involved dangerously indefinite commitments quite disproportionate to the real security that these commitments gave. Those who took that view were persuaded that States, conscious of their own pacific purposes, would be wise to refrain from such commitments which might draw them into a war in which their own vital interests were not threatened, and that therefore States should not bind themselves to intervene in conflicts unless they themselves were directly attacked.

That is the conflict of philosophy of which your Lordships are very well aware, because in one form or another it has constantly been debated in this House. I have no doubt that in considering these two theses the judgement of many has been influenced by the estimate that they place, rightly or wrongly, upon the probability of direct attack. If it were possible, in their judgement, to rate that probability low, then that low probability of direct attack had to be weighed against what might seem to them the greater risk of States being involved in conflicts that were not necessarily arising out of their own concerns. But if and when it becomes plain to States that there is no apparent guarantee against successive attacks directed in turn on all who might seem to stand in the way of ambitious schemes of domination, then at once the scale tips the other way, and in all quarters there is likely to be found immediately a very much greater readiness to consider whether the acceptance of wider mutual obligations, in the cause of mutual support, is not dictated, if for no other reason than the necessity of self-defence. His Majesty's Government have not failed to draw the moral from these events, and have lost no time in placing themselves in close and practical consultation, not only with the Dominions but with other Governments concerned, upon the issues that have suddenly been made so plain.

It is not possible as yet fully to appraise the consequences of German action. History records many attempts to impose a domination on Europe, but all these attempts have, sooner or later, terminated in disaster for those who made them. It has never in the long run proved possible to stamp out the spirit of free peoples. If history is any guide, the German people may yet regret the action that has been taken in their name against the people of Czechoslovakia. Twenty years ago that people of Czechoslovakia recovered their liberties with the support and the encouragement of the greater part of the world. They have now been deprived of them by violence. In the course of their long history this will not be the first time that this tenacious, valiant, and industrious people have lost their independence, but they have never lost that which is the foundation of independence—the love of liberty. Meanwhile, just as after the last War the world watched the emergence of the Czech nation, so it will watch to-day their efforts to preserve intact their cultural identity and, more important, their spiritual freedom under the last and most cruel blow of which they have been the victims.

36

THE ITALIAN OCCUPATION OF ALBANIA

13 April 1939

[On March 31st, 1939, following upon the German occupation of Prague, the British Government assured Poland that, in the event of any action which clearly threatened Polish independence and which the Polish Government considered it vital to resist with their national forces, they would feel themselves bound at once to lend the Polish Government all support in their power. This unilateral guarantee was replaced a week later by an agreement for mutual assistance.

In the middle of March Rumania was reported to have received from Germany a demand that she should cease to export grain, oil, cattle, and foodstuffs to any other country than Germany. The terms of the trade agreement between the two countries on March 31st fell short, however, of these alleged demands.

On Good Friday Italy invaded Albania, a country to which it had been bound by defensive alliance since November, 1927, and on Easter Sunday there were disquieting reports of Italy's intention to occupy the Greek island of Corfu. The events in Albania and the measures taken by the British Government were recounted in similar terms by Mr. Chamberlain in the House of Commons and by Lord Halifax in the House of Lords, in an extraordinary session of Parliament.]

Government Statement

MY LORDS, it would perhaps be convenient if I reminded your Lordships as shortly as I may of the historical sequence of events that have taken place since we last met and which have occasioned widespread disquiet and uneasiness in Europe, and in the Eastern Mediterranean in particular. It is just a week since my right honourable friend the Prime Minister made a statement in another place on the subject of Albania. In that statement he said that, two days before, His Majesty's Ambassador at Rome had drawn the attention of the Italian Minister for Foreign Affairs to rumours concerning the concentration of Italian ships and Italian transport at Bari and Brindisi. He then mentioned the suggestion which, according to Count Ciano, the King of Albania had made on March 8 regarding the strengthening of the existing Treaty of Alliance between Italy and Albania and the difficulties which had taken place in the ensuing discussions, the nature of which was not quite plain, and the Prime

Government Statement Minister added that, according to Count Ciano, Italian interests had been threatened.

Italian warships appeared off the Albanian coast early on April 6, and Italian residents were taken on board. The same evening Italian troops left Bari and Brindisi for Albania. Your Lordships will appreciate that communications with Albania have been difficult, and His Majesty's Government are still awaiting a full report on the recent events from His Majesty's Minister at Durazzo. In the meantime we have received Italian and Albanian accounts of the earlier events of April 7, but, as regards the latter part of that day and subsequent happenings, there is little but the official Italian news. The occupation of Albania began in the early hours of April 7, when Italian ships disembarked at Santi Quaranta, Valona, Durazzo, and San Giovanni di Medua—and, if I might interject, I would say that no one act in this business can have more shocked religious sentiment everywhere than the fact that it should have been initiated on the day which to most Christians is the most sacred day of the year. The accounts vary of the amount of resistance offered, but it seems clear that by the afternoon of Good Friday the four coast towns had been occupied by Italian forces. King Zog and apparently the Albanian Government left Tirana during the night of April 6–7 and, according to Italian sources, their departure was the signal for an outbreak of disorders in the capital. Italian troops seem to have entered Tirana on April 8 (Saturday), and the town was visited that day by Count Ciano. During the same day King Zog and Queen Geraldine, who was, as the House knows, only able to be moved in circumstances of extreme difficulty, arrived on Greek territory, where they were hospitably received by the Greek Government.

Those, my Lords, are the bare facts of the Italian occupation of Albania so far as they can be disentangled from conflicting accounts. A similar divergence of testimony is also evident when we come to examine the circumstances of the occupation. On April 4 Count Ciano informed His Majesty's Ambassador in Rome that on March 8 King Zog had suggested to the Italian Government the strengthening of the

Government Statement

Italo-Albanian Alliance. On March 20 Count Ciano said the King had asked that troops should be sent to Albania for use, it was alleged, against Yugoslavia. This proposal the Italians had refused, and, shortly afterwards, they had submitted a scheme for a reinforced alliance in accordance with King Zog's earlier suggestion. The scheme put forward did not, according to Count Ciano, modify the existing juridical status of Albania, and was not accompanied by an ultimatum. Count Ciano stated that it was then that King Zog had started mobilizing and displaying a hostile attitude towards Italian interests. It was not the Italian wish to change the *status quo* in Albania, but their interests the Italian Government felt bound to protect. In another communication made to the Foreign Office on April 5, it was stated that the Albanian authorities had begun to organize anti-Italian demonstrations by organized bands which threatened Italian residents throughout the country. Reports indeed from His Majesty's Minister at Durazzo went to confirm the fact that some demonstrations of an anti-Italian character had taken place in the early days of April.

That is in substance the Italian account of the circumstances of those weeks and days. The Albanian account is different. On April 8 I received the Albanian Minister, who stated that the Italian Government, having endeavoured to force upon the Albanian Government the acceptance of proposals incompatible with the independence, sovereignty, and integrity of the country, attempted to impose their will by an ultimatum. To this ultimatum, which was unanimously rejected by the Chamber of Deputies, the Albanian Government replied with a clear-cut refusal; whereupon, according to the Albanian communication, Italian troops, under cover of an intense bombardment by the Navy and Air Force, made an attack on the four Albanian ports early on April 7. The Albanian Minister stated that he had as yet no details of the Italian proposals, but, according to reports which His Majesty's Minister at Durazzo said were current at the time in Albania, they appeared to have included Italian administrative control on a very extended scale and the occupation by Italian troops of certain strategic

Government Statement

points of importance, and it seems probable that these proposals might have opened the door to extensive Italian immigration. A representative of King Zog confirmed this view in conversation with His Majesty's Minister and the Ministers of France and the Balkan Entente. He added that a Commission which had been appointed to study the proposals had reported that the proposals were intended to establish a virtual protectorate, damaging alike to the independence, the sovereignty, and the integrity of Albania; and when the King had inquired of the Italian Minister what would be the result if he refused to entertain these proposals, he had been informed that that would entail real danger to Albania. None the less, His Majesty had rejected the proposals and declared that if necessary he would resist by force, and the Albanian Minister, when I saw him on April 8, concluded by appealing to His Majesty's Government to do their utmost in aid of a small nation desperately trying to defend its own territory.

These accounts of course differ very greatly from one another, and it is doubtful, I think, whether even now we are in full possession of all the facts. It was in these circumstances that on April 7 the British Ambassador in Rome was instructed to state to Count Ciano—whilst I myself on the same day used the same language to the Italian Chargé d'Affaires—that on the information then at my disposal it seemed to me that the situation was likely to raise in an acute form the whole question of the maintenance of the *status quo* in the Mediterranean which formed, in our opinion, so important an element in the Anglo-Italian Agreement of April 16 last year. The Adriatic was certainly a part of the Mediterranean area, and the Italian Government could not therefore claim that His Majesty's Government were not concerned. On the same day, April 7, Lord Perth had seen Count Ciano, who said that the Italian Government fully intended to respect the independence and integrity of Albania and the *status quo* in the Mediterranean area.

On April 9, Easter Day, the Ambassador again saw him and said that, although His Majesty's Government had taken note of these assurances, they were deeply concerned at the

Government Statement

reports which had reached them of the sudden invasion of Albania. They could hardly believe that, if the situation between Italy and Albania was as had been described, the differences between the two Governments were incapable of solution by negotiation. Nor could they easily understand how it was possible to reconcile the Italian landing on the Albanian coast with the maintenance of that country's independence and the integrity of her frontiers. Lord Perth reminded Count Ciano that both Governments were pledged under the Anglo-Italian Agreement to the *status quo* in the Mediterranean area, and informed him that His Majesty's Government felt themselves to be entitled to the frankest and fullest explanation not only of the present developments in the immediate Albanian situation and their previous history, but also of the future intentions of the Italian Government. Lord Perth was also instructed to add that the explanations proffered up to date had caused His Majesty's Government profound misgivings and that they would in no way satisfy public opinion in this country.

When pressed by Lord Perth as to what were Italian intentions in regard to the future, bearing in mind the definite assurances which the Italian Government had already given, Count Ciano said that that would depend upon the wishes of the Albanian people. It would appear from the latest news that the Albanian Provisional Administrative Council has now offered the Crown of Albania to the King of Italy. We must no doubt await the answer of the Italian Government to this offer, but whatever may be the technicalities of the position I must frankly state that His Majesty's Government find extreme difficulty in reconciling what has happened in Albania with the preservation of the national sovereignty of Albania as contemplated by the Anglo-Italian Agreement.

But it is not only the future of Albania which is at stake. As was natural and inevitable, unmistakable signs of disquiet and uneasiness have been manifested not only in the adjacent areas but in other countries bordering on the Mediterranean or included in the Balkan peninsula. On Easter Eve I received the Italian Chargé d'Affaires after dinner, when he

Government Statement

made me a communication from Signor Mussolini to the effect in part that the neighbouring countries, Yugoslavia and Greece, were perfectly calm, and that therefore it was clear that Italy was not intending to cause trouble in neighbouring countries. Later in the course of our interview Signor Crolla drew attention to reports that, according to his information, the English Sunday Press was likely to make various suggestions as to possible courses of British action, including British occupation of Corfu. On this point he assured me that the Italian Government were certainly not going to threaten Greek independence, and that any British occupation of Corfu would create the most dangerous reactions. I at once told Signor Crolla that he could dismiss from his mind, and his Government could dismiss from theirs, the idea that the British Government had any intention of occupying Corfu. That was not the sort of thing we did, but the British Government, I said, would certainly take a very grave view if anybody else occupied it.

I conveyed to the Greek Minister on Easter Sunday morning the assurance given by the Italian Chargé d'Affaires the night before—namely, that Greece and Yugoslavia were calm, and it was therefore clear that Italy meant to give no trouble to neighbouring countries, and that the Italian Government had no intention of threatening Greek independence. I also told the Greek Minister the exact terms of my reply to the Italian Chargé d'Affaires the night before on this subject of the rumoured occupation of Corfu. I saw the Italian Chargé d'Affaires again the next morning, on Easter Sunday, and with him I reverted to the statement that he had made to me the previous evening regarding the calm existing in neighbouring countries, and I said that, according to my information, in view of reports that were in circulation, there was anxiety that the Italian Government intended to occupy Corfu. Signor Crolla said that this was the first time he had ever heard a hint of such action, and he had no hesitation in saying that in his view it was absolutely impossible that it should be correct, since it would be a flagrant contradiction of what on the authority of Signor Mussolini he had told me the night before. On his own responsibility, therefore, Signor Crolla gave me an assurance that this was not the Italian intention. Corfu, he said, was a vital strategical point for the Italians, and the Italian Government could not allow foreign occupation other than Greek of the island. In his own opinion the rumours that might have been disturbing Greece or ourselves must be the reaction to the rumours that it was the British intention to occupy the island.

I told the Italian Chargé d'Affaires that I naturally welcomed this personal assurance on his part, but it was right to leave him in no doubt that, if any Italian action of the sort were ever in contemplation, it must be a matter of the gravest concern to His Majesty's Government; that it was vital that there should be no misunderstanding between our two Governments on this point, and I should be very glad to know that the Italian Government had made their own the assurance which on his own responsibility he had given to me. I added that it would be of even more value if the same assurance could at once be repeated by the Italian Government to the Greek Government. Accordingly, the same evening, the Italian Chargé d'Affaires called upon me with a further message from Signor Mussolini to the effect, among other things, that he had already given the most ample assurance to the Greek Government confirming that the Italian Government intended to base their relations with Greece on a cordial and solid friendship; and that he had sent new instructions to the Italian Chargé d'Affaires in Athens to assure the Greek Government that all rumours concerning the Italian hostile intentions to Greece were false, inasmuch as Italy intended to respect in the most absolute manner the territorial and insular integrity of Greece. That information was at once telegraphed to His Majesty's Minister in Athens, who was instructed to impart it without delay to the Greek Government. I subsequently learned that the Italian Chargé d'Affaires in Athens conveyed to the Greek Government on April 10 the assurances promised by Signor Mussolini.

I shall refer to that in one moment, for a reason that will become plain. Apart from other considerations—to which, as I say, I shall recur—one question which I think will be present to your Lordships' mind is the relation that all these

Government Statement

events hold, and ought to hold, towards the Anglo-Italian Agreement. I am very well aware that there are those who say that the Anglo-Italian Agreement has now clearly proved valueless and that accordingly, in whatever may be the appropriate form, it should be denounced. They would argue, I think, that inasmuch as the spirit of the Anglo-Italian Agreement had been broken, there was no purpose in attempting, by something like artificial respiration, to keep alive a body from which the spirit had departed. My Lords, I can very readily understand that attitude and that argument, but I take a somewhat different view. As we are all very well aware, the ground covered by the Anglo-Italian Agreement was a wide one and included many very diverse questions. It certainly was the idea of His Majesty's Government that it should be a contribution to peace, and I do not suppose that there is any one of your Lordships who would not feel that no one should say a word to make the preservation of peace—if the state in which we are living can rightly be described by that name—more difficult. We should therefore, I think, weigh carefully all the considerations that are involved.

It is quite obvious that assurances have only the value of the good faith by which they are inspired and of the faith which they command in those to whom they are given. Everybody can form his own judgement in regard to this or that point connected with these assurances. For myself, I cannot doubt that the great mass of thinking opinion in this country and the world over will be greatly influenced in their final judgement of the worth of the Anglo-Italian Agreement by the test of its operation in the matter of the withdrawal of Italian troops from Spain. Accordingly, in the course of the recent communications made in Rome, Lord Perth was instructed to inquire the intention of the Italian Government in this connexion; and Signor Mussolini caused the Ambassador to be informed, and sent the same information to myself through the Italian Chargé d'Affaires, that the evacuation of Italian troops was being arranged and would be effected as soon as the victory parade in Madrid had taken place. In reply to a further inquiry, Count Ciano informed Lord Perth on April 9 that when the troops went, Italian aeroplanes and

Government Statement

pilots would go also. His Majesty's Government have taken due note of these fresh assurances, which, of course, confirm those which they had received before. I need only add that the Government have always regarded the evacuation of Italian volunteers from Spain as a vital element in the Agreement, and they look forward accordingly to its early fulfilment.

I need not emphasize to your Lordships the disturbing effects of such events as I have described on international confidence. There is no dispute about the special position and the special interests that Italy has enjoyed in Albania. These things were expressly recognized by the Council of Ambassadors many years ago, and, so far as I know, they have never been challenged. But, whatever may be said as to that, there can be no doubt as to the general effect produced in all quarters by Italian action. It is not necessary for me to take up your Lordships' time by stating at length what must be the judgement of His Majesty's Government on these events. That judgement has been shared by the overwhelming mass of opinion in this country, by most of the States of Europe, and by the United States of America. By its effect of weakening confidence in the pledged word, such action as that recently taken by Italy encourages, for one thing, the circulation of wild rumours and helps to keep the world in a state of continual disturbance and anxiety, a state in which the conduct of peaceful commerce and industry and the development of ordinary life become impossible.

A few minutes ago I gave your Lordships a somewhat detailed account of the reports connected with and arising out of Corfu. Those reports of Italian intentions may well have been just as unfounded as the reports attributing similar intentions to ourselves. The fact, however, that they should have gained currency and caused real anxiety is the measure of extent to which confidence has again been shaken and faith in the value of international undertakings again undermined. It is quite impossible for the plant of confidence to flourish if its roots are suffering perpetual violence. I know very well that some rumours at these times are put into deliberate circulation. Others are the natural product of the atmosphere of suspicion

Government Statement

and fear which these events are bound to create; but in the last twelve months many reports have come true, and it must therefore be the duty of law-loving peoples, who desire to see international engagements respected, to prepare themselves for all events. If those who occupy the position of Dictators are at times disposed to gird at the indecision and divisions of others, I venture to think that they themselves have done more than anyone else to provide the cure. They have, I think, achieved for us, and, if we may believe general report, for the French also, what it seemed difficult for us to achieve for ourselves—namely, national unity.

In these circumstances His Majesty's Government feel that they have both a duty and a service to perform, by leaving no doubt in the mind of anyone as to their own position. I therefore take this opportunity of saying, on their behalf, that His Majesty's Government attach the greatest importance to the avoidance of disturbance, by force or threats of force, of the *status quo* in the Mediterranean and the Balkan Peninsula. Consequently they have come to the conclusion that, in the event of any action being taken which clearly threatened the independence of Greece or Rumania, and which the Greek or Rumanian Government respectively considered it vital to resist with their national forces, His Majesty's Government would feel themselves bound at once to lend the Greek or Rumanian Government, as the case might be, all support in their power. We are communicating this declaration to the Governments directly concerned, and to others, especially Turkey, whose close relations with the Greek Government are known. I understand that the French Government are making a similar declaration this afternoon.

In authorizing those who speak for them to make this declaration to-day, as also to make a corresponding declaration a week or so ago concerning Poland, His Majesty's Government are fully aware of the gravity of the decisions thus recorded. But they have taken this course after full reflection and consideration, in the belief that, as things stand to-day, a perfectly clear definition of their attitude in certain events, from which in no case could we probably stand aside, would render these events less likely.

37

THE PRINCIPLES OF INTERNATIONAL RELATIONS

19 April 1939

[The extinction of Czechoslovak independence prompted the British Government to approach, in the latter part of March 1939, the Government of the U.S.S.R. with a suggestion that a joint declaration against aggression should be signed by Britain, France, Poland, and the U.S.S.R. With the same object in view President Roosevelt addressed an appeal to Herr Hitler and Signor Mussolini on April 14th asking them whether, in the interests of world peace, they were willing to give assurances that their armed forces would not attack or invade the territory or possessions of various named independent nations.

The following speech was made by Lord Halifax in the House of Lords in reply to an inquiry from Lord Cecil as to whether the Government could make any general statement concerning the foreign policy of the country and the steps they thought it possible and desirable to take with a view to the maintenance of an enduring peace.]

MY LORDS, the principal aims of the foreign policy of His Majesty's Government may be summed up in a very few words. They are the maintenance of peace in the world, and the protection of the persons, the property, and the legitimate interests of British subjects abroad. In the pursuit of these aims His Majesty's Government have sought to apply certain principles which, in their opinion, and until recently I think in the opinion of all civilized countries, ought to govern the relations between sovereign States; and these principles were those contained in the Preamble to the Covenant of the League.

And there are also other principles which are implied in the Covenant itself, such as respect for the territorial integrity and the political independence of sovereign States, the substitution for the use of force in the settlement of international disputes of the methods of conciliation and so on, and the reduction and limitation of armaments. Now it is quite evident that the international machinery which was devised to apply these principles has failed of its purpose, and if we were to apply ourselves to finding the reason why it has failed, we should I think have to examine at some length all the history of the last twenty-five years. It was certainly not only the machinery which was at fault, but also, I think we must admit, the will of States to make it work effectively; and no country I think is entirely free from responsibility.

Certain criticisms have been directed against the policy of His Majesty's Government, and the fundamental part of that criticism seemed to me to be something to this effect, that, had the League of Nations been kept in full vigour and energy, it would have been easy to have utilized its machinery for doing exactly what the Government are now seeking to do. That seems to me to beg the question. The whole trouble is that it has unfortunately proved impossible to keep the League in full vigour and energy, and I certainly would not admit that it was the fault of His Majesty's Government by any particular action or inaction of theirs that this state of affairs had been reached. After all, three of the most powerful nations in the world have seceded from the League, and they have not only seceded from the League but they have flatly abjured the very principles of consultation, co-operation, and negotiation on which the League as a structure was based. I do not think that even now there would be more than a very few who would contend that His Majesty's Government ought in these last years to have attempted to play the role of a general moral High Commissioner for the entire world within the limits of a system which was not, and never has been, universal.

It has been claimed, and I think truly claimed, that the international system was both too rigid and not rigid enough, and by that I mean this. It did not, on the one hand, provide always adequate means of redressing grievances, and at the same time did not provide sufficient guarantees for the security of individual States. It followed that the States with real or imagined grievances broke away from the international community and resorted to force to achieve what they held to be their rights, while other countries were not prepared to take the risks involved in taking action in all cases to uphold the principles of the Covenant on questions in regard to which, rightly or wrongly, they did not consider their own vital interests to be immediately involved.

It has been one of the tragedies arising from that process of disintegration that the dissatisfied countries have come to reject those principles by which international society was intended to be governed, so that to the constant conflict of national interests has now been added a far more dangerous conflict of ideas. And there is now no accepted or common currency in the terms of international intercourse. We do not mean the same thing when we use the same words. The ideas of justice, the ideas of respect for treaties, the value of pledges, for one reason or another are differently interpreted in the interests of national ambition, and claims are held to be identical with rights. With all that has gone the invention of new doctrines to justify policies of expansion; claims of race or the like are made to cover and justify the application of force; and all the time truth is obscured and darkened by violent propaganda.

So far as His Majesty's Government are concerned, they have endeavoured to avoid by all means in their power this debasement, as I term it, of international relations and this conflict of ideologies—to use a word that is hateful to me. They tried to do that both by precept, which is most annoying to the people to whom the precept is addressed and is indignantly resented, and also by example, for instance in the matter of disarmament, which has merely encouraged the employment of force. We have endeavoured to arrive at a general settlement of international grievances, and, in the face of a great deal of criticism, tried last September to effect by negotiation the solution of an outstanding European problem in the hope that that would lead, on the basis of the understandings then reached, to the settlement of other problems. Well, frankly, my Lords, those hopes, as we know, have been disappointed, and one of the difficulties of the present position is that when His Majesty's Government offer negotiation they are accused of weakness, and when they show a disposition to defend their interests or the principles upon which international society, as we think, depends, they are accused of aggressive designs.

Despite those difficulties, and while not neglecting any of the steps that were necessary to make the defensive position of this country secure, His Majesty's Government continued to work for international understanding, and were ready to continue along this path until it became clear, after the German military action against Czechoslovakia, that the essential basis of mutuality—I emphasize that: of mutuality—for such a policy at this moment did not appear to exist. But we should never wish to abandon any efforts that could promise any hope of success, if those efforts could win a response from the other side and be mutual in character.

It became apparent that, unless our efforts were able to secure support in other quarters, they were only liable to be interpreted as a sign of weakness, which brought its own dangers. In the speech that I made on March 20[1] I tried to set out at some length the circumstances which in my judgement seemed to render necessary new action to meet new facts. The steps which His Majesty's Government have taken to forestall further attempts, if such should be made, to dominate and control Europe have been explained as they have been taken. It is therefore not necessary for me to go into any detail about them to-day, but I wish with your Lordships' permission to make two general observations.

First of all, those steps are purely defensive in their nature, and are defensive of the independence and liberties of States who may feel themselves threatened. It is quite fantastic to suggest that the consultations upon which we have been engaged, and the guarantees which we have given, cover any aggressive design on our part. The cry of 'encirclement', by which I suppose it is intended to suggest that the purpose of His Majesty's Government is to throttle the legitimate aspirations of other peoples or even to engage in a preventive war, has no doubt been raised for obvious purposes. But if my voice should reach so far, I should be prepared, on the authority of His Majesty's Government, now or at any time to give the most solemn undertaking I could that no such idea would ever find place in British policy; for not only would it be the extreme of folly, not only would it lack any

[1] No. 35 in this collection.

colour of morality, but it would be entirely foreign to the whole trend of British thought, which rests essentially upon the desire to live and let live in the world.

We are sometimes asked how we reconcile our professions with the possession of the greatest Empire in the world. My answer is that it is precisely because we have applied our principles of freedom to the various nations which compose the British Commonwealth that that Commonwealth is so flourishing and so widespread to-day. It has been the aim of His Majesty's Government all through, within the British Empire, to give the freest play possible to the conditions and the necessities of individual territories and to their aspiration for self-government. We have not sought to restrain economic or political development in any part of the Empire, but, on the contrary, to foster the gradual growth of self-governing institutions. Therefore it is in the same order of thought that we have no desire to restrain the natural growth or the natural prosperity of any other nation. Whatever may be the effect of the policies of other Governments upon the condition of their own subjects, it is the constant desire of His Majesty's Government, as it should surely be of every other, to promote conditions in the world in which the common man may be able to find means of subsistence and contentment.

The second general observation that I would make is that the efforts which His Majesty's Government are making to resist further aggressive actions involve no departure from the principles of policy which I have tried to lay down. On the contrary it would be our hope that the policy that we are pursuing will in time lead to a reaffirmation of those principles, and a return from the technique of aggression to methods of friendly discussion and negotiation. In that endeavour His Majesty's Government are anxious to work in close association with all peace-loving countries, who, like themselves, are determined to preserve the independence of sovereign States and, so far as they can, to resist attempts by other Powers to impose their will by force of arms.

If a country accepts the same principles of international relationships, and has the same willingness to work for the maintenance of peace, the internal political organization of that country is not a matter of concern to His Majesty's Government. They are not influenced by the fact that a country is authoritarian, or the reverse, in its political philosophy, but they are influenced by the declared objects of its external policy. In saying that I have not absent from my mind the position of the Soviet Union. Lord Strabolgi referred to the speech recently delivered by Mr. Stalin, and he asked if I could give him any information as to the progress of the negotiations in which we had been engaged with Moscow. I do not think there is anything that I can say at the present time beyond the fact that we are engaged in active pursuit of these negotiations, and that I have every hope that recognition of the different points of view of which we each have to take account will enable us to make the progress that we all desire, on the matters to which those negotiations are being directed.

The particular purpose to which the conversations that have been held have been directed has been the situation and facts in Europe, but I should not exclude the possibility of conversations being more widely extended, although they have not been so up to now. Our attitude in regard to these matters is not, as your Lordships are aware, always shared by other countries, and it is not therefore an easy problem; but, as I have said, we are not prepared ourselves to reject, on grounds of any abstract ideology, the co-operation which any country is willing to offer, so long as it does not seek to impose its own political conceptions on other countries which do not want them.

The noble Viscount who moved the Motion asked whether that kind of defensive plan to which I have referred is all that His Majesty's Government have in their mind. Beyond the immediate necessities, whether created by obligations or by interest, by which we are bound, is there, he seemed to ask, no more positive programme which His Majesty's Government propose for themselves and the world at large? Shall we be satisfied if we are able to secure a cessation of those sudden and unprovoked attacks on foreign territory which have shocked world opinion? Are we to be satisfied with that? After all, to do that would be no negligible achievement, for it is only when confidence is restored, and security assured, that discussion and negotiation can come back to their own.

The noble Viscount spoke very truly when he said that it was not possible to cast the world into a permanent mould, or to arrest the peaceful evolution of peoples and States. Therefore, what we all desire to see established, if we can, is a comprehensive system against aggression, but with facilities for peaceful change, excluding no one who wishes to come into it. That is true; but if we are interested in practical achievement, we must first, I submit, apply ourselves with all the strength and determination we can command to the immediate concrete problem before us. Remoter ideals and indefinite commitments must induce, I suggest, no vagueness in our major plans. On that I venture to say that His Majesty's Government can speak with a clear conscience, for no nation and no Government has pledged itself so wholeheartedly—with, indeed, what was on the part of its people a kind of religious fervour—to the system of international relationships which was embodied twenty years ago in the League Covenant. That effort failed, for reasons to which I have already made allusion; and it was indeed quite natural that so long as the aggression seemed remote, or of comparative insignificance, and so long as the collective system seemed to be based on abstract hypotheses or theory, so long nations should hesitate to commit themselves to what they were bound to recognize were ultimately measures of hostility in conditions which it was impossible to determine in advance.

I, unlike some, have never quarrelled with the conception of collective security, but I have quarrelled with the interpretation of it by those who rely upon it as a kind of magic touchstone when the conditions for its practical realization did not, in the circumstances of the time, exist. I always took the view that to do so was dangerous self-delusion. We cannot tell to-day what the future may hold, but if we are indeed faced with an attempt at what Mr. Gladstone, I think, called 'unmeasured aggrandisement', then an immediate and instantaneous reaction on the part of those countries who, feeling themselves menaced, will naturally get together, is inevitable. In that situation, and when the independence of certain smaller States in Europe seemed to be threatened, His Majesty's Government have gone to great lengths in assuring their support for the defence of that independence.

The noble Viscount stigmatized that policy as a 'piecemeal' policy. I think that is less than just. We have to work with the material at our disposal and to rally, if we may, the forces of those countries which resent, and are prepared to resist, a policy based only on force. If a structure collapses it cannot be rebuilt all in a moment, and it is not helpful to belittle the progress made in the early stages of rebuilding because the whole building does not immediately appear. He expressed anxiety lest the present policy of His Majesty's Government should have the effect of dividing the world more and more into two camps of a *bloc* alliance against another *bloc*. Is that really quite a fair presentation of the facts? Is not the world already, by no fault of our own, so divided, and would he not feel that we were therefore right to rally and organize those who think and feel as we do in defence of our beliefs and aspirations?

I would hope that our policy might be regarded as an approach to a permanent solution, a necessary first step. That certainly would be the manner in which I would regard it myself. The noble Viscount himself has given some indication of the permanent policy he has in mind, in which the main elements would be machinery for peaceful change based on some system of collective security. With regard to the latter, I have already pointed out both what I believe to be its possibilities and its limitations; and, as things are to-day, the necessary conditions for the full application of such a system simply do not exist. They may be built up again, but I think that the process is likely to be a gradual one, which can only be brought about by a change of outlook in several of the major Powers.

As regards machinery for peaceful change, no one would agree more wholeheartedly than I do that that might be the key, could we but find it satisfactorily, to most of our difficulties. But it is a great deal easier to state that objective than it is to find the means of achieving it. During twenty years of the League's existence, a great part of which were more leisured for speculation and thought than these years are, no completely satisfactory solution was found by those who devoted much thought and energy both to the foundation of the League and to examination of that problem. And yet a solution of it is essential, if we are to be realists in the world, and there is no question to which, if only we could get general co-operation of nations, international effort could more profitably and usefully be directed.

I apologize for keeping your Lordships so long, but what I have said will, I hope, show that it has not been from any disbelief in the ideals either of international justice or of collective security that His Majesty's Government have come to a policy, onerous enough but not unlimited, which we believe to be the nucleus round which may be enlisted the support of all peace-loving States. But while that side of our policy has of necessity been forced into prominence by recent events, we are always ready to take our part in more positive endeavour, not only to restrict force, but to promote enduring peace. Our record in that respect, I think, will bear examination by all who complain that we have obstructed the development and expansion of growing nations. I think the facts simply will not support the fantastic notion that the British Empire is a great treasure-house whose bounty is selfishly exploited and jealously locked.

I do not argue that now, because the facts are familiar enough to us. But the vast export of raw materials to industrial countries is there for all to see. There has been no difficulty for any country to get raw materials within the British Empire, except where countries have deliberately rationed themselves in order to provide for war industry. We have, both at Geneva and elsewhere, offered to discuss further concessions should any preferences that might exist be shown to place undue restriction on international trade. By some that offer was accepted; but it received little, if any, response in those quarters where we are charged with hoarding possessions and monopolizing markets. Methods other than those of free discussion and negotiations have been unhappily preferred, leaving us with no option but to continue to increase our strength, and make ourselves fit beyond all question, if need be, to carry out our undertakings. Any other course, from the examples before us and as things stand at this moment, might well risk the destruction of the independence of European nations one by one, until at last different races and different cultures were swallowed up in an imposed uniformity alien to the whole spirit of European development.

Therefore that was the danger that we felt bound to resist, and that not because we have any wish to thwart the natural opportunities of other peoples, but because by such means we hope that we may succeed in the creation of conditions by which the voice of reason may be heard once more, calling the great Powers to join hands in reconstruction and forgo courses that might lead to disaster. And certainly this country will neglect no approach, no suggestion to this end; for, as well as our defence policy, we have constantly present to our minds the positive desire to extend what Lord Salisbury called 'the neighbourly view of foreign politics'. Those words naturally lead me to add my word of thanks for the recent initiative of the President of the United States, for he has made his own the ideal of good-neighbourly relations between States. As has been already made clear, His Majesty's Government find themselves in essential agreement with the outlook on international relationships which he has expressed with great clarity of language and with the immense authority at his command. I have no doubt at all that millions of people in all countries will trust that his initiative may have a successful outcome.

One word more and I have done. The noble Viscount said that the people of this country demand that our foreign policy should have a basis of morality. I profoundly agree with him. If in the last resort you are to ask people, as he said, to make sacrifices and to hazard their lives, they will never willingly do that for any cause that fails to appeal to the highest elements in their nature. I have endeavoured to make clear that our policy has such a basis as that. It is founded on the principle that the rights of smaller States shall not be set aside by the stronger, that force shall not be the deciding factor in the relations between peoples, and that negotiations shall not be overshadowed or overborne by constraint. And there is something deeper than that. The historian and the philosopher can speak with authority on the diverse strands which are woven into the pattern of our culture. These strands run far back into the past, and derive from many countries and many epochs; but whatever the historian or the philosopher may conclude, I cannot doubt that at the foundation of our civilization are the moral values which have been gradually set up through the influence of Christianity, and by the observance, however imperfect, of the principles of Christian thought and action which have for centuries been the strongest single element in European life. Nor can I doubt that, unless Europe is prepared to return to these principles, we are not likely to make much progress either in personal or international relations. I would only add this last sentence, that if war ever came to the world it would, so far as the people of this country are concerned, only be because they would feel that there was no other way of defending causes and values which to them are more important than life itself.

38

NEGOTIATION

8 June 1939

[Negotiations between the British and Soviet Governments, undertaken with the object of securing a declaration of mutual assistance if either country were involved in hostilities through support given by it to the victims of aggression, were carried on throughout May 1939, and were the subject of more than one statement by Mr. Chamberlain in the House of Commons. They entered on a new phase when Mr. William Strang, a representative of the British Foreign Office, was sent to Moscow on June 12th. Meanwhile Mr. Chamberlain was able to announce on May 12th that the British and Turkish Governments had agreed that, in the event of an act of aggression leading to war in the Mediterranean area, they would be prepared to co-operate and to lend each other all the aid and assistance in their power. And on May 22nd Dr. Salazar, speaking for the Portuguese Government, declared the determination of his country to fulfil faithfully the duties of the Anglo-Portuguese Alliance.

The following speech was delivered by Lord Halifax in a debate in the House of Lords on a motion of Lord Snell, who called attention to the foreign policy of His Majesty's Government, and moved for Papers.]

MY LORDS, in the negotiations on which we have been engaged we have endeavoured to take account of the special situation of each country with which we have been in contact, not binding ourselves to any uniform pattern, but, so far as we can, trying to make a practical approach to the practical problem with which we had to deal.

The House, I am sure, will understand if I cannot give detailed particulars of discussions that are still in progress, for, great as are the advantages of responsible Parliamentary inquiry, it must be admitted that excessive pressure for premature information is some handicap in the handling of foreign relations, and perhaps places us at no small disadvantage in comparison with the countries which do not enjoy the blessing of free institutions. Provided that Parliament is, as I hope it is, broadly satisfied as to the purpose His Majesty's Government have in view, and the wide principles by which they are trying to achieve it, I do not doubt that both here and in another place there will be a disposition to exercise reasonable patience and restraint. In most departments of life it would be in the highest degree embarrassing for the parties concerned if each offer and counter-offer were to be trumpeted abroad before the final solution were reached.

As regards Poland, the House will recall the declaration made in the House of Commons by the Prime Minister in agreement with the Polish Foreign Minister on April 6. By that declaration the assurance given by His Majesty's Government to Poland was made reciprocal pending the conclusion of a permanent Agreement between the two countries. It is my hope that this permanent Agreement will shortly be concluded. Our assurances to Rumania and Greece, as the House knows, are unilateral in form, and at present require no further definition. These assurances, as the House will remember, will operate, as in the case of Poland, if there should be a clear threat to the independence of Rumania or of Greece which the Rumanian or Greek Government respectively consider it vital to resist with their national forces. As regards Turkey, the first stage of the negotiations with the Turkish Government was brought to a successful issue just a month ago, on May 12, and your Lordships will recollect the declaration that was made by both Governments in regard to the Agreement then reached. The further consultations for which that declaration provided are being actively pursued, and I have very little doubt that before long I shall be able to announce to your Lordships' House that they have been successfully completed. The attitude of friendly co-operation which the Turkish Government have adopted throughout these discussions has been a source of the greatest satisfaction to His Majesty's Government, as it has been to the whole country, and I think it is the best augury for the consolidation of peace in the Mediterranean area and South-Eastern Europe.

Now I come to the negotiations with the Soviet Union. Since the statement that was made by the Prime Minister in another place some little time ago, I have had the advantage of personal discussions with French Ministers in Paris and at

Geneva, as well as the continuance of my conversations with the Russian Ambassador in London. As a result of these discussions, joint Anglo-French proposals were made to the Soviet Government which, in our view, met in all essentials the points on which there had been difficulty. The Soviet Commissar for Foreign Affairs, in a public comment on these proposals, has indeed recognized that they do in substance go far to meet the preoccupation of his Government. But there remain one or two difficulties to be resolved, and your Lordships will be aware of the statement on the position as it stands to-day made by my right honourable friend in another place yesterday.

The main point of difficulty is the position of the Baltic States. Throughout all these discussions His Majesty's Government have been guided by the desire, not only to take account of the particular circumstances of the Government with which they were negotiating, but also to have regard to the situation and the wishes of third countries; and we have never attempted, and we should not think it right to attempt, to thrust assurances on countries which did not want them, or to take any step which might compromise in other quarters the relations of those countries which only desire to maintain their own neutrality inviolate. While your Lordships, I am sure, would give full weight to that consideration, at the same time it must be recognized that from the point of view of their own security the Soviet Government cannot be disinterested in the independence of their neighbours; and I hope that we may be able to find means by which that difficulty, and any others which may arise in the adjustment of the general points on which there is now, I think, no difference between the three Governments, will be resolved, and the greatest effect given to the general principle of mutual support against aggression by which the agreement we seek to reach is inspired.

We thought it of importance that, for the purpose of these negotiations, His Majesty's Ambassador in Moscow should be as fully informed as possible as to what was in His Majesty's Government's mind, and, accordingly, we had hoped to ask him to come back for a day or two for consultation with us. We had indeed asked him to do so, but yesterday it appeared, unluckily for him, that he had succumbed to the fashionable evil of influenza, and, therefore, as the Prime Minister stated yesterday, in order to accelerate the negotiations we are proposing to send a representative of the Foreign Office to Moscow to convey to His Majesty's Ambassador there full information as to the attitude of His Majesty's Government on all outstanding points, and I so informed the Soviet Ambassador this morning.

I have tried to give, in a brief form, some account of action taken by His Majesty's Government in the last few weeks which represents a fresh departure of great significance in British foreign policy, and before I leave this subject I would say one word about an engagement, somewhat similar in purpose and in character, which was concluded, I think, in the fourteenth century, and which has successfully withstood the changes and chances of 500 years of European politics. I refer, of course, to our alliance with Portugal. On May 22 the President of the Council, Dr. Salazar, took the opportunity to declare that the alliance between our two countries remained one of the unchanging principles of Portuguese policy. As the Prime Minister at once informed Dr. Salazar in a personal message, this declaration was received with the liveliest satisfaction both by His Majesty's Government and by the British people, and His Majesty's Government, on their side, reaffirmed their determination to fulfil with complete loyalty their obligations under the alliance. I am happy to think that these mutual assurances, following on the visit of a British Military Mission to Portugal, have contributed to consolidating still farther the alliance which has bound our two countries, as Atlantic and as Colonial Powers, for so many centuries, and which will, in the view of His Majesty's Government, continue to be a potent instrument in the cause of world peace.

I want now to make one or two general observations that are suggested by the summary of the negotiations which I have given to the House. I have no doubt that we must all be constantly reminding ourselves in these days of the danger of using any language of exaggeration, or of jumping too hastily at insecure conclusions. Above all, we must be sensible of the extreme importance of doing our utmost to understand the point of view of other nations and of getting them to understand our own. British policy seems to ourselves straightforward and plain, but it is perhaps not difficult to imagine how differently it may appear to many thinking people in Germany. There must be many such who are not less shocked than ourselves at the treatment of the Jews, and realize that, whatever Germany may have felt about relations between Germany and Czechoslovakia as they were left by Munich, to attempt to solve that problem by the destruction of Czech independence was—to state it in moderate terms—both unwise and wrong. But, feeling all this, such people in Germany may, in the light of post-War years, feel too that Germany would never in fact have secured consideration for claims that seem to her people eminently reasonable and just, unless she had been prepared to back them by threat of force. And it is no long step from this for the patriotic German to accept the gospel sedulously preached to him that British policy consists in the blocking of any and all of Germany's legitimate aspirations, whether racial, political, or economic.

There, to my mind, emerges the really dangerous element in the present situation, which is that the German people as a whole should drift to the conclusion that Great Britain had abandoned all desire to reach an understanding with Germany, and that any further attempt at such a thing must be once for all written off as hopeless. Now, my Lords, I am very well aware that in some quarters everything that this country has lately done is maliciously and untruly labelled as provocative and is condemned as only calculated to bring more close the disaster that all peoples everywhere desire above all things to avoid. But to us the British policy and British opinion wear a very different guise. The British people I think have constantly sought, and would still earnestly desire if they thought it possible, to reach such an understanding with Germany as might not only assist a settlement of particular questions but might also place the relations of the two countries upon a secure footing of mutual confidence. They have been very ready to admit many mistakes made both at and after the conclusion of the War, and there was a widespread desire to rectify what might legitimately be rectified and to enter into an era of genuine friendship with the German people. That desire found practical experience, for example, as is now forgotten, in the successful negotiations for the evacuation of the Rhineland before the time laid down in the Peace Treaty.

It was quite inevitable that events since 1933 should have profoundly disturbed the development of friendly Anglo-German relations. After the occupation of the Rhineland the German Chancellor assured the world that the period of surprises was over. After the *Anschluss* with Austria he said that Germany had no territorial demands to make in Europe. Then came the German action in regard to the Sudeten German problem in Czechoslovakia—culminating in Munich—last year. British opinion was inevitably disturbed, but according to its habit was prepared to do its best to understand, if not to accept, the German point of view. Treaty provisions were certainly being torn up, but Herr Hitler had repeatedly given to the world the assurance that Germany did not want to incorporate non-Germans within the Reich, and that seemed to be a guarantee of limitation upon Germany's aims in foreign policy. But on these events followed first the attack on the Jews in November of last year, which shocked the conscience of the world, and finally the destruction of the independence of Czechoslovakia by a lightning military occupation.

There seemed here something much more than a fresh departure in German policy. Above everything, there was a staggering blow that was levelled at confidence and at the value of the pledged word in international relationships. And to many people, certainly to our own, it seemed no unreal fear that made them wonder whether they might not be faced with a first step in an attempt to dominate the world by force, and made them feel themselves standing on the threshold of conditions in which no country could feel that its security and its independence might not at any time be threatened. Therefore it was almost overnight that there was an immediate and instinctive drawing together on the part of many countries to meet what appeared a great potential danger. The reaction in France was precisely the same, and no more tragic or disastrous error could be made than to suppose that because the French and British peoples are by nature tolerant and disposed to settle differences by discussion, by compromise, they are therefore less resolute, less vigorous, and less resilient than any other people. M. Daladier in recent speeches has expressed in language of quite unmistakable clarity the spirit which I believe to animate without exception to-day the whole French people; and I think it should now be equally clear that the people of this country are not less ready and not less determined than their friends across the Channel to make whatever contribution is necessary to uphold their way of life and to defend their position in the world.

If indeed it is true that in no country do the leaders cherish sinister designs of imposing settlements under pressure of overwhelming force, then not one of our engagements will ever be called into operation. The way is open to new opportunities by which all may benefit and the nations can rapidly emerge from the atmosphere of doubt, uncertainty, and fear in which for these last months they have been obliged to dwell. I am encouraged to say that by some words that were used by Signor Mussolini in the speech he made at Turin on May 14. Millions, he said, were asking whether we were on the road to war or peace, and his own answer was that there were at present no questions which would justify a war which by the logical development of events would become a universal war. If these problems are to be resolved by negotiation, there must be goodwill on both sides. There must be a readiness on each side to make allowances for the point of view of the other, and there must be give as well as take. Furthermore, there must be the conviction on both sides that the word of the other will be kept. Is it too much to hope that in this twentieth century of the Christian era it should be possible for the peoples of Europe and for their leaders to achieve these pre-conditions and so eliminate 'aggression' from the vocabulary of Europe?

There are a great many points at issue between European countries, and I should despair of their settlement if I were to consider only the polemical utterances on both sides. I refuse to accept at its full face value everything that is written or said in other countries, just as I would expect the Governments and peoples of those countries to ignore some irresponsible expressions of opinion in this country. If one may try to extract some comfort from a recent disaster[1] that in these last days has overshadowed all our thoughts, I would observe that it was significant that among the first messages of condolence to be dispatched to His Majesty the King on behalf of the people for whom they speak were the messages from the German Chancellor and Signor Mussolini. It is easy to say that those messages are the perfunctory expressions of international courtesy; but may it not be that one may see in them also an illustration of the readiness of great peoples, behind and beneath whatever may be the political differences of the moment, to meet each other upon the common basis of humanity? Nothing, in my view, would be more tragic than if through avoidable misunderstanding they were to abandon hope of such genuine co-operation as might offer the greatest contribution in all history to the peace of Europe.

If there is one thing certain in this uncertain world, it is that Great Britain and France, and, I may safely say, the countries with which they have been in consultation, will never commit any act of aggression or attempt by indirect means to undermine the independence or security of any State. So far from wishing to embarrass Germany in the economic field, we know that a truly prosperous Germany would be good for all Europe and be good for us. So far from wishing to obstruct settlements of problems which now or hereafter may appear likely to disturb the international order, our one desire is to throw all our weight in the scale of peaceful settlement. The day has gone by when the independence of European nations can be destroyed by unilateral action, and it is clear that any attempt to do so will meet with wide and resolute resistance. But provided the inde-

[1] The loss of the submarine *Thetis*.

pendence of nations is recognized, His Majesty's Government are not only willing but anxious to explore the whole problem of economic *Lebensraum*, not only for Germany but for everybody, for all European nations.

That brings me to the possibility of a conference. I venture to express some doubt whether a conference by itself, whatever may be its appeal to our natural feelings and emotions, offers any remedy. It has often been said that no conference can succeed that has not been carefully prepared beforehand, and that a conference which fails only makes a difficult situation worse. I am quite sure that we have to admit that there is great force in those ideas. But I have no hesitation in saying that, if there ever seemed to be elements of a real settlement, His Majesty's Government would advocate it, and we should be prepared to make the best contribution that we could to bring it to a successful result. Any of Germany's claims are open to consideration round a table, and Great Britain is only anxious, as I have said, to see rival claims adjusted on a basis that might secure lasting peace. But I repeat that we are concerned to see that these needs are settled by negotiation and not by force, for on no other terms than those can international life go on.

It may perhaps be thought that the action which His Majesty's Government have so far taken is only negative: that we have, so to speak, set up a number of notice-boards with 'Danger' written on them but have not made any constructive proposals which might make the boards unnecessary. I venture to say that that is a superficial view. In these recent months His Majesty's Government, in co-operation with other Governments, have been engaged upon the urgent and immediate task of trying to keep the peace, on which the future of all European countries depends. But if, as we hope, we succeed in reaching calmer waters, His Majesty's Government are under no illusion as to the necessity for devising positive plans for the future. Nobody could suppose that, even if it be appreciated that further acts of aggression against the independence of European States would be resisted, if necessary by force of arms, it would be satisfactory or even possible for Europe to settle down as long as its

Governments are divided into potentially hostile groups, and for nations to remain in a kind of uneasy equilibrium while their peoples were slowly impoverished by the burden of armaments and the stagnation of trade that must assuredly result. His Majesty's Government must therefore certainly wish to reach a point at which international differences can be made the subject of calm and unprejudiced negotiation.

Do not let us underrate the difficulties. In most of the problems which call for treatment to-day there is the most difficult of all human adjustments to make—namely, between conflicting claims, each of which can fairly be said to rest upon some foundation of equity but neither of which can be completely met if regard is had to the case, not less strong, upon the other side. In such cases it is quite clear that no just settlement can be reached unless both parties desire it. Here and elsewhere we are all prone to think that our judgement is as just as Solomon's, and we do not always remember that it is proverbially difficult to judge the case of another quite as fairly as one's own. But even if human judgement is always fallible, and perhaps will never be in a position to dispense perfect justice, yet we can, I think, generally manage to feel and see fairly plainly what is unjust. No settlement that it was sought to impose unilaterally by force without proper consideration of the claims on the other side could be described as just, and I think that those who seek to build a just world are bound to resist things by which justice is plainly disregarded and denied.

It may well be that there are questions for which at any particular moment, having regard to the temper of the times and the temper of those concerned, there is no immediate solution. In such cases I suppose it is the duty of statesmanship to work for such a *détente* as may make a real change in the atmosphere through which an approach to the problem has to be made. That will, of course, be eminently unsatisfying to the champions of importunate and imperative demands. But reasonable people everywhere will, I think, feel that, however difficult it may be to get a settlement which will completely suit both sides, it is certainly true that no settlement by negotiation can be worse than, or as bad as, a settlement achieved by war. And this feeling will be immeasurably stronger if in a particular question at issue there is no hardship or oppression which clamours for an immediate redress.

People are apt to say in these days that war is unavoidable. I do not share that view. It is true that there are delicate problems in Europe which are only too likely to lead to war if roughly handled, and there are men who have it in their sole power to precipitate a conflict. The danger always is that, for whatever reason, their judgement should mislead them as to the nature of the risk they are running and as to both the purpose and the temper of those against whose convictions they may at any time be moved to act. There must be no misunderstanding. If the issue were ever to be joined, I have no doubt at all about the ultimate outcome, whatever might be the varying fortunes of war or the duration of the struggle. But I find it difficult to believe that, with the certain prospect of resistance, with the awareness of the fearful consequences which must follow, with the knowledge of the desire of all peoples for peace, and the readiness of all peoples to see matters settled by negotiation, those who might feel tempted to risk the arbitrament of war would not feel—if they might once convince themselves of the good faith of those with whom they have to deal—that it was wiser and more profitable to resolve by negotiation the difficulties which inevitably arise in adjusting the claims and satisfying the needs of a constantly changing world.

[Four days later, on June 12th, Lord Halifax supplemented the foregoing speech, which had been variously interpreted. Speaking again in the House of Lords he said:]

I do not wish this afternoon to emphasize one part or another of what I said a few days ago in order to counter any misreading of its sense or purpose, and I have no doubt at all that it has been very well understood by those who have read it as a whole. I would venture with respect to say that it is a sign of some confused thinking to suggest that my speech implied some change in British policy. On the contrary, it was a perfectly frank attempt to get people here and elsewhere to face the realities of the situation. . . . There are two things as I see them. First, we must make plain that British policy, while making no threats and while concealing no ulterior designs, does want to make it quite clear to the world that if force is used to-day those who use it must count on force being met by force. The spirit of the people of these islands to-day is far stronger, more robust and united than even in 1914; and the one thing foreign machinery of propaganda always fails to mention—and the reason is obvious enough—is that not one of our engagements will ever function if there in fact exists nowhere any forcible disturber of the peace.

The second point, which I should certainly wish to see kept clearly before the people of this country, is that, if there is no attempt or intention to resort to force, then the whole influence of this country, which is not negligible, will be thrown, and in my judgement will be vitally thrown, on the side of reaching fair settlements by negotiation. And I agree that, to reach the point of negotiation, both sides must mean the same thing. That must be an essential condition, in my mind, for the success of any negotiations on which we hope one day the nations of Europe will be prepared to enter.

It is not always easy to judge accurately all intentions, and our judgement must largely depend on the words spoken and the acts done by those who control the policy of other countries. But there are, as I see it, the two alternatives at present standing for choice before the world, and I should be well content if I thought this debate had the effect of focusing the attention of all whom it might reach on the incalculable advantage of changing the dangerous, threatening, and sinister methods of arbitral force for the methods of negotiation and peaceful settlement.

39

THE PURPOSE OF BRITISH POLICY. III

21 June 1939

[The Military Training Bill, imposing compulsory military service upon all men between the ages of twenty and twenty-one, passed its third reading in the House of Commons on May 18th, 1939.

On June 21st Lord Halifax was the principal guest at the annual dinner of the 1900 Club, held at Grosvenor House. His speech is printed from a text supplied by him.]

THE one thing that makes the British Empire unique in history is that the whole driving force of it has been liberty. In liberty it has discovered the secret of unity, and through liberty it has been able to reconcile essential unity with that wide diversity which has enabled peoples of all sorts to bring all their varied gifts of tradition, thought and culture to that single end that they feel to be the expression of them all. . . . Exactly the same thing underlies foreign policy to-day. Nothing interests people so much at the present time as foreign policy, and rightly so. That is not only because they feel it involves issues of peace or war but because they feel that in foreign policy to-day are being tested out the great issues that are vital to our way of life.

. . . . .

Has British policy changed during recent months? In one sense, yes. I said in the House of Lords[1] after the occupation of Prague something that was by nature a platitude, but is perhaps worth reminding ourselves of. Broadly speaking, there have been since the War two conflicting theses as to the best method of avoiding conflicts and establishing security.

First of all, there was the view that security could be attained through machinery for consultation, conciliation, and arbitration, with, behind it, the sanction of collective force. There was the other view that indefinite commitments involved dangers out of proportion to the real security which those commitments gave; and consequently from that argument flowed a tendency towards isolation and against

[1] Page 247 above.

entangling alliances, as they were called, where immediate or vital interests were not threatened.

The inclination to believe in one or other of these two depended on the estimate of the dangers that were involved on the one hand of extending commitments or on the other of an ultimate attack on the vital interests of the nations concerned. I ventured to say in the House of Lords that, when it became plain that there was no apparent guarantee against successive attacks directed in turn on all who might seem to stand in the way of ambitious schemes of domination, then at once the scale tipped and in all quarters there was likely immediately to be found a much greater readiness to consider the acceptance of wider obligations for mutual support. That is exactly what has happened.

In that sense there has been a change, but in another sense—and in a more real sense—there has been no change. The main purpose of British policy remains the same, and the principles that inspire it are in no way altered. What have changed are the circumstances and conditions in which the purpose comes to be pursued and the principles have to be applied.

I may in one or two sentences restate as I see them the principles on which that policy must to-day be based. We fully recognize that the world does not remain static. The whole of human life is based on change. What does not change is dead. But unless change can be orderly, human life is impossible and ends by being itself destroyed. Therefore our purpose is, while always ready to admit the necessity of the adjustment of conflicting claims in a changing world, to declare in plain language our opposition to methods of force. We feel that if nations were to live always under no law but the law of might, their life would exist only under constant threat, and on those terms life becomes intolerable. Accordingly we have been, and are, working to unite with ourselves those who feel the same—not with any intention hostile to any other nation, but with a single and perfectly clear resolve to throw all we can into the scales on the side of law as opposed to lawlessness in Europe.

We have accordingly given certain guarantees to European

States, and all those arrangements are devised with the sole object of assisting those States to maintain their independence in the event of its being threatened, and to resist attempts, if such should be made, to dominate them. We are now, and not, as Mr. Churchill has said, without incurring criticisms in some quarters, engaged in negotiation with the Soviet Government with a view to securing their co-operation along the same lines and with the same objective. We believe that in this field the Soviet Government have the same interest and the same objective that we have ourselves. As is not uncommon, the search for the exact formula presents difficulties, but with the conviction that we aim at the same thing, and if we can succeed in dispelling the forces of mistrust, I am confident that we shall succeed in reaching agreement.

We have gone farther than many would have thought right in the endeavour to find agreement; and I think that, if we have so far failed, we can truly feel that it has not been our fault. We have made repeated attempts to persuade others to join in constructive approach on the basis of mutual efforts to strengthen the foundations of peace. At the very time of the destruction of the independent existence of Czechoslovakia we were on the edge of important talks between British and German industrialists actively supported by the Board of Trade.

But just as it takes more than one to quarrel, so, I am afraid, it takes more than one to make friends. If every attempt that we make to improve relations is construed as weakness and is made the ground for new and more bitter attack, it is surely hardly to be wondered at if many people form the conclusion that the only argument which those who seem to rely on force are likely to understand is that others should be not less ready themselves to use force in self-defence.

I do not know who it was who first invented the term 'peace front'. But it is a precise expression of our purpose. It contains no design hostile to any other country, and it means that our action springs solely from the conviction that in spite of all the misrepresentation that was to be expected, it is the best insurance to-day for world peace.

That action has not been taken without full consideration and review of all the issues that are involved. It was to be foreseen that many attempts, persistent and ingenious, would be made to weaken the resolution of the British people. Wild rumours from many quarters would be set in constant circulation, and attempts to sow suspicions and to breed infirmity of purpose would be made in this quarter or in that. But I think all that technique, if it be employed, will fail, and it will fail for this reason: that the British people have now reached a point where the three indispensable elements of a consistent policy are present.

Those three elements, in my judgement, are, first, that to a greater extent than at any time during recent years the country is united. How much that means both at home and abroad, nobody, I think, is in a better position than the Foreign Secretary to say. Secondly, I think, the country is clear in its own mind what is the great end to which its policy ought to be directed. And, lastly, it knows that it is strong and getting stronger.

You see in many directions the expression and the result of these elements in operation. Is it not significant how the country has in the last few weeks accepted in peace provision for compulsory military training without any impairment of national unity? To anyone who knows our people and the strength of their common tradition, based in part on the geographical accident of being an island, in part based on the recollection of Cromwell, and who remembers how long that measure of compulsory service was postponed in the crisis of the Great War for fear of impairing national unity, surely that event is one of profound significance. So, too, is the spirit in which our young men are coming forward willingly and only glad to have the opportunity clearly shown to them of rendering service to their country.

A great responsibility rests upon this country. I have repeatedly said that responsibility is twofold—the prevention of war and constructive efforts for peace. I cannot believe British policy ought ever to let go either one or the other. That great responsibility rests upon our people, and to-day it is assuredly not less than it has ever been. I am convinced that our people will not be unworthy of it. Above all, I cannot doubt—and here I end as I began—that the British people will be true to their own spirit of liberty and that, by being true to their own spirit of liberty, they will be serving the cause of liberty throughout the world.

40

THE PURPOSE OF BRITISH POLICY. IV

29 June 1939

[On June 29th, 1939, Lord Halifax was again the principal speaker at the annual dinner—ninth in the series—of the Royal Institute of International Affairs. His speech has been published by the Institute as a separate pamphlet.]

WHEN I look back to the speech which I delivered at the Chatham House Dinner in June a year ago,[1] I am conscious, as we all are, of the great changes that have taken place. A year ago we had undertaken no specific commitments on the Continent of Europe, beyond those which had then for some considerable time existed and which are familiar to you all. To-day we are bound by new agreements for mutual defence with Poland and Turkey; we have guaranteed assistance to Greece and Roumania against aggression, and we are now engaged with the Soviet Government in a negotiation, to which I hope there may shortly be a successful issue, with a view to associating them with us for the defence of States in Europe whose independence and neutrality may be threatened. We have assumed obligations, and are preparing to assume more, with full understanding of their causes and with full understanding of their consequences. We know that, if the security and independence of other countries are to disappear, our own security and our own independence will be gravely threatened. We know that, if international law and order is to be preserved, we must be prepared to fight in its defence.

In the past we have always stood out against the attempt of any single Power to dominate Europe at the expense of the liberties of other nations, and British policy is therefore only following the inevitable line of its own history, if such an attempt were to be made again. But it is not enough to state a policy. What matters is, first, to convince the nation that the policy is right, and, secondly, to take the steps necessary

[1] No. 27 in this collection.

for that policy to succeed. I believe that at no time since the War has there been such national unity on the main essentials of our foreign policy as to-day, and that with this spirit of unity goes a deep and widespread determination to make that policy effective. But I believe too that among all classes of our people who, in virtue of their common citizenship, are being called upon to defend their country, and the causes for which it stands, there is an increasing desire to look beyond the immediate present, and to see before them some goal for which they would willingly sacrifice their leisure and, if need be, their lives.

We are already asking for great sacrifices from all ages and classes in the call for national service, and in one way and another every man and woman has a part to play, and I know is prepared to do so. The immense effort that the country is making in equipping itself for defence at sea, in the air, and on land is without parallel in peace time. We have an unchallengeable navy. Our air force is still undergoing an expansion which has outstripped all expectations of a few months ago and has now nothing to fear from any other. I have little doubt that its personnel are in spirit and in skill superior to all others. Our army, once derided, but which survived to prove its worth so that it made a boast of that derision, is, no doubt, small in comparison with that of some other countries. But, as happened once before, we are creating here also a powerful weapon for the defence of our own liberty and that of other peoples. With every week that passes, that effort gains momentum, and on every side of life—political, administrative, industrial—we have abundant evidence of how firmly this national effort is driven and supported by the people's will. Behind all our military effort stands the British people, more united than ever before, and at their service their wealth and industrial resources. These again are the object of contemptuous reference, but they are upheld by the labour, skill, and courage of our people. None of this formidable array of strength will be called into play except in defence against aggression. No blow will be struck, no shot fired. Of the truth of that, everyone in this country is convinced, and I believe that most people in other countries really accept it in spite of what propaganda dins into their ears to the contrary. What now is universally accepted in this country, but may not be well understood everywhere, is that, in the event of further aggression, we are resolved to use at once the whole of our strength in fulfilment of our pledges to resist it.

These great changes in our national life could not indeed be brought about, were they not backed by deep conviction, which is immensely strengthened by what we hear and read almost daily from other parts of the world. We are often told that, though once we were a great nation, our ways are now old fashioned, and that our democracy has no life in it. We read the mischievous misrepresentations of our actions and of our motives, which some people in countries holding a different international philosophy from our own think fit to make. We read them with resentment, knowing that they are false and knowing that those who make them know it too. These things do not pass unnoticed here, nor, I may say, do provocative insults offered to our fellow countrymen farther afield.[1] I can say at once that Great Britain is not prepared to yield either to calumnies or to force. It may afford some satisfaction to those who have pronounced our nation to be decadent to learn that they themselves have found the cure—and that most effective. For every insult that is offered to our people, every rude challenge that is made to what we value and are determined to defend, only unites us, only increases our determination and strengthens our loyalty to those others who share our feelings and our aspirations. Over a large part of the world the old standards of conduct and of ordinary human decency, which man had laboriously built up, are being set aside. Things are being done to-day which we can hardly read without amazement, so alien are they to our conception of how men should deal with their fellow men. Rules of conduct between nations are overridden with the same callous indifference as rules of conduct between man and man.

The first thing, therefore, which we have to do is to see

[1] The reference is to the blockade by the Japanese of the British Concession in Tientsin and the maltreatment of British subjects there.

that our own standards of conduct do not deteriorate. On that point there must be—and I know there is—complete national unity. We respect our fellow men. We know that without that there can be no real self-respect either for individuals or in the long run for nations. The day that we lose our respect for our fellow men, our democracy would have lost something on which its vitality depends, and would justly become what our critics like to think it, namely moribund and dead, for it would indeed have lost the right to live. If then we hold fast to these principles, what is the application of them to our foreign policy? At a time when our aims are being constantly misrepresented, it is perhaps well to restate them boldly and with such plainness of speech as I can command. And I would try to deal briefly both with our aims in the immediate present and our aims in the future; what we are doing now and what we should like to see done as soon as circumstances make it possible.

Our first resolve is to stop aggression. I need not recapitulate the acts of aggression which have taken place, or the effect which they have had upon the general trust that European nations feel able to place in words and undertakings. For that reason and for that reason alone we have joined with other nations to meet a common danger. These arrangements we all know, and the world knows, have no purpose other than defence. They mean what they say—no more and no less. But they have been denounced as aiming at the isolation—or as it is called the encirclement—of Germany and of Italy, and as designed to prevent them from acquiring the living space necessary for their national existence. I shall deal with these charges to-night, and I propose to do so with complete frankness.

We are told that our motives are to isolate Germany within a ring of hostile States, to stifle her natural outlets, to cramp and throttle the very existence of a great nation. What are the facts? They are very simple and everybody knows them. Germany is isolating herself, and is doing it most successfully and most completely. She is isolating herself from other countries economically by her policy of autarky; she is isolating herself politically by a policy that causes constant anxiety to other nations, and culturally by her policy of racialism. If you deliberately isolate yourself from others you can blame nobody but yourself; and so long as this isolation continues, the inevitable consequences of it are bound to become stronger and more marked. The last thing that we desire is to see the individual German man, or woman, or child suffering privations; but if they do so, the fault does not lie with us, and it depends on the German Government and on the German Government alone whether this process of isolation continues or not, for any day it can be ended by a policy of co-operation. It is well that this should be stated plainly so that there may be no misunderstanding here or elsewhere.

I come next to *Lebensraum*. This word, of which we have not heard the last, needs to be fairly and carefully examined. Every developed community is, of course, faced with the vital problem of living space. But the problem is not solved simply by acquiring more territory. That may indeed only make the problem more acute. It can only be solved by wise ordering of the affairs of a country at home, and by adjusting and improving its relations with other countries abroad. For nations expand their wealth, and raise the standard of living of their people, by gaining the confidence of their neighbours and thus facilitating the flow of goods between them. The very opposite is likely to be the consequence of action by one nation in suppression of the independent existence of her smaller and her weaker neighbours. And if *Lebensraum* is to be applied in that sense, we reject it and must resist its application. It is noteworthy that this claim to 'living space' is being put forward at a moment when Germany has become an immigration country, importing workers in large numbers from Czechoslovakia, from Holland, and from Italy to meet the needs of her industry and agriculture. How then can Germany claim to be overpopulated? Belgium and Holland, and to a less extent our own islands, have already proved that what is called overpopulation can be prevented by productive work. The wide spaces and the natural resources of the British Empire and of the United States of America were not able to save them from widespread distress during the great slump of 1929 to 1932. Economically the world is far too closely knit together for any one country to hope to profit itself at the expense of its neighbours, and no more than any other country can Germany hope to solve her economic problems in isolation. It is no doubt impossible at present for us to foresee the day when all trade everywhere will be completely free. But it is possible to make many arrangements, given the opportunity, which would greatly enlarge the area of freedom, and through co-operation—and we, for our part, are ready to co-operate—there is ample scope for extending to all nations the opportunity of a larger economic life with all that this means, which is implied in the term *Lebensraum.*

If the world were organized on such lines, neither Germany nor Italy need fear for her own safety, and no nation could fail to profit from the immense material benefits which the general application of science has brought within universal reach. But no such society of nations can be built upon force, in a world which lives in fear of violence and has to spend its substance in preparing to resist it. It is idle to cry peace where there is no peace, or to pretend to reach a settlement unless it can be guaranteed by the reduction of warlike preparations, and by the assured recognition of every nation's right to the free enjoyment of its independence. At this moment the doctrine of force bars the way to settlement, and fills the world with envy, hatred, malice, and all uncharitableness. But if the doctrine of force were once abandoned, so that the fear of war that stalks the world were lifted, all outstanding questions would become easier to solve. If all the effort which is now devoted to the senseless multiplication of armaments, with the consequent increase of insecurity and distrust, were to be applied to the common peaceful development of resources, the peoples of the world would soon find an incentive to work together for the common good; they would realize that their true interests do not conflict and that progress and well-being depend upon community of aim and effort. The nations would then be in a position to discuss with real promise of success both political grievances and economic difficulties, whether in the international or colonial field.

This brings me to say something about the principles of our colonial administration. There was a time when in the British Empire, as elsewhere, colonies were regarded merely as a source of wealth and a place of settlement for Europeans. You have only to read any of the colonial literature of those days to see for how little counted the rights and welfare of the natives. But during the last half-century a very different view has gained ground, a view which has been finely expressed in Article 22 of the Covenant, namely that the well-being and development of 'people not yet able to stand by themselves under the strenuous conditions of the modern world' is 'a sacred trust of civilization'.

That trust has been steadily fulfilled since the War in the case of the mandated territories, on which the operation of the provisions of Article 22 of the Covenant has conferred immense benefits; and the British Commonwealth, I think, is fully aware of the heavy responsibility resting upon it to see that, through respect for these principles, continuity and development is assured to the native populations. The mandatory system, in fact, derives from exactly the same inspiration as that which governs British colonial policy. We have applied the same principles to India and Burma, where they are now steadily at work on a scale that twenty or thirty years ago would have seemed far beyond the bounds of reasonable expectation. Within the last few years we have seen the transformation of Eire into a separate and independent member of the British Commonwealth, enjoying with our other partners of the Empire full Dominion status. For many years we tried, as the phrase went, to hold Ireland, under the mistaken belief, which is to-day invoked to justify the subjection of Czechoslovakia, that it was indispensable to our national security. But we have now realized that our safety is not diminished but immeasurably increased by a free and friendly Ireland. And so both here and in every country for which we have been responsible we have steadily moved in one direction. The whole picture is a significant and faithful reflection of British thought, projected into political form, and expressing itself, through history and now, in the development of institutions. We recognize, as the

United States have recognized, that self-government should be the ultimate goal of colonial policy, a goal which is near or distant according to the capacity of the peoples concerned to manage their own affairs. In one of your own studies, *The Colonial Problem*, the type of research which enhances the reputation of Chatham House, you have considered the question whether colonies pay. You drew attention to the benefits of cheap imports which the consumers of a country possessing colonies obtain as the result of the relatively low cost of production of certain commodities in colonial territories. But under an international system under which the present trade barriers were to a great extent abolished, these benefits, already shared as they are to a considerable extent by many countries not possessing colonies, would be shared still more widely. On all sides there could be more free and more ready access to markets and raw materials of the world; wider channels of trade down which would flow the goods which nations require to buy and sell. Such are some of the possibilities within everybody's reach.

How does all this affect our wider problems? One of the most significant facts in world history is the extent to which the principle of trusteeship has come to be adopted in the British Commonwealth during the last thirty years, and there is surely something here that can be used for the great benefit of mankind. Can we not look forward to a time when there may be agreement on common methods and aims of colonial development, which may ensure not only that the universally acknowledged purpose of colonial administration will be to help their inhabitants steadily to raise their level of life, but also that colonial territories may make a growing contribution to the world's resources? On such an agreed foundation of purpose we hope that others might be prepared with us to make their contribution to a better world. If so, I have no doubt that in the conduct of our colonial administration we should be ready to go far upon the economic side, as we have already done on the political side, in making wider application of the principles which now obtain in the mandated territories, including, on terms of reciprocity, that of the open door. Whatever may be the difficulties of the colonial problem, or of any other, I would not despair of finding ways of settlement, once everybody has got the will to settle. But unless all countries do in fact desire a settlement, discussions will do more harm than good. It is impossible to negotiate with a country the leaders of which brand a friendly country as thieves and blackmailers and indulge daily in monstrous slanders on British policy in all parts of the world. But if that spirit gave way to something different, His Majesty's Government would be ready to pool their best thought with others in order to end the present state of political and economic insecurity, and, if we could get so far, what an immense stride the world would have made! We should have exorcized the anxiety which is cramping and arresting business expansion, and we should have brought back an atmosphere of confidence among nations and assurance for the future among the youth of this and every other European country. These would be tremendous gains which would brighten the whole horizon, but they would only be the first step. Our next task would be the reconstruction of the international order on a broader and firmer foundation. That is too large a topic for me to embark upon this evening, but I should like to commend it to your thinking.

We must ask ourselves how far the failure of the League was due to shortcomings in the Covenant itself, or how far it was the absence of some of the greatest countries at every stage of its history that has crippled both its moral authority and strength. Is it, I would ask, beyond the political genius of mankind to reconcile national individuality with international collaboration? Can human purpose rise high enough to solve the riddle? An examination of the history of the Covenant may perhaps disclose that some of its obligations were too loose and others too rigid. It has been suggested, for instance, that some system of specific regional guarantees for the preservation of the peace would be more effective than the indefinite but universal obligations of Articles 10 and 16, and it is not impossible that the grouping of the Powers as it exists to-day, instead of dividing Europe, might be so moulded as to become the embryo of a better European system.

That is one side of the problem. But it is not enough to devise measures for preventing the use of force to change the *status quo*, unless there is also machinery for bringing about peaceful change. For a living and changing world can never be held in iron clamps, and any such attempt is the high road to disaster. Changes in the relations, needs, and outlook of nations are going on all the time. And there is no more urgent need, if we are ever to find a workable system of international organization, than to invent peaceful means by which such changes can be handled. To-day when the European nations, forgetful of their common civilization, are arming to the teeth, it is more important than ever that we should remind ourselves of the essential unity of European civilization. European minds meet across political frontiers. With the same background of knowledge, with the same heritage of culture, they study the same problems; the work of the great masters of science, of literature, and of art is the common property of all peoples; and thinkers in every land exchange knowledge on equal and friendly terms. Truly is a divided Europe a house divided against itself, and our foreign policy must therefore constantly bear in mind the immediate present and the more distant future, the steps we are now taking and the goal to which they are meant to lead.

Ladies and gentlemen, I have strained your patience, but if you will allow me a few moments more I will endeavour to pick up the threads of my thought and perhaps make one or two points more explicit. British policy rests on twin foundations of purpose. One is determination to resist force. The other is our recognition of the world's desire to get on with the constructive work of building peace. If we could once be satisfied that the intentions of others were the same as our own, and that we all really wanted peaceful solutions —then, I say here definitely, we could discuss the problems that are to-day causing the world anxiety. In such a new atmosphere we could examine the colonial problem, the problem of raw materials, trade barriers, the issue of *Lebensraum*, the limitation of armaments, and any other issue that affects the lives of all European citizens.

But this is not the position which we face to-day. The

threat of military force is holding the world to ransom, and our immediate task is—and here I end as I began—to resist aggression. I would emphasize that to-night with all the strength at my command, so that nobody may misunderstand it. And if we are ever to succeed in removing misunderstanding and reaching a settlement which the world can trust, it must be upon some basis more substantial than verbal undertakings. It has been said that deeds, not words, are necessary. That also is our view. There must be give and take in practical form on both sides, for there can be no firm bargains on the basis of giving something concrete in return for mere assurances. None of us in these days can see very far ahead in the world in which we live, but we can and we must always be sure of the general direction in which we wish to travel. Let us, therefore, be very sure that whether or not we are to preserve for ourselves and for others the things we hold dear depends in the last resort upon ourselves, upon the strength of the personal faith of each one of us, and upon our resolution to maintain it.

41

RUSSIA AND DANZIG

3 August 1939

[On April 28th, 1939, Herr Hitler made a speech in the Reichstag stating that Poland had rejected a demand from Germany for the incorporation of Danzig in the Reich. At the same time he denounced the Anglo-German naval treaty of 1937 and the non-aggression agreement which he had made in 1934 with Poland on the plea that this had been infringed by Poland's pact with Great Britain. Mr. Chamberlain made the British attitude plain in a statement delivered to the House of Commons on July 10th. 'Recent occurrences in Danzig', he said, 'have inevitably given rise to fears that it is intended to settle her future status by unilateral action, organized by surreptitious methods, thus presenting Poland and other Powers with a *fait accompli*. In such circumstances any action taken by Poland to restore the situation would, it is suggested, be represented as an act of aggression on her part. . . . If the sequence of events should, in fact, be such as is contemplated on this hypothesis, the issue could not be considered as a purely local matter involving the rights and liberties of the Danzigers but would at once raise graver issues affecting Polish national existence and independence. We have guaranteed to give our assistance to Poland in the case of a clear threat to her independence which she considers it vital to resist with her national forces, and we are firmly resolved to carry out this undertaking.'

On June 28th Lord Halifax and Mr. Chamberlain announced in Parliament that it had been agreed between the British and Japanese Governments that conversations should take place in Tokyo with the object of effecting a full settlement of the various questions relating to present conditions in Tientsin. On July 24th the result of the discussions was given in statements made simultaneously by the Prime Minister and by Lord Halifax. The British Government recognized that the Japanese forces in China had special requirements for the purpose of safeguarding their own security and maintaining public order in the regions under their control, and stated that they had no intention of countenancing any acts or measures prejudicial to the attainment of those objects.

Before Parliament rose for the August recess Lord Halifax surveyed in the House of Lords the position of foreign affairs. After defending the Tokyo formula he proceeded as follows.]

MY LORDS, I must say something about Russia. His Majesty's Government have taken the lead in endeavouring to organize a combination of resistance against aggression, and the fact that the principal portion of blame for every difficulty or delay falls on them shows indeed that their leading role is generally acknowledged. If the world were just, His Majesty's Government would receive the lion's share of credit for whatever has been achieved; but as the world, or the people in it, is or are not always just, His Majesty's Government make no complaint at all of shouldering the greater part of the blame for real or imaginary failures. The basis of British policy has been, as your Lordships are aware, close co-operation with France in defence of interests that are common, as was explicitly laid down in the declaration made so long ago as the beginning of February by my right honourable friend the Prime Minister in another place. It was starting from that point that His Majesty's Government offered their guarantee to Poland and Rumania, and undoubtedly by doing that they made a substantial contribution to the security of Russia; and it was in view of the fact that they felt obliged at that time to act promptly, with, I think I can say, the approval of the overwhelming mass of opinion in this country, that they did not make their action dependent on receiving any counterpart then and there from the Soviet Government.

The present negotiations with Russia have as their object the strengthening of the forces against possible aggression, and noble Lords will no doubt realize that to provide an instrument which will cover every possible contingency is a very complicated task which must inevitably give rise to certain divergencies of view. Moreover the problem is further complicated by the necessity of trying to provide for the new technique of indirect aggression. His Majesty's Government and the French Government and the Soviet Government are in full agreement on the necessity of trying to make such provision, but the differences which have arisen relate to the precise form in which this elusive shadow of indirect aggression can be brought to definition. Our common object is to find a formula which may cover what may rightly be regarded as indirect aggression without in any way encroaching on the independence and the neutrality of other States, and it is no secret that the proposals that the British and French

Governments have made have appeared to the Soviet Government insufficiently comprehensive, whilst the formula favoured by the Soviet Government has seemed to His Majesty's Government and the French Government to go too far in the other direction.

The delays which have occurred have risen not only from the complexity of the problem in hand, which affects the rights and interests of a very large number of States. I rather doubt whether even noble Lords, and I am quite sure still more of the general public outside, fully realize all that is involved in negotiations of this character. It is quite true that an interim agreement such as those made with Poland and with Turkey can be concluded relatively quickly; in the case of both these countries, the formal agreements are still under discussion. I have been asked whether our agreement with Poland included a definition of indirect aggression and, if it did, why it was not possible to transplant that definition into the Russian Agreement. The answer is that the formal agreement with Poland is still being agreed; it is still not concluded; and the arrangement on which we have been working and are working with Poland does not, I think, refer to indirect aggression, and for the simple reason that our guarantee to Poland rested upon a perfectly simple, precise, but rather different basis. Our guarantee to Poland was made operative in the event of Polish independence being clearly threatened and the Polish Government feeling it necessary to resist.

The Soviet Government, in contra-distinction from what we were able to do with Turkey and Poland, preferred to proceed without any intermediate stage to the conclusion of a formal agreement. The terms of that formal agreement naturally have required careful consideration, and it was inevitable that there was a great deal of discussion to be done on the drafting. The fact that we had to agree any modifications and alterations with the French Government necessarily and inevitably involved a certain measure of additional time expenditure. It has been assumed in some quarters that, had His Majesty's Government been represented by a Cabinet Minister instead of an Ambassador, a quick agreement would have been secured. One should remember the Washington Naval Conference in 1921, when His Majesty's Government were represented by a most distinguished Minister, the late Lord Balfour. Although the ground for that Conference had been prepared with the utmost diligence through diplomatic channels, it took no less than three months there to secure agreement. In the present case I understand M. Molotov is obliged at every stage to consult his Government, and the same would have applied to any British representative, whether in the Cabinet or out of the Cabinet, who had been on our behalf conducting the negotiations for His Majesty's Government in Moscow.

The fact that His Majesty's Government and the French Government have decided to dispatch Military Missions to Moscow—I think they leave the day after to-morrow—before full agreement has been reached on the political issues, may be held, I hope, to be the best evidence of the bona fides and determination of His Majesty's Government, and concrete evidence not only of our interest to bring these negotiations to an early and successful conclusion but of our belief that that step will facilitate outstanding discussions on political issues which will proceed simultaneously with the military discussions.

I must say a word or two in regard to another subject. That is Danzig. But I do not know that I want to say very much. Your Lordships will recollect that the Prime Minister in another place on July 10 last set out the attitude of His Majesty's Government in a statement which, in some quarters there may be surprise to learn, I had some hand in drafting. I do not want to quote parts of that statement, because it was a balanced whole, and still less would I wish to quote it all to your Lordships, but I would only say this in regard to it. Its terms were, I think, clear; they were precise and they were certainly carefully weighed; and I do not wish to say to-day anything in any way to weaken whatever may be held to be their effect or their value. But I would say one word in reply to a suggestion that an international force should be established in Danzig. The fact that I do not think that the installation of an international force in Danzig at this moment would be a practical and useful step in all the circumstances, does not mean that His Majesty's Government are not watching the situation most closely or that they are not fully alive to the possible repercussions or developments in that quarter upon the future of European peace.

May I say before I leave that part of the world a few words in regard to Poland and more particularly the Anglo-Polish financial negotiations to which reference has been made? As your Lordships know, discussions with the Polish delegation have covered two separate matters. The first relates to export credits; and I am glad to say that an agreement was signed yesterday for the guarantee of export credits to Poland up to an amount of rather over £8,000,000 in order to facilitate the purchase in this country by the Polish Government of material necessary for their defence. Discussions have also been taking place on the possibility of a cash loan to Poland by His Majesty's Government and the French Government acting jointly, and along with all members of your Lordships' House I greatly regret that it was not found possible to reach agreement as to the conditions on which such a loan might be made available in time for Parliament to be asked to pass the necessary legislation before we rise. The difficulties that were in the way were, as has been stated in another place, technical difficulties, and it would not I think be in the public interest to discuss them; but I may add just this, that the difficulties that arose were not difficulties in connexion with the purchase of arms by Poland in countries other than the United Kingdom. There has been some misconception on that point, and I think it is worth making that plain. I would also add that these difficulties have in no degree—I think I can safely say this—impaired the relations of complete confidence that exist between the Governments of the two countries.

. . . .

As we rise for our Recess, much as I should like to do so I cannot encourage anyone to feel complacent about the situation in which the world finds itself. I do not think that anxiety is confined to the people of this country. It is felt by the people, I think, in all countries. Therefore we cannot be complacent, for that would not be, as I see it, in accordance with the facts and the possibilities as we believe them to exist to-day. Indeed, it may well be that the next weeks or months may prove critical. The policy of His Majesty's Government is, I hope, sufficiently clear and so generally accepted that I need not recapitulate it. I myself tried to define it in the speech which I made something over a month ago.[1] To that speech I have nothing to add, and from that speech I have certainly nothing to withdraw. Only those for whom, as for the Bellman in *The Hunting of the Snark*, the degree of truth is directly dependent upon verbal repetition would think any useful purpose was served by my saying it again. I venture to think that misunderstandings are more often the child of speech than of silence. Accordingly I would add this. We have tried to make the position of this country crystal-clear. We have no aggressive designs; our alliances and understandings have not been framed with any aggressive intent. We have, however, sought to define the double purpose of British policy as regards, on the one hand, our attitude towards aggression by others, and on the other our willingness, if force and threat of force were abandoned, to join in the constructive establishment of a peaceful order.

There can, I think, be no mistake now as to where this country stands. We have taken our own precautions, and we have done everything possible, by organizing the forces of peace, to strengthen the deterrents to war. It only remains for us—and this would be my special request as this House approaches the time of its rising—to keep calm and, so far as we may, to keep united; to avoid exaggerated attention to rumour, and to be neither over-confident nor over-pessimistic. For I suggest that a united nation which both knows exactly where it stands and knows itself to be strong can meet the future, whatever it may hold, with confidence.

[1] No. 40 in this collection.

42

THE DANZIG CRISIS. I

24 August 1939

[The immediate cause of the dispute between the Polish Government and the Danzig Senate which resulted in German aggression against Poland was the position of the Polish Customs officials in Danzig. The question was capable of solution by negotiation, but discussions had hardly started when an official announcement made in Berlin and in Moscow on August 22nd that Germany and the U.S.S.R. were about to sign a pact of non-aggression caused the British Cabinet to be immediately called together. In a statement issued after their meeting the Cabinet announced that they had no hesitation in deciding that the pact would in no way affect their obligations to Poland which they were determined to fulfil. The Prime Minister immediately sent a personal letter to Herr Hitler on August 22nd, making the British position clear, to which Herr Hitler replied on August 23rd. Parliament was summoned to meet on August 24th for the purpose of passing through all its stages the Emergency Powers (Defence) Bill. On the Houses assembling, Lord Halifax made, in the House of Lords, the following statement, and one on similar lines was given to the House of Commons by Mr. Chamberlain.]

MY LORDS, I am glad to accede to the invitation of the noble Lord opposite, and perhaps your Lordships will forgive me if I make a statement of somewhat greater length than is customary in answer to a formal question. It will perhaps be of some usefulness if I sketch in a word or two the background of the international developments which have led to the recall of Parliament. The events of this year are fresh in all our minds, and the cumulative effect of them had been to lead many countries of Europe to feel themselves confronted with an attempt on the part of Germany to dominate and control their destiny, and there were few which had not reason to fear that their liberties were in greater or less degree in danger. As a matter of history, successive British Governments have felt obliged to resist attempts by a single Power to dominate Europe at the expense of others, and the imposition of one country's will by force of arms. This country has stood for the maintenance of the independence of those

States who both valued their liberties and were ready to defend them, and has endeavoured to uphold the principle that changes which must inevitably take place in the relations between nations can and should be effected peacefully and by free negotiation between those concerned.

His Majesty's Government accordingly entered into consultation with the countries who felt themselves to be more immediately threatened, for the sole purpose of concerting resistance to further aggression if such should be attempted. His Majesty's Government at the same time endeavoured to make clear their attitude both by word and deed so that no doubt might anywhere exist as to the policy which they were determined to pursue. They introduced compulsory service and made efforts unprecedented in times of peace to expand and equip the armed forces of the Crown and to place both the civil and military defences of the country in a state of full preparedness. The declarations of policy which have been made in this House and in another place have sought to set out both general principles of British policy and also the attitude of His Majesty's Government to particular questions, such as Danzig, which have from time to time held the forefront of the stage. The declarations which were thus made and the action which was taken met, I think, with the general approval both of Parliament and people.

Government Statement.

Before the Adjournment early this month my right honourable friend the Prime Minister said that the situation, in which the accumulation of the weapons of war was going on at such a pace, was one which could not but be regarded with anxiety. He referred to the bad feeling which was being created by poisonous propaganda, and said that if that could be stopped and if some action could be taken to restore confidence in Europe, there was no question which should not be capable of solution by a peaceful means. Of such action, however, there has unhappily been no sign, and since the House adjourned the international situation has deteriorated, until to-day we are confronted with the imminent peril of war.

At the beginning of August further differences arose

Government Statement.

between the Polish Government and the Danzig Senate concerning the position and functions of the Polish Customs inspectors in the Free City. These differences were relatively unimportant in themselves, and in an atmosphere of less tension would no doubt have been capable of being settled amicably, as similar differences have been settled in the past. Discussion of the questions at issue was in fact proceeding at the end of last week. But while efforts were being made to set the machinery of negotiation in motion, the German Press opened a violent campaign against the Polish Government. This campaign, as noble Lords may have noticed, was not confined solely, or even principally, to the question of Danzig. On this question it was stated that there could be no compromise: Danzig must return unconditionally to the Reich. With it was linked the question of the so-called Corridor, and the attack on Poland has extended to cover the general attitude and policy of the Polish Government, and in particular the position of the German minority in Poland.

In regard to the German minority I would say this. Every country must be concerned to secure just treatment for minorities, and must naturally feel particular interest in minorities allied to it by race. No one in this country, certainly, would wish to defend conditions under which such treatment was denied to any minority section; but if causes of complaint exist, let them not be made the ground for such embitterment of the atmosphere as must make any settlement a hundred times more difficult, but let them be fairly and dispassionately brought to examination, so that before the public opinion of the world some ground may be established for their consideration and redress. It is impossible to ignore the fact that the accusations against Poland bear a strong resemblance to the accusations made last year against Czechoslovakia, and it is right also to remember that there is a large Polish minority in Germany, of whose treatment the Polish Government also bitterly complain.

Of the general attitude of Poland it must be admitted, I think, that in the face of a campaign which appears to threaten not only their independence of action, but also the existence of Poland as a nation, the declarations of the Polish

Government Statement.

leaders have been firm but quite unprovocative. I am confident that they have been, and are at all times, ready to discuss the differences between themselves and Germany, if they could be reasonably certain that the discussion would take place under free conditions, without the menace of force, and with assurance that the results of the discussion would be loyally and permanently observed. If at times the Polish newspapers have replied in kind to the onslaught of the German Press, this has not been reflected in the attitude of the Polish Government. Concurrently with the Press campaign there has been much active military preparation in Germany, and that country is being placed on a footing of complete readiness for war. At the beginning of this week there were indications that German troops were moving towards the Polish frontiers, and, in the face of what was obviously becoming a very menacing situation, His Majesty's Government decided that the time had come when they must seek the approval of Parliament for further measures of defence.

That, in outline, was the situation when on August 22—the day before yesterday—it was officially stated in Berlin and Moscow that negotiations had been in progress, and were to be at once continued, for the signature of a non-aggression pact between the Soviet Union and Germany. I do not conceal the fact that this announcement came as a surprise to His Majesty's Government. For some time past there had been rumours of a change in the relations between the German and Soviet Governments, but no hint of such a change was conveyed by the Soviet Government to His Majesty's Government or the French Government, with whom they were in negotiation; and on July 31 last the Prime Minister remarked in another place that His Majesty's Government were showing a great degree of trust, and a strong desire to bring their negotiations with the Soviet Government to a successful issue, when, before any agreement had been finally reached on political matters, they agreed to send a Military Mission to Moscow to discuss military plans. The Military Missions of France and this country reached Moscow on August 11, and the conversations

Government Statement. were proceeding to all appearance on a basis of mutual confidence; and it is certainly disturbing to learn that, while these conversations were taking place, the Soviet Government were secretly negotiating a pact with Germany for purposes which, on the face of it, were inconsistent with the objects, as we had understood them, of their foreign policy.

I would not now pass any final judgement on this matter. That would be premature until we have had time to consult with the French Government as to the meaning and the consequences of the agreement, the actual text of which has been published this morning. But one matter forces itself upon the immediate attention of His Majesty's Government. They had to consider what effect this changed situation should have on their policy. In Berlin the agreement was somewhat cynically welcomed as a great diplomatic victory which removed the danger of war, since, so it was alleged, Great Britain and France would no longer fulfil their obligations to Poland; and His Majesty's Government felt it their first duty to remove this dangerous illusion. It should be recalled, if it is not in mind, that our guarantee to Poland was given before any agreement with Russia was in prospect, and without condition that such agreement should be reached. His Majesty's Government therefore at once issued a statement that their obligations to Poland and other countries remained unaffected; and throughout these days, as noble Lords will imagine, we have been in close and constant contact with the French Government, whose attitude is identical with our own. Our obligations rest on the agreed statements which were made in this House and in another place, and which are binding. Effect is being given to them in treaties, which are in an advanced stage of negotiation, and these treaties will formally define the mutual obligations of the parties, but they neither add to nor subtract from the obligations of mutual assistance which have been already accepted.

Certain necessary measures of precaution have already been taken. Some of these measures have already been announced, and other steps will be taken, as judged necessary, as soon as the legislation is passed, which I understand it is proposed to invite your Lordships to consider this after-

Government Statement.

noon. There is another action which has been taken to-day in the financial sphere. Your Lordships will have seen the announcement that the bank rate, which has remained for a long time past at 2 per cent., has to-day been raised to 4 per cent. The House will recognize that this is a normal protective measure, which is adopted for the purpose of defending our resources in a period of uncertainty. There is, in this connexion, a contribution to be made generally by British citizens. The public can best co-operate by reducing, so far as possible, any demands which involve, directly or indirectly, the purchase of foreign exchange; next, by scrupulously observing the Chancellor of the Exchequer's request that capital should not at present be sent or moved out of the country; and finally, by holding no more foreign assets than are strictly required for the normal purpose of business.

My Lords, I have said that His Majesty's Government have tried to make their position quite clear; but, in order that no possible doubt might exist in the mind of the German Government, His Majesty's Ambassador in Berlin was instructed yesterday to seek an interview with Herr Hitler and to give him a message on His Majesty's Government's behalf. The object of this message to the German Chancellor was to restate our position and to make quite sure that there was no misunderstanding. His Majesty's Government, as I have suggested, felt that that was all the more necessary having regard to the reports which we had received as to the military movements in Germany and as to the then projected German–Soviet Agreement. My right honourable friend the Prime Minister, therefore, on behalf of His Majesty's Government made it plain, as had indeed been made plain in the statement issued after the meeting of the Cabinet on Tuesday last, that, if the case should arise, His Majesty's Government were resolved and prepared to employ without delay all the forces at their command.

On numerous occasions the Prime Minister has stated his conviction, which is shared, I would suppose, by all people of this country, that war between the British and the German peoples—admitted on all sides to be the greatest calamity that could occur—was not desired either by our people or by

Government Statement. the German people. And the Prime Minister further informed the German Chancellor that we did not see that there was anything in the questions arising between Germany and Poland which could not and should not be resolved without the use of force, if only a situation of confidence could be restored. We have expressed our willingness to assist in creating the conditions in which such negotiations could take place. It was obvious that the present state of tension created great difficulties, and the Prime Minister expressed the view that, if there could be a truce on all sides to Press polemics and all incitements, a suitable condition might be established for direct negotiations between Germany and Poland upon the points between them. The negotiations could, of course, also deal with the complaints made on either side about the treatment of minorities.

The German Chancellor's reply includes what amounts to a restatement of the German thesis that Eastern Europe is a sphere in which Germany seeks to have a free hand; if we or any other country having less direct interests choose to interfere, the blame for the ensuing conflict will be ours. The British position is that we do not in any way seek to claim a special position for ourselves; we do not think of asking Germany to sacrifice her national interests; but we do insist that the interests of other States should be respected. We cannot agree that national interests can only be secured by the shedding of blood or by the destruction of the independence of other States; and unfortunately events such as those of last March make it difficult to accept assurances, even now repeated, about the limitations of German interests. Herr Hitler has often said that he has fought for a better Anglo-German understanding, but it has, as we see it, been the acts of Herr Hitler himself that have time and again destroyed our earnest and sincere endeavours to that end. As regards relations between Germany and Poland, the German Chancellor has referred again to the situation at Danzig, drawing attention to the position of that city and of the Corridor, and to the offer which he made only this year to settle those questions by methods of negotiation. The allegation that it was our guarantee to Poland that decided

Government Statement.

the Polish Government to refuse the proposals then made has been repeatedly refuted. That guarantee was not in fact given until after the Polish refusal had been conveyed to the German Government.

My Lords, in view of the delicacy of the situation I would refrain at this time from any further comment upon the communications which have just passed between the two Governments. Catastrophe has not yet come upon Europe, and we must, therefore, still hope that reason and sanity may find means to reassert themselves. As to the military measures that we have taken, it must be remembered that Germany has already an immense number of men under arms, and has also made military preparations of all kinds on a vast scale. The measures taken in this country have so far been only of a precautionary and defensive kind, but no threats will affect our determination to do what is necessary to prepare the country for any emergency. I would with emphasis repudiate any suggestion that the measures we are taking imply a contemplated act of menace on our part. Nothing that we have done or propose to do constitutes a threat to any of Germany's legitimate interests. It is no act of menace to prepare oneself to help one's friends to defend themselves against the use of force.

In a speech that I made some six weeks or two months ago to the Royal Institute of International Affairs[1] I tried to set out in terms which were fortunate enough to meet with almost unanimous approval the twin foundations of purpose on which British policy rests. The first was a determination to resist force, and the second was the recognition of the world's desire to get on with the constructive task of building peace. And if we could once, as I said, be satisfied that the intentions of others were the same as our own, and that we all really wanted peaceful solutions, then, I said, we could discuss all the problems that were causing the world anxiety. That definition of the policy of His Majesty's Government stands. Our object is, and has been, to build an international order based on mutual understanding and mutual confidence; but that order can only rest on the basis of certain moral

[1] No. 40 in this collection.

Government Statement.

principles which are widely recognized to be essential to the peaceful and the orderly life of nations, and among those principles I place high the renunciation of forcible solutions and the respect for the pledged word in international relationships. And, fundamentally, it is those principles which are to-day in danger, and it is those principles which we consider it vital to try and protect.

There are some who say that the fate of European nations is no concern of ours, and that we should not look far beyond our own frontiers. But those who thus argue forget, I think, that in failing to uphold the liberties of others we run great risk of betraying the principle of liberty itself, and with it our own freedom and independence. We have built up a society with values which are accepted not only in this country but over vast areas of the world. If we stand by and see these values set at nought, the security of all those things on which life itself depends seems, to my judgement, to be undermined, and that is a fundamental matter on which I scarcely think that there will be any difference of opinion. I have no doubt that those with whom rest the issues of peace and war will measure their responsibilities to present and future generations before precipitating a struggle in which many nations of Europe must immediately be involved, of which the duration cannot be foreseen, and by which even those who stand aside from active participation will be vitally and dangerously affected. And I would earnestly hope that in face of all the certain consequences of a resort to force, and before any step is taken which cannot be retraced, reason may yet prevail. His Majesty's Government have noted with warm appreciation the appeal for peace made by King Leopold after the meeting at Brussels yesterday in the name of the heads of the Oslo States. It will be evident from what I have said that His Majesty's Government share the hopes to which that appeal gave such moving expression, and earnestly trust that effect may be given to it.

My Lords, in this moment of anxiety I trust that the ground on which His Majesty's Government have determined to take their stand will meet with the approval of all parties in this House. I believe it will, and I do not doubt that the Government may rely on the support of the whole country in any measures necessary to defend the cause of just dealing between the nations and to preserve secure the place of honourable freedom in the world.

43

THE DANZIG CRISIS. II

29 August 1939

[The Anglo-Polish agreement for mutual assistance was signed on August 25th, 1939. It provided that, if either party should become engaged in hostilities with a European Power in consequence of aggression by that Power, the other party would at once give all possible support and assistance to the victim of aggression. On the same day Herr Hitler informed Sir Nevile Henderson, British Ambassador to the Reich, that the problem of Danzig and the Polish Corridor must be solved, but that after its solution he would approach England once more with a large comprehensive offer. The British Government's reply, delivered on August 28th, expressed willingness to discuss the German Chancellor's proposals for a general understanding when once the differences between Germany and Poland were peacefully composed, and their opinion that a reasonable solution could be effected on lines safeguarding Poland's essential interests. In the meantime appeals for peace had been broadcast by the King of the Belgians on August 23rd and by the Pope on the following day. President Roosevelt appealed on August 25th to Herr Hitler and to the President of Poland to solve their differences by direct negotiation, by submission to arbitration, or by the procedure of conciliation. President Moscicki expressed his willingness to negotiate; Herr Hitler made no response. On August 28th the King of the Belgians and the Queen of the Netherlands put out a joint offer to mediate in the dispute, an offer that was welcomed by the French and British Governments.

When Parliament met again on August 29th, the developments in the situation during the preceding five days were recounted by Mr. Chamberlain in the House of Commons and by Lord Halifax in the House of Lords.]

Government Statement. MY LORDS, since the debate on August 24 the international situation has not substantially changed. The position remains one of great anxiety and danger, but, until hope must be finally abandoned, there is still hope that reason may prevail. I gave the House on August 24 some account of the message which was sent to Herr Hitler by my right honourable friend the Prime Minister on August 23 and of the reply which had been received by him. On August 25 Herr Hitler invited His Majesty's Ambassador in Berlin to call upon him and asked him to transmit a further message to His Majesty's

Government. Herr Hitler also suggested that Sir Nevile Henderson should fly back to London and personally report upon the communication which had been made to him. The communication was received here late on August 25, and Sir Nevile Henderson came to London on the afternoon of the following day. His Majesty's Government have now studied the German Chancellor's communication with all the care and the attention which it demanded, and His Majesty's Ambassador left yesterday afternoon for Berlin bearing with him a considered reply. He saw Herr Hitler late last night.

Government Statement.

I should be glad if I could disclose to the House the fullest information as to the contents of the communications exchanged with Herr Hitler; but I hope noble Lords will understand that, in a situation of such extreme delicacy, and when issues so grave hang precariously in the balance, it is not in the public interest to publish these communications or to comment on them in detail. I am, however, able to indicate in quite general terms some of the main points with which they deal. Herr Hitler was concerned to impress upon His Majesty's Government his wish for an Anglo-German understanding of a complete and lasting character. On the other hand, he left His Majesty's Government in no doubt of his views as to the urgency of settling Polish-German questions. His Majesty's Government have frequently stated their desire to see the realization of such an Anglo-German understanding, and, as soon as circumstances permit, they would naturally welcome an opportunity of discussing with Germany the several issues a settlement of which would have to find place in any permanent agreement. But everything turns upon the manner in which the immediate differences between Germany and Poland can be handled and the nature of the proposals which might be made for any settlement. For we have made it plain that our obligations to Poland, cast into formal shape by the agreement signed on August 25, will be carried out. But, as noble Lords will remember, His Majesty's Government have said more than once publicly that German-Polish differences should be capable of solution by peaceful means.

Government Statement.

Meanwhile, the first prerequisite, if there is to be any chance of useful discussions, is that the tension created by frontier clashes and by reports of incidents on both sides of the border should be diminished. His Majesty's Government accordingly hope that both Governments will use their best endeavour to prevent the occurrence of such incidents, the circulation of exaggerated reports, and all other activities that result in dangerous inflammation of opinion. His Majesty's Government would hope that if an equitable settlement of Polish-German differences could be reached by free negotiation, this might in turn lead to a wider agreement which would accrue to the lasting benefit of Europe and of the world at large.

I need not discuss in detail the background of events against which the communications between His Majesty's Government and Herr Hitler have been taking place. Further military preparations have been made in many European countries, there have been many incidents of the kind to which I have just referred, and there has been more interference with the existing Polish position in Danzig. On the other hand, there have been moving appeals from many quarters for a peaceful solution. The position, therefore, at this moment is that we are awaiting a further reply from Herr Hitler which every member of the House will hope may not close the door to peace.

In this moment of anxiety, His Majesty's Government have not neglected to take all steps which seem necessary to place this country in a state of complete readiness for all eventualities. These steps cover all the three Services and the wide range of civilian defence. The air defence of the country is now in a state of instant readiness. The whole of our Fighting Fleet is ready at a moment's notice to take up the dispositions which would be necessary in war. The appropriate instructions have already been issued to merchant shipping on the various routes, and the necessary preparations have been made for expediting the completion of the mobilization of the Regular Army and the embodiment of the Territorial Army, if this should prove necessary.

Instructions to complete the organization of civil defence measures have been sent to the local authorities with whom the main responsibility lies. Noble Lords will have seen that a rehearsal of the arrangements for evacuating school children was carried through yesterday. In general, I think I can assure your Lordships that, thanks to public co-operation on all sides, all this action is proceeding smoothly and well, and that all preparations have been made to ensure that effect can be given to further precautionary measures as rapidly as possible as soon as these are found necessary.

I hope the House may feel, from what I have said, that during these last anxious days His Majesty's Government have done their best faithfully to pursue the policy which commands the practically unanimous support of the people of this country. We have sought to be absolutely firm in loyalty to our obligations, but, while determined to maintain any undertakings that we have given, we have thrown our whole influence upon the side of resolving these dangerous issues by negotiation rather than by force, which must immediately bring such incalculable consequences. Your Lordships will believe that the responsibility and the strain are not too light; but His Majesty's Government have been constantly helped by the knowledge that in these matters they were speaking for a country that was absolutely united and that was itself facing the unknown future with complete steadiness and resolution. That attitude will, I have no doubt, be maintained; and I would only appeal to all those who speak or write in public to remember that on them, as on us, lies a great responsibility.

44

THE GERMAN INVASION OF POLAND

1 September 1939

[The British reply sent to Herr Hitler on August 28th, 1939, announced the readiness of the Polish Government to enter into direct negotiations with the Government of the German Reich. Herr Hitler replied on the evening of the following day (Tuesday, August 29th) that his Government were prepared to accept the British proposal for direct discussion. Germany never had any intention, he added, of touching Poland's vital interests or of questioning the existence of an independent Polish State. They therefore accepted the British Government's offer of their good offices in securing the dispatch of a Polish emissary to Berlin and counted upon his arrival on the following day. The German Government, it was said, would immediately draw up proposals for a solution acceptable to themselves and would, if possible, place them at the disposal of the British Government before the arrival of the Polish negotiator.

The German proposals comprised sixteen points of which the principal were the return of Danzig to the Reich, and the holding of a plebiscite to decide whether the Corridor should belong to Poland or to Germany. Herr von Ribbentrop, German Foreign Minister, read them out to the British Ambassador at Berlin, on the night of Wednesday, August 30th, under the circumstances recounted by Lord Halifax in the following speech. He stated that the terms were not being communicated to the British Government officially, as it was already too late owing to the failure of the Polish negotiator to arrive. In the evening of Thursday, August 31st, the proposals were broadcast by the German official wireless with the intimation that they had been rejected by the Polish Government, to whom they had, however, never been communicated.

At dawn of Friday, September 1st, German troops invaded Poland, and Herr Hitler issued a proclamation to his Army declaring that the Polish State had refused the peaceful settlement of relations and had appealed to arms. The Polish Ambassador in London promptly called at the Foreign Office and informed Lord Halifax that Poland had been invaded, her open cities bombed, and her independence threatened, and that she was therefore compelled to invoke the Anglo-Polish Agreement. The steps taken to honour that Agreement were reported to Parliament that same evening. When the House of Lords met at six o'clock Lord Halifax at once rose to make the following statement, which was similar to one made by Mr. Chamberlain in the House of Commons.]

MY LORDS, the conditions under which your Lordships

meet are very grave. I do not know whether your Lordships have yet had opportunity—I rather fear you may not—to study the documents that have been laid this afternoon and that will be published in the Press to-morrow; but, when you do, you will, I think, see quite clearly how the negotiations leading up to the present situation have developed. As was stated the other day in the reply of the President of Poland to the President of the United States, the Polish Government have been prepared to enter into direct negotiations with the German Government, and His Majesty's Government were authorized by the Polish Government to state in their communication to the German Government on August 28 that the Polish Government were willing to enter into such discussions on the basis that had been proposed by His Majesty's Government. Again, last night in Berlin, the Polish Ambassador sought an interview with the German Foreign Minister, Herr von Ribbentrop, and repeated the assurance of the Polish Government's readiness to negotiate the questions in dispute with the German Government on a free and equal basis. I understand that immediately after that interview he endeavoured to communicate with his Government but was unable to do so, because communications between Berlin and Warsaw had been cut, and at dawn this morning—so His Majesty's Ambassador at Warsaw has reported—German troops advanced over the frontier. It is perhaps worth mentioning that we have received an official and most categorical denial from the Polish Government that the Polish forces committed any act of aggression last night as reported by the German News Agency.

Government Statement.

The German broadcast of the sixteen points last night contained the sentence 'In these circumstances the Reich Government considers its proposals rejected', and it is therefore worth while examining what those circumstances were. The proposals of the German Government had in fact never been communicated to Poland at all. His Majesty's Ambassador saw Herr von Ribbentrop on Wednesday evening—the night before last—and urged that, when the German proposals were ready, Herr von Ribbentrop should invite the

Government Statement.

Polish Ambassador to call and should hand him the proposals for transmission to his Government. Thereupon, as the Ambassador reported, in his own words, 'In the most violent terms Herr von Ribbentrop said that he would never ask the Polish Ambassador to visit him', but he hinted that if the Polish Ambassador asked him for an interview it might be different. This was on Wednesday night, which according to the German statement of last night is now claimed to be the final date after which no negotiations with Poland were acceptable. The inference would seem plain, and the inference would seem to be that Germany claims to treat Poland as in the wrong because, although the Polish Ambassador was in touch with the German Foreign Minister last night—Thursday—Poland had not by Wednesday night entered upon a discussion with Germany of a set of proposals of which the Polish Government had never heard.

Not only that, but the text of these proposals had never been communicated to His Majesty's Government before we heard them on the German wireless last night. When our Ambassador on Wednesday night, August 30, or in the early hours of Thursday morning, saw Herr von Ribbentrop, the latter, as our Ambassador telegraphs, produced a lengthy document which he read out in German aloud, at top speed, and our Ambassador naturally supposed that after this reading he would be furnished with a copy of the document; but, when he asked Herr von Ribbentrop for the text of these proposals, the reply he received was that it was now too late, as the Polish representative had not arrived in Berlin by midnight. Consequently, until the German broadcast last night our Ambassador was only able to furnish us with an outline from recollection of Herr von Ribbentrop's reading.

I think from those facts—and I have tried to state them as shortly and as plainly as I can—it is clear that the true facts are not as stated on the German wireless, but that the text of the German proposals was not, before it was broadcast, communicated either to Poland or to Great Britain, and noble Lords and those outside can draw their own deductions. The rulers of Germany appear to have conceived of a negotiation between themselves and Poland as nothing

Government Statement.

more than the summoning of a plenipotentiary of the Poles to Berlin at twenty-four hours' notice, to discuss terms not previously communicated to them; and I am bound to say that such a position, with the examples of the Austrian Chancellor and the President of Czechoslovakia before them, was not one which I think the Polish Government could readily be expected to accept. And thus, in those circumstances, when the German Chancellor issued this morning a statement that 'the Polish State has refused the peaceful settlement of relations which I desire'—my Lords, of those issues and of those doings the world will judge. The language used by the German representatives, the documents, and above all, I think, the action of the German Government, speak for themselves.

As regards the actual terms concerning Danzig and the Corridor, now published, it would naturally have been primarily for the Polish Government to express their opinion upon their full significance. His Majesty's Government can only say this, that in their view, had the German Government been sincerely anxious to negotiate a settlement, they would surely have submitted these terms to the Polish Government, giving them time to consider whether or not they could fairly be held to infringe Poland's vital interests, which the German Government, in their communication to the British Government of August 29, had declared their intentions of respecting.

I saw the Polish Ambassador at 10.30 this morning. He told me that according to his information German troops had crossed the Polish frontier at four points, and that several Polish towns had already been bombed. I immediately asked the Counsellor of the German Embassy, the Chargé d'Affaires, to see me. I told him that His Majesty's Government had received these reports, and I inquired of him whether he had himself received any information or had any communication from his own Government for His Majesty's Government. The Counsellor replied that he had neither received information nor instructions to make any communication, and I told him that we were, I feared, faced with a situation of which I could not exaggerate the gravity.

I added that the Cabinet was meeting this morning, and

Government Statement. that any further communication we had to make in the light of these events would be addressed to his Government. His Majesty's Ambassador in Berlin has now been instructed to make the following communication to the German Government:

'On the instructions of His Majesty's Principal Secretary of State for Foreign Affairs I have the honour to make the following communication. Early this morning the German Chancellor issued a proclamation to the German Army which indicated clearly that he was about to attack Poland. Information which has reached His Majesty's Government in the United Kingdom, and the French Government, indicates that German troops have crossed the Polish frontier, and that attacks upon Polish towns are proceeding.

'In these circumstances, it appears to the Governments of the United Kingdom and France that by their action the German Government have created conditions (namely, an aggressive act of force against Poland threatening the independence of Poland) which call for the implementation by the Governments of the United Kingdom and France of the undertaking to Poland to come to her assistance.

'I am accordingly to inform your Excellency that, unless the German Government are prepared immediately to give His Majesty's Government satisfactory assurances that the German Government have suspended all aggressive action against Poland and promptly to withdraw their forces from Polish territory, His Majesty's Government in the United Kingdom will, without hesitation, fulfil their obligations to Poland.'

It is thus that we reach the end of all the efforts and the hopes of these last weeks, and I do not suppose that any man has ever laboured more devotedly for peace than my right honourable friend the Prime Minister; and no stronger proof, in my judgement, could be afforded of the fact that the present situation has been forced upon this country, than that it should be to him of all men that it falls to lead our country, if so it be, into war. Anyone who reads these documents and who knows the instinctive desire for understanding common, I believe, both to the German and the British peoples, can measure the tragedy that is involved by the totally unjustifiable action taken this morning by the German leaders, and first and foremost by the German Chancellor, on whom in history surely an overwhelming responsibility will lie.

So far as His Majesty's Government are concerned, I cannot think of anything that we have left undone or that, looking back, one would wish to have done differently. It has been a source of great satisfaction to us to know that Signor Mussolini also was using all his influence in an endeavour, up to the last moment, to save the peace. Our conscience, I think we can say, is clear. As will be seen from the documents, when your Lordships have time to study them, we have made it absolutely plain to the German Government what the consequences of such action as they have taken must be; and there is indeed only one thing that I can think of that we might have done to save the peace, but which I think would have been an action quite impossible for this country, with any regard to its principles or to its honour, to take, and that one thing would have been to have pressed the Polish Government to submit to methods of intimidation, on which basis alone were the German Government apparently willing to discuss their proposals; in other words, that once again Europe should agree to be held to ransom by the naked menace of force.

If one thing has been made clear it is, I am afraid, that the German Government were not prepared to lay force aside. This problem of Danzig and the Corridor has been present for twenty years. When it suited Germany in 1934 to be on good terms with Poland, the Danzig question faded out, and only during the last five months has it been deliberately aggravated and inflamed. And although it only took the German Government a few weeks to rouse feeling to fever-pitch, it was, to say the least, unreasonable to make the presence of a Polish plenipotentiary within twenty-four hours a condition of any negotiation, and to expect those negotiations to be conducted on the basis of proposals which the Polish Government had not at that time had any opportunity of seeing. It is surely partly in the light of that action that the proposals themselves fall to be judged. Certainly we must all have learnt that so long as engagements are to be freely broken without notice, and so long as force is to be the arbiter of international disputes, we were bound to look forward to a new crisis every six months, and to see one country after another made the object of this menace of force. And that, I think, is the answer to those who, here or elsewhere, might ask why this country should interest itself in a dispute which did not apparently or immediately concern it. My right honourable friend the Prime Minister answered this in other words when he said in another place a few days ago that, if war came, we should not be fighting merely on the issue raised by the position of some far-off city in a foreign land, but for principles on which all international life finally depends, and apart from which, I think, no international life is tolerable.

45

THE EVE OF WAR

2 September 1939

[Signor Mussolini made a last-minute attempt to avert war between the Great Powers. Having received replies from France and from Great Britain favourable in principle to his proposal for a Five-Power Conference, he informed Herr Hitler, on the morning of Saturday, September 2nd, 1939, that there was still a possibility of calling a conference. Herr Hitler replied that he did not reject a conference absolutely, but that he wished to know whether the note presented to Berlin by France and Britain on the previous day had the character of an ultimatum, since in that event all negotiation would be useless. His question was referred that same afternoon to the British and French Governments, who replied that the note was in the nature of a warning, and was not to be considered as an ultimatum. The two Governments considered, however, that before any conference could meet, Herr Hitler should evacuate the Polish territory he had invaded. That evening similar statements on the position of affairs were made by Mr. Chamberlain in the House of Commons and by Lord Halifax in the House of Lords.]

Government Statement.

MY LORDS, His Majesty's Ambassador in Berlin was received by Herr von Ribbentrop at 9.30 last night when he delivered the warning message which was read to the House yesterday. Herr von Ribbentrop replied that he must submit the communication to the German Chancellor. The Ambassador declared his readiness to receive the Chancellor's reply, but up to the present no reply has been received. It is possible that delay has been due to a proposal which has meanwhile been put forward by the Italian Government that hostilities should cease and that there should then immediately be a conference between the five Powers—Great Britain, France, Poland, Germany and Italy.

While appreciating the efforts of the Italian Government, His Majesty's Government for their part would not find it possible to take part in a conference whilst Poland is being subjected to invasion. Her towns are under bombardment, and Danzig has been made the subject of a unilateral settlement by force. His Majesty's Government will, as stated yesterday, be bound to take action unless the German forces are withdrawn from Polish territory. They are in communi-

Government Statement.

cation with the French Government as to the limit of time within which it would be necessary for His Majesty's Government and the French Government to know whether the German Government were prepared to effect such withdrawal. If the German Government should agree to withdraw their forces, then His Majesty's Government would be willing to regard the position as being the same as it was before the German forces crossed the Polish frontier, that is to say, the way would be open to discussion between the German and Polish Governments of the matters at issue between them, on the understanding that the settlement arrived at was one that safeguarded the vital interests of Poland and was secured by an international guarantee. If the German and Polish Governments wished that other Powers should be associated with them in the discussion, His Majesty's Government for their part would be willing to agree.

There is one other matter to which allusion should be made in order to make the present situation perfectly clear. Yesterday Herr Forster, who on August 23 had, in contravention of the Danzig Constitution, become the head of the State, decreed the incorporation of Danzig in the Reich and the dissolution of the Constitution. Herr Hitler was asked to give effect to this decree by German law. At the meeting of the Reichstag yesterday morning a law was passed for the reunion of Danzig with the Reich. The international status of Danzig as a Free City is established by a treaty of which His Majesty's Government is a signatory, and the Free City was placed under the protection of the League of Nations. The rights given to Poland in Danzig by treaty are defined and confirmed by agreements concluded between Danzig and Poland. The action taken by the Danzig authorities and the Reichstag yesterday is the final step in the unilateral repudiation of these international instruments, which could only be modified by negotiation. His Majesty's Government do not therefore recognize either the validity of the grounds on which the action of the Danzig authorities was based, the validity of this action itself, or of the effect given to it by the German Government.

46

WAR WITH GERMANY

3 September 1939

[On the morning of Sunday, September 3rd, 1939, the Foreign Office announced that Germany had been informed that, unless satisfactory assurances from the German Government should have reached His Majesty's Government in London by eleven o'clock, a state of war would exist between the two countries from that hour. At a quarter past eleven the Prime Minister broadcast a declaration announcing that no reply had been received from Berlin, and that consequently this country was at war with Germany. Parliament met at noon, and in the House of Lords Lord Halifax recounted the events of the past few hours.]

Government Statement.

MY LORDS, the House will recall the communication to the German Government that we made on September 1 and which I reported to your Lordships; and in that communication, your Lordships will remember, we instructed His Majesty's Ambassador in Berlin to inform the German Foreign Minister that, unless the German Government were prepared immediately to give His Majesty's Government satisfactory assurances that the German Government had suspended all aggressive action against Poland, and were prepared promptly to withdraw their forces from Polish territory, His Majesty's Government in the United Kingdom would, without hesitation, fulfil their obligations to Poland. That communication was made more than thirty-six hours ago, and at 7.30 last night, when your Lordships met, I was still not in a position to report any reply received from the German Government. But I repeated that His Majesty's Government would be bound to take action unless the German forces were withdrawn from Polish territory, and I added that we were in communication with the French Government as to the limit of time within which it would be necessary for His Majesty's Government and the French Government to know whether the German Government were prepared to effect such withdrawal.

In view of reports reaching His Majesty's Government of intensified action against Poland, His Majesty's Government

Government Statement.

concluded that the situation admitted of no further delay. Accordingly we sent a telegram to the Ambassador last night instructing him to ask for an interview with the Minister for Foreign Affairs in Berlin at nine o'clock this morning, and to make to him or, if he was not able to receive him, to a representative of the German Government, the communication which I will read to the House in one moment. We added that, if the assurance referred to in that communication was received, the Ambassador was to inform me by any means at his disposal before 11 a.m. to-day. If on the other hand no such assurance was received here by 11 a.m., we should inform the German representatives in London that a state of war existed as from that hour and the Ambassador in Berlin would act accordingly.

This was the communication that we instructed His Majesty's Ambassador to make:

'Sir,

In the communication which I had the honour to make to you on September 1, I informed you, on the instructions of His Majesty's Principal Secretary of State for Foreign Affairs, that unless the German Government were prepared to give His Majesty's Government in the United Kingdom satisfactory assurances that the German Government had suspended all aggressive action against Poland and were prepared promptly to withdraw their forces from Polish territory, His Majesty's Government in the United Kingdom would, without hesitation, fulfil their obligations to Poland.

Although this communication was made more than twenty-four hours ago, no reply has been received, but German attacks upon Poland have been continued and intensified. I have accordingly the honour to inform you that unless not later than 11 a.m. British Summer Time to-day, September 3, satisfactory assurances to the above effect have been given by the German Government and have reached His Majesty's Government in London, a state of war will exist between the two countries as from that hour.'

We had a telegram from the Ambassador to say that he had carried out those instructions this morning at 9 a.m., the communication being received on behalf of the Minister for Foreign Affairs. I am in a position to indicate that the French Ambassador in Berlin is at this moment making a similar communication to the German Government accompanied also by a definite time limit in accordance with the arrangement made between His Majesty's Government and the French Government. No reply having been received from the German Government accepting the conditions of His Majesty's Government, a state of war now exists between this country and Germany, and passports have been handed to the German Chargé d'Affaires in London.

Government Statement.

47

THE PURPOSE OF THE STRUGGLE

7 November 1939

[The campaign in Poland ended in the rapid conquest of that country by Germany. This was facilitated by the action of the Soviet Republic, whose troops invaded Poland on September 17th, 1939. Warsaw fell on September 27th, and on September 28th the German and Soviet Governments made a partition of Poland. In the meantime British war aims had been defined by Mr. Chamberlain in the House of Commons on September 20th as being to redeem Europe from the perpetual and recurring fear of German aggression and to enable the peoples of Europe to preserve their independence and liberties. The German peace proposals were outlined by Herr Hitler in the Reichstag on October 6th. The French answer to them was given by M. Daladier on October 10th in a broadcast address to the French nation. France, he said, would not lay down her arms until she had received guarantees for security. Two days later Mr. Chamberlain defined the British Government's attitude by saying: 'Either the German Government must give convincing proof of the sincerity of its desire for peace by definite acts and by the provision of effective guarantees of its intention to fulfil its undertakings, or we must persevere in our duty to the end.' On November 7th the following broadcast was made by Lord Halifax.]

FOR more than two months we have been at war with Germany. During that time my memory has often taken me back to the moving statement which the Prime Minister broadcast to the nation on Sunday morning, September 3, a quarter of an hour after we declared war. You will remember his final words: 'It is the evil things we shall be fighting against—brute force, bad faith, injustice, oppression and persecution; and against them I am certain that the right will prevail.'

These words were said at a tragic and solemn moment for our country, for France and Poland, and for the whole civilized world; and at the time they were spoken, and since, they have more and more seemed to answer the two questions that, with growing insistence, were likely to present themselves to thoughtful minds. The first of these questions is: What is the real purpose of our struggle? and the second is: May we in fact feel secure that through victory in this conflict of physical force we can achieve it?

What is the real purpose of our struggle? That many people are seeking an answer to this question is evident from the desire expressed in so many quarters that the Allied countries should define with greater precision what are sometimes called 'war aims'. In general terms the answer has been plainly given. We are fighting in defence of freedom; we are fighting for peace; we are meeting a challenge to our own security and that of others; we are defending the rights of all nations to live their own lives. We are fighting against the substitution of brute force for law as the arbiter between nations, and against the violation of the sanctity of treaties and disregard for the pledged word.

We have learned that there can be no opportunity for Europe to cultivate the arts of peace until Germany is brought to realize that recurrent acts of aggression will not be tolerated. It must accordingly be our resolve, not only to protect the future from the repetition of the same injuries that German aggression has inflicted on Europe in these last few years, but also, so far as we can, to repair the damage successively wrought by Germany upon her weaker neighbours. And that purpose must be the stronger as it is reinforced by knowledge of the cruel persecution of causes and persons at the hands of ruthless men in Germany.

In general it is no business of one nation to interfere with the internal administration of another, and history has plenty of examples of the futility of such attempts. The British are particularly reluctant to interfere in other people's business—provided always that other people do not seek to interfere in theirs. But when the challenge in the sphere of international relations is sharpened, as to-day in Germany, by the denial to men and women of elementary human rights, that challenge is at once extended to something instinctive and profound in the universal conscience of mankind. We are, therefore, fighting to maintain the rule of law and the quality of mercy in dealings between man and man and in the great society of civilized States.

We foresaw, indeed, that the time might well come when

we should have to fight for these saving graces of our earthly commonwealth. Some months ago—it seems many months ago now—I spoke at a dinner at Chatham House with what I was told was unusual frankness.[1] Among other things I said this: 'Over a large part of the world the old standards of conduct are being set aside. Things are being done which we can hardly read without amazement. Rules of conduct between nations are being overridden with the same callous indifference as rules of conduct between man and man.' And I added something that is always to be remembered, if we are to pursue this struggle in the spirit that can alone support the price that it is likely to exact: 'We ourselves must see,' I said, 'that our own standards of conduct do not deteriorate, because the day that we lose our respect for our fellow men our democracy will have lost something on which its vitality depends.' I spoke then at a time when I hoped—as we all did—that somehow or other war might be honourably averted. That hope was disappointed. Faced with evil things, as the Prime Minister truly said we are, there are only two courses open. You must either defy or you must acquiesce. And acquiescence is dishonour.

As I look back to those days in which we all walked in the dark valley of decision, I can feel no doubt in my own conscience that only with supreme dishonour could we in fact have averted war. *Now*, supreme dishonour, as well as the supreme folly, lie with the aggressor. The supreme dishonour of the German Government is laid open to the world. We and those who are fighting side by side with us—men of our race from every quarter of the world; peoples owing the same loyalty to the Crown; our French and Polish allies—we are all united, in the will, and under Providence we have the power, to prove also the supreme folly with which the German Government has moved to its own destruction.

That brings me to my second question. May we in fact feel secure that through victory in this conflict of physical force we can achieve our purpose? In other words, after victory, what then? What kind of a better future is it, for

[1] The speech is given as no. 40 in this collection.

which we may be content to make sacrifice and not count the cost? The Prime Minister has stated that we seek no vindictive peace, that we have no territorial ambitions for ourselves, and that we should feel the future to hold little hope unless the new peace settlement might be reached through the method of negotiation and agreement. But we are determined, so far as it is humanly possible, to see to it that Europe shall not again be subjected to a repetition of this tragedy. With this purpose in view we shall use all our influence, when the time comes, in the building of a new world in which the nations will not permit insane armed rivalry to deny their hopes of fuller life, and future confidence not be for ever overborne by grim foreboding of disaster.

The new world that we seek will enlist the co-operation of all peoples on a basis of human equality, self-respect, and mutual tolerance. We shall have to think out again many things that lie at the root of international contacts—social, political, and economic—and find means of reconciling the necessity of change in a constantly changing world with security against the disturbance of the general peace through resort to violence. To this order that we shall seek to create, all nations will have their contribution to make, and a great responsibility, both in thought and action, will rest upon our people.

We, not less than others, have our lesson to learn from past failures and disappointments. We have no idea what the shape of the post-war world will be; we do not know the circumstances in which hostilities will end, or the materials which will lie to our hands in building the edifice of peace. There are some who believe that the new order can only come through surrender in some measure by the nations of their sovereign rights in order to clear the way for some more organic union. But if it is thus hoped to create a more truly international system out of independent States, we must learn the lessons of the past. No paper plan will endure that does not freely spring from the will of the peoples who alone can give it life. Nor will it avail for one people alone to see a vision that has no message for their neighbours. International, like national, institutions must have deep roots, and if they are to grow must have, like everything else, a soil that suits them.

There is a cynical saying that it is often the task of the wise to repair the harm done by the good. When this war is over, we shall have to see to it that wisdom and goodwill combine for the immense task that will await us. When, or how, we may be able to feel that our objects have been attained, it is in no man's power to say. But provided we are, in fact, convinced that both our decision and the general direction of our course are right, we need have no anxiety about the issue. I am confident that if the British people can maintain their own standards of purpose and conduct throughout this war, we shall, with God's will, be the better equipped in spirit to play our part in ordering a better future. For in this matter, as indeed in all life, it is finally the spiritual side that counts.

To many it seems strange that we should look to force, with all its suffering, to bring redemption. It is, of course, profoundly true that the things of the spirit can only finally be conquered in the spiritual sphere, and that physical force is not of itself able to destroy the evil which is the source of war. We need not deny the limitations set to what physical force alone can do, but the recognition of this truth should never blind us to the fact that if, for fear of the tragedy of war measured in human lives broken and destroyed, we rest inert before action which we hold evil, we are surely surrendering to annihilation the expression of spiritual values which have inspired and guided all human progress. Certainly we are not alone in these beliefs and aspirations. Across the seas, the peoples of the Empire; across the Channel, France, twice our ally in war within a generation; and in all parts of the world, many nations which are not involved in the present conflict—all these have sensed the threat to standards and values that are theirs not less than ours.

This road which we intend to travel may be a long one. A great Englishman, Francis Bacon, once spoke of 'the good hours of the mind'—those hours in which we strengthen ourselves to take high resolutions and to face grave dangers.

Between them lie long periods of everyday existence, in which the spell of the 'good hours' often fades, and life again seems drab and uninspired. The old Christian writers were keen observers of human nature when they placed this sort of paralysing boredom[1] among the deadly sins.

And the way of salvation is just to carry on, which is often the most difficult thing of all to do. The stimulus of great events is not there; and it is not easy to keep in mind the need for doing with all our might what lies ready to our hand. We have time to ponder our own grievances, and to reflect on how much better we could do someone else's job. The right to grumble is almost traditional with the British race, who do it supremely well; and it is a mark of freedom, as compared with Germany, where grumbling is quite likely to land you in a concentration camp. The impulse to grumble is not wholly bad. It may spring from an honest desire to improve things; it may avert or repair mistakes, and it can bring together different points of view. So let us keep our freedom; but let us use it to the greater strengthening of our purpose.

And we must always remember that our enemies will not be slow to make the most of anything that they can represent as evidence of divided purpose and weakening resolution. It is our duty here—just as much as it is the duty of the men on active service—to stand united, firm, unshakable, in mind and heart. On this will certainly depend our power to meet the challenge in the present struggle, and, when that is over, to answer the call to work worthily for the future of mankind.

[1] Accidie.

48

WAR AND PEACE AIMS

5 December 1939

[The German peace proposals of October 6th, 1939, were followed up a month later (November 7th) by a joint appeal to the belligerents from the King of the Belgians and the Queen of the Netherlands and an offer to facilitate peace negotiations. King George VI and President Lebrun replied on November 12th, referring to the public statements that had been made regarding the aims of their two Governments. Although their replies did not close the door to mediation, the German Government announced three days later that they considered the matter closed. An address on war and peace aims was broadcast by Mr. Chamberlain on November 26th. Our war aim, he said, was to defeat the enemy. Our desire when we achieved our war aim would be to establish a new Europe in which fear of aggression would have ceased to exist, adjustments of boundaries would be settled by conference, goods and services would be freely interchanged, each country would have the unfettered right to choose its own form of internal government, and armaments would be gradually dropped. It would be necessary, he added, to have some machinery capable of guiding the development of the new Europe in the right direction.

Between September 28th and October 10th the Soviet Government concluded pacts of mutual assistance with Estonia, Latvia, and Lithuania, under which each of those countries agreed to allow the U.S.S.R. to establish naval bases and aerodromes within their territories. Negotiations were also begun with Finland on October 9th. Soviet demands included the leasing of the port of Hangö as a naval base and the cession of a portion of the Karelian isthmus. But Finland proved less compliant than her neighbours, and consequently the Soviet Government, after denouncing the treaty of non-aggression signed in 1932, invaded Finland on November 30th.

On December 5th Lord Snell called attention in the House of Lords to the recent declaration by the Prime Minister respecting the war and peace aims of His Majesty's Government, to the essential principles of a satisfactory and lasting peace, and to the urgent need for a wisely planned programme of national economies and social reconstruction. Lord Halifax wound up the debate.]

MY LORDS, the distinction that my right honourable friend the Prime Minister drew the other day between peace and war aims is generally admitted to be valid, and I think that what he said in that connexion has secured a very general approval. . . . The general purposes for which we have taken up arms are perfectly clear. They have been, as I think, defined as far as it is possible for the Government to define them. I really do not think there is any difference of opinion in any quarter now as to their general substance. It is quite possible that some may put the emphasis differently and that, as circumstances change, these may from time to time lead to some variety of expression. But the fundamental purpose remains. . . .

Perhaps I may for the sake of clarity, however, repeat and summarize in the briefest possible fashion what our purposes appear to me to be. We desire peoples who have been deprived of their independence to recover their liberties. We desire to redeem the peoples of Europe from this constant fear of German aggression, and we desire to safeguard our own freedom and security. It is quite true to say that we do not seek aggrandizement and we do not seek to redraw the map in our own interests, and still less—although I recognize what can be said about the increasing difficulty of maintaining this position in the hearts of our people as the war goes on—are we moved by any spirit of vengeance. On the contrary, if Germany is able to restore the confidence which she has destroyed, we aim at a settlement which will encourage her to take her rightful place in Europe; and we wish to create an international order in which all peoples, as we hope, secure under the reign of law, can determine their political and economic life free from the interference of their more powerful neighbours. To this end we would be willing to give our best, in full co-operation with other nations, including Germany, to the work of reconstruction, political and economic, for only so do we believe that the ordered international life of Europe can be preserved.

Now, my Lords, that general framework—and it has been said over and over again—will be found in the speeches of members of His Majesty's Opposition just as much as in speeches of those who speak for His Majesty's Government, and in the views expressed in statements made on behalf of the Dominions. It will be found in the declaration of M. Daladier and of French leaders of all parties, and I do not believe it would meet with dissent in any Allied quarter. These declarations in my judgement may fairly claim to represent what the terms of the Motion describe as 'the essential principles of a satisfactory and lasting peace'. It may well be that the sacrifices that this war must be expected to impose may lead—and I most devoutly hope that they will lead—to an appreciation of Christian values, and lead all men to seek to give more practical application to them in the life of our people. If such are our peace aims and if, perhaps more important, that is the spirit in which we would wish to see them realized, it is perhaps not difficult to see the answer to another question that many people pose, which is the same question in other words.

What are the precise terms, it is asked, upon which this country would be willing to stop the war to-day? His Majesty the King the other day, in answering the peace proposals of the King of the Belgians and the Queen of the Netherlands, said that it was not his wish nor that of his Government for the war to continue a day longer than was necessary. On what conditions, then, would this country lay down arms? The answer to that question was given by M. Daladier in the speech he made a few days ago. He said that France—and he might have added the United Kingdom—would lay down her arms when she could treat with a Government whose signature could be trusted. She would treat when the wrongs caused to weaker nations could be righted and lasting security established. And he went on to indicate that France must have confidence that this security would endure.

A great many people write to me, as no doubt to many of you, suggesting that an armistice should be proclaimed and a conference summoned. They say: 'You will have to have a conference some time; why wait till after the war? Why not have it before you have to pay all the price that war exacts?' The success of any conference depends upon the conditions of its meeting. The conference method was followed in September 1938. We were willing to follow it again immediately before this war, if Germany would abandon her intention of invading Poland and would withdraw her troops. Why, in fact, did not the Munich conference secure lasting peace in Europe? Agreement was reached, the most solemn assurances were given, but only six months afterwards Herr Hitler changed his mind; and, as he has so often shown, he can always find excuses satisfactory to himself to justify action which completely contradicts assurances given earlier. That kind of right-about-turn after such solemn undertakings does show that no conference can be securely counted successful unless that habit of disregarding assurances is abandoned. That is a fundamental reversal of what has hitherto been German policy, and it is little use deluding ourselves with wishful thinking about the results to be achieved by conference until the primary lesson has been learnt by those who would take part in it—namely, that force is a bad plan. There is no evidence yet that the German Government have learnt that primary lesson.

Therefore, my Lords, I suggest to you that the two prerequisites for a conference are, first, evidence that the German Government were willing to accept terms which would correspond to the purposes for which we took up arms—and everybody knows what those were—and secondly, security that any settlement reached would be respected. On any other basis a conference, in my judgement, would achieve nothing and would be only likely to enable the leaders of Germany to make their people believe that on the whole the old method of force had not worked too badly. The aim of showing that aggression had failed would not have been achieved, and the world would in consequence be left in the same precarious and intolerable suspense as we have all known during these last years.

The tale of evil consequence that has flowed from the German example and practice of aggression grows. In the last two days we have witnessed what has been universally condemned as an inexcusable act of aggression by one of the largest upon one of the smallest but most highly civilized nations of Europe: their open towns bombarded, their women and children mutilated and done to death, on the pretext that a nation of under 4,000,000 had hostile designs against one of 180,000,000. The British people, themselves deeply committed in a struggle against aggression, have, I think, experienced two deep emotions: they have been profoundly shocked by the circumstances of the Soviet attack, and they have profoundly admired the magnificent resistance of the Finns. This matter is forming the subject of an appeal to the Council of the League of Nations at the end of this week, to be followed, as I understand, by a meeting of the Assembly on Monday. On that occasion His Majesty's Government, by whomever represented, will make their position plain.

There are two comments that I would make on this unhappy extension of the conflict, and the first is this. The Russian attack on Finland seems to me to be a direct consequence of German policy. By the agreement which he thought would give him a free hand to attack Poland, it would seem that Herr Hitler bartered what was not his property to barter—the liberties of the Baltic people. The sequence of events has shown how wide is the damage once the floodgates are opened. I know that historical parallels can often be pushed too far, but your Lordships will perhaps forgive me if I remind you of the famous passage in which Lord Macaulay condemns the action of Frederick the Great, because it is not without significance to these events:

> 'Till he (Frederick the Great) began the war, it seemed possible, even probable, that the peace of the world would be preserved. . . . To throw all Europe into confusion for a purpose clearly unjust was no light matter. . . . England was true to her engagements. The voice of Fleury had always been for peace, but the selfish rapacity of the King of Prussia gave the signal to his neighbours. The whole world sprang to arms. . . . The evils produced by his wickedness were felt in lands where the name of Prussia was unknown, and in order that he might rob a neighbour whom he had promised to defend, black men fought on the coast of Coromandel and red men scalped each other by the Great Lakes of North America.'

That is not quite irrelevant to the passage of events to-day.

Earlier in the year we had tried to improve our relations with Russia, but in doing so we had always maintained the position that rights of third parties must remain intact and be unaffected by our negotiations. Events have shown that the judgement and the instinct of His Majesty's Government in refusing agreement with the Soviet Government on the terms of formulae covering cases of indirect aggression on the Baltic States were right. For it is now plain that these formulae might well have been the cloak of ulterior designs. I have little doubt that the people of this country would prefer to face difficulties and embarrassment rather than feel that we had compromised the honour of this country and of the Commonwealth on such issues.

The other observation that I wished to make was this. Germany used to complain of encirclement, and I remember saying in the summer[1] that if encirclement there was, it was Germany herself who was responsible for it. I little thought when I spoke that we should so soon see Germany extending this operation of self-encirclement in a direction that must surely give the German people food for anxious thought upon the future issue of it.

In the face of these events we have increasing awareness of the perils that threaten European society as a direct consequence of German policy. I have heard it suggested that immediate peace on almost any terms would be desirable in order to save Western civilization from worse perils. I venture to think that view is short-sighted. Its fallacy is exposed to my judgement and to my heart by events in German-occupied Poland. Noble Lords will have seen the account issued in the last few days by the Polish Government of the terrible acts of oppression and savagery that have been perpetrated there, and which are condemning daily thousands of Poles to misery and many to death. Nor does that stand alone. We hear much, but we do not hear all, of the tyranny in Prague; and we hear much, but I have no doubt again we do not hear all, of the veiled menace to other countries who as yet preserve their independence and their neutrality intact. These considerations are surely relevant in forming a judgement upon the conduct of the war.

We have recently received protests from certain neutral countries about the measures which we have taken by way of reprisal against German exports, which will, it is claimed, harm neutral interests. These protests will be answered

[1] Page 290 above.

with full detail. It is undeniable that hostilities are bound to involve some loss to all countries, but His Majesty's Government have not exceeded the rights given to them by international law. We do our best to apply our policy with restraint and consideration. We try to alleviate hardships to neutral trade, and nothing that we have done on the sea has brought into peril a single life of any neutral citizen. But Germany has ruthlessly violated neutral rights and destroyed neutral life by indiscriminate sinking of neutral as well as belligerent ships, whether by submarine action or by illegal mines. Her policy clearly threatens both the liberties of neutral countries and the fundamental principles on which their life, just as much as our own, is founded. It is in that light that we have a right to ask neutral countries to judge the actions which are forced upon us through the methods by which the German Government makes war.

It is such considerations as those that have brought our people and their Allies to their present resolve to see this war through. They understand well enough what is at stake. They do not expect an easy victory. They do not underrate the skill and the power and the determination of their enemy. Nor do they count on an early collapse on the enemy's home front. But they do know the quality of their own resolution, and they know that the recognition of the issues at stake will keep that resolution both united and intense. There are some, whom we may honour even if we cannot applaud, who feel that it is both futile and wrong to attempt to exorcize the evil spirits loose in the world to-day by the use of physical force; and if we could be exclusively concerned with what is passing in the non-material sphere we might, I should suppose, all be of one mind. But where physical force is invoked for the destruction of values, moral and material, upon which our very life depends, it is in the last resort only by physical force that the ravages of the evil spirit can be resisted and contained.

But I most whole-heartedly agree that resistance would not by itself achieve our purpose unless, when it had opened the door to the positive work of reconstruction, we were able to enlist much practical wisdom in that great task. The Prime Minister referred to this subject in his broadcast address the other day. We do not of course know, as yet, what will be the conditions in which peace is made. It has already been said that a new order in Europe can only come through surrender in some measure by the nations of their sovereign rights in order to clear the way for some more organic union. No paper plan will endure that does not freely spring from the will of the peoples that can alone give it vigour and life; and international, like our own national, institutions must be very securely and deeply anchored on reality. I often think that some, in reflecting on the future of these things, are inclined to yield to thoughts of schemes that I cannot myself believe to be immediately practicable. We must build our Utopia course by course on foundations that are themselves well laid and solid.

Much emphasis has been placed, and rightly placed, upon the thought to be given to the economic side of international collaboration in the future. I would not say more to-day than that His Majesty's Government fully appreciate and recognize the importance of all those issues. It may well be that, from working together to solve concrete problems and difficulties arising in finance and in trade, closer political understanding may spring and may develop. But here again, in considering the future of economic as well as of political collaboration, we must not only keep in line with our Allies and with the Dominions, but also we have to consider the views and the interests of many nations themselves to-day non-belligerent. But if we bear these considerations in mind, then we may hope, I think, to get security, and then the reconstruction will, in the words of the Motion, be 'wisely planned'.

I have only one more word to add. When we see, as we do see wherever we look to-day, the rank growth of the doctrine of brute force in the world, and when we picture to ourselves how, if unchecked, this must choke all the other plants upon which the human race depends for its sustenance and its health, most of us, I think, instinctively recognize that there can be no merely temporary truce or patched-up armistice that would bring no real relief. My Lords, our people are sometimes slow to grasp the full implication of events, or to draw deductions which force upon them the necessity for grave decisions, but their judgement is shrewd and astonishingly sure; and it is just because they have come to see with perfect clarity how impossible life is to-day on the conditions created by the present rulers of Germany, that there is no inconsistency between their passionate desire for peace and their deep determination to see this struggle through until their purpose is attained.

49

THE PROGRESS OF THE WAR

20 January 1940

[Throughout the winter of 1939–40 the war remained stationary on the Western Front, where the British Expeditionary Force had taken their place in the line from October 1939, under the command of the French Commander-in-Chief. On sea the Germans endeavoured to counter the Allied blockade by unrestricted submarine warfare and by the illegal sowing of mines. Two of their pocket battleships raided commerce in the South Atlantic. One, the *Deutschland*, regained German waters after sinking the British armed merchant cruiser *Rawalpindi*, on November 26th, south-east of Iceland. The other, the *Admiral Graf Spee*, was encountered off the River Plate on December 13th by the British cruisers *Exeter*, *Ajax*, and *Achilles*. She was severely damaged, forced to take refuge in Montevideo harbour, and four days later was scuttled by her own crew. Unity of military command was supplemented by the setting up of an Anglo-French Co-ordinating Committee to ensure common action in the air, munitions and war materials, oil, food, shipping, and economic warfare.

War continued in Finland. In pursuance of a resolution taken at a special meeting of the Assembly of the League of Nations on December 14th, States Members were invited to render assistance to Finland, and the U.S.S.R. was expelled from the League. The British Government informed the Secretary-General of the League that they intended to give to Finland all the assistance in their power.

In the preface to a German White Book issued on December 12th, in which he set out to prove that Britain alone had caused the war and desired it in order to destroy Germany, Herr von Ribbentrop stated the German aim to be the military annihilation of its enemies and afterwards the safeguarding of the living-space that belongs to the German people against any future threat. On Christmas Eve the Pope addressed the College of Cardinals and enumerated five postulates for a just and honourable peace: (1) All nations had a right to life and independence. (2) Peace must be founded on disarmament. (3) Juridical institutions must be constituted to ensure the loyal application of agreements and, if necessary, to revise them. (4) Attention must be given to the just demands of nations and of racial minorities. (5) Rulers and peoples must become imbued with the spirit of moral justice.

The following speech, delivered by Lord Halifax at Leeds, is printed from a text supplied by him.]

WE are under no illusion about the war. We know how great are the issues—the liberty and independence of our country and Commonwealth, and of all European States. We do not underrate the strength of our enemy or the sternness of the struggle upon which we are engaged. We realize that to secure victory in that struggle will require all the energy and resolution we can command.

There is a profound difference between a dictator and democracy in this business of making war. A dictator enjoys initial advantages. His preparations and policy can be made in complete secrecy. The people have no part in that policy. They do not know what it is, and they cannot place themselves in opposition to it. The dictator's actions appear as the expression of a single will. In democracy there is no surrender of private judgement; no suppression of outside contacts; no sinister coercion by secret police. Admittedly, this increases the difficulty of any Government in the time of preparation and planning; but when trouble comes, the fact that the people know, and the people have approved, invests decision with the overwhelming force of free judgement and united will. It is this unity of moral purpose, which Herr Hitler rates so low, that will be the principal cause of his defeat. The strain of modern war is great, but there is no doubt in my mind that it will be borne more easily by the man who is in it from conviction than by the man who is in it by coercion.

One of my predecessors at the Foreign Office, Sir Austen Chamberlain, in a written instruction to the permanent staff, emphasized that decisions of foreign policy were taken by reasonable men moved by the best motives on the basis of the information available. It must therefore be assumed, he argued, that reasonable men outside the Foreign Office, if they shared the same information, would reach the same conclusion; and he therefore urged that, if our foreign policy was to be understood and was to receive public support, the fullest information possible should be given. It is in this spirit that I want to speak this afternoon.

There is no need to recall the history of the last years during which Europe watched, waited, and wondered, much as we wait through sultry, heavy days for the breaking of the storm. I became Foreign Secretary at the end of February

1938. A fortnight later the German Army marched into Austria. Two months later came the crisis over the alleged preparations of Germany to attack Czechoslovakia. Whatever may be the exact truth of those days, the immediate anxiety aroused was the measure of the extent to which, even then, the German Government had succeeded in destroying confidence. All through the summer there was the operation of the now familiar technique by way of preparation for the real offensive which culminated in the crisis of September 1938.

The Munich settlement gave Germany all she immediately wanted. In applying the Agreement, every contentious point was decided in Germany's favour. Yet it became quite clear at once that Herr Hitler was profoundly dissatisfied. In private, he inveighed against the Agreement and against those of his advisers who had stood on the side of peace. In public, he began within a few days to attack this country in speeches; and the German newspapers closest to the German Ministry of Propaganda launched a violent press campaign against this country. It became rapidly evident that Herr Hitler objected to the procedure of settlement by negotiation and that, if we may judge by all the evidence, he resented having been baulked of a war over Czechoslovakia. During several stages of the discussions which preceded Munich, Herr Hitler made it clear that he was anticipating with relish the opportunity of chastizing Czechoslovakia. He was also disillusioned because he had hoped that after Munich we should be lulled into security and close down upon our own rearmament, making no attempt to compete with Germany, with the consequence that Germany would have been left in possession of what Herr Hitler himself described as the mightiest armaments the world has known. In that position he could have made himself the dictator not only of Germany but of Europe.

There was, however, still some reason to believe that, having vented his annoyance, he would nevertheless abide by the settlement he had signed; but we all know what happened. Within six months of the signature of the Munich Agreement, in defiance of many solemn promises, he annexed the remainder of that unhappy country. A forceful incorporation of millions of another race showed the whole world, as in a flash, that here was no question of German right, but the symptom of real purpose—German domination; and that struck at something very deep in the hearts and minds of the British people the world over.

The instinct of our people has always driven them to resist attempts by any one nation to make itself the master of Europe. They have always seen in any such attempt a threat both to their own existence and to the general cause of liberty in Europe. I have no doubt that the history of the nineteenth century proves them to have been right. Just look back. During that time, thanks to the command of the seas, the power of Great Britain was unchallenged, and it was no coincidence that that century saw a great development of liberty throughout the world.

There is no more striking instance to be found of the different uses to which great strength can be put than that which is provided by this country and Germany. No small nation has ever regarded our sea power as a menace to its orderly and legitimate development. Not so with Germany, for no sooner did the land and air forces of Germany regain their strength after the last war than a kind of trembling began to run through the smaller States of Europe, and all Germany's neighbours felt that not only their liberty, but possibly their very existence, was threatened by it. Therefore I say without hesitation that, if the British people have been right before in resisting the domination of Europe by any one Power, they are doubly right to-day.

The occasions of war are not always their fundamental cause. It is quite true that the case of aggression on Poland was covered by our formal commitment to Poland; but it was not Poland in itself, but the whole picture of German policy as by then it had been revealed, that first of all caused that commitment to be given, and, secondly, caused it to be honoured with practical unanimity in this country when the time came. It has been suggested that we might perhaps have stood aside and allowed Germany to do what she liked in the east and south-east of Europe, and that we might have reached an understanding with Herr Hitler by which Germany would not challenge British or French vital interests. We have always been willing to recognize the special interest Germany had in those parts of Europe which, for geographical or economic reasons, occupied for her a special importance, and in which she was therefore entitled to claim such special interest. But once it became clear that the purpose of German policy was domination by the absorption of non-German peoples, then it was to my mind overwhelmingly plain that we were once again faced by the identical challenge of history, which no number of Herr Hitler's assurances could disguise.

And, you remember, in his speech at Danzig on October 7 last, Herr Hitler defended himself against the charge that he had broken his word in the course of his various raids on other nations. His defence was significant of his thought. 'I object strongly,' he said, 'when a foreign statesman says that I break my word because I have now carried out these revisions. On the contrary, I have carried out my solemn word, which I pledged to the German people, to put an end to the Versailles Treaty.' In other words, any breach of trust in Herr Hitler's view is justifiable if it helps him to realize his aims. And in the same way, I have not the slightest doubt that, if we had shaped our policy on Herr Hitler's assurances that he did not intend to attack our interests, we should certainly have been told in due course, after he had broken his word and reduced the British Empire to his will, that he was merely carrying out the intention that he had publicly and frequently proclaimed—openly in *Mein Kampf*—to make the German people the rulers of the world, and that we had no legitimate complaint.

Therefore I think we should indeed have been very blind not to recognize that all the signs pointed to his purpose being much bigger than Poland; and that, when he had cleared up and strengthened his position in the East, he would have been in good shape to tackle what are the main obstacles to his larger ambitions, namely, the British Empire and France. And it is also true to say that experience has shown that understandings with Herr Hitler are regarded by him only as stepping-stones to the realization of the Nazi ambitions. They do not mean to stop there. They are useful pausing points before getting to the next stage. The Anglo-German Naval Treaty was ruthlessly swept away as soon as it had served its purpose of encouraging the British people to think that an understanding with Germany was possible. The Polish Agreement was cancelled without notice as soon as Herr Hitler thought the time had come to settle his accounts with Poland; and I am forced to believe that any other agreement with Herr Hitler would have been equally provisional. Therefore, in my own mind, quite apart from the moral considerations, no salvation for the British Empire was to be found by bartering the liberties of other nations against the continuance of our own.

And I would like to carry that argument one stage farther. I think that even if we had been able to reach an understanding with Germany, it is quite clear that the Nazi Government have no scruple whatever in abandoning their friends for a political purpose which Herr Hitler thinks more important for Germany. The fate of Finland proves it. Germany assisted Finland to maintain her independence in 1918. Now that independence is threatened by a brutal and totally unprovoked aggression, for which Germany, by one of the most cynical acrobatic feats of political history, which has brought new dangers to European society, must bear her own full and heavy share of the blame. The Finnish people, who have shown the world the power that springs from unity of purpose, have gained our profoundest admiration, and I am quite certain many and earnest prayers all over the world are going up for their success. It would not be in the public interest to disclose the measures which the Government are taking and have taken to fulfil their undertaking to give assistance to Finland. But you can rely on the Government to see to it that our undertaking to help her is not remaining, and will not remain, an idle expression of academic or formal sympathy.

There is thus no doubt about the issues on which the struggle between Britain and Germany is joined. The essence of the clash is that the basis of German policy is, plainly, force. As Herr Hitler frankly confessed, in his view 'the weak have no right to live'. The British Commonwealth of Nations is designed on a conception that is wholly different. We have learned by experience that unity can best be born of liberty and cannot be artificially created by coercion. Look at the results of the two methods as we see them in operation to-day. In Austria, Bohemia, Moravia, and Poland you see Germany being compelled to drain her reserves of military strength by sending divisions to hold down by force the territories which she has incorporated in the Reich. Divisions are moving, too, in the British Commonwealth. But in our case they are divisions of free men from the free Dominions overseas, moving of their own free will to take their places in the fighting line beside us.

We know that there is no freedom in Germany, but many do not realize in this country how far the individual has been deprived of every single right he formerly possessed. There is no Constitution. Pastor Niemoeller is acquitted by the regular court and picked up by the secret police; trade unions have been dissolved; families are broken up or compelled to migrate to work in different parts of the country; property is seized at the caprice of the local dictator. Against these proceedings the individual has no right of appeal and no legal remedy whatever. Now what goes on in Germany is doubtless primarily the concern of the German people. What does concern us vitally is the openly declared intention of the Nazi party to apply to foreign policy the tactics and principles which brought them to power in Germany.

In the preface to the recently published German White Book on the origin of the war, Herr von Ribbentrop—on whose shoulders before the tribunal of history will rest a heavy responsibility for this war—declares the German war aim to be our military destruction. After this military destruction, with the prospect of loot accompanying it, would come the defeat of all the things we stand for—the preservation of a standard of decency and fairness in international relations; the idea of justice between man and man; and the ideal of liberty ultimately based upon the Christian teaching of the eternal value of every human soul. You will have been impressed, as I was, by the words in which His Holiness the Pope, in his address to the cardinals at Christmas, spoke of these things far better than I can hope to do; but I have no hesitation in saying that I would a hundred times sooner be dead than alive in a world under the heel of Nazi government.

The war certainly has not developed as many people expected. It is not surprising that one of the consequences of that should have been much criticism of the Government. Some people say that we have taken a lot of action and imposed many restrictions that experience shows to have been quite unnecessary, and merely evidence of bureaucratic red tape which we all instinctively dislike. Why all this expenditure, trouble, and interference over evacuation, black-outs, and rationing?

As regards expenditure, it may interest you to know that drastic action has been taken by the Treasury, and special machinery set up to ensure that we get value for the vast sums we are now forced to spend. In this machinery, business men are associated with Government representatives. The result of their work has already been to effect considerable reductions in various directions. And it is worth noting that these economy measures have been adopted now, at this comparatively early date, and not, as twenty-five years ago, after the war had been going on a long time.

As regards the war-time restrictions, we are under no illusion about the inconvenience and hardship they cause. Just as we often reproach ourselves for carrying a macintosh when it does not rain, so we are now inclined to say that the course of the war has shown that these elaborate precautions were unnecessary. I suggest to you that no one could know before the war started that they were going to be unnecessary yesterday, and no one can say to-day that they are going to be unnecessary to-morrow. Certainly no Government could have taken the chance of being wrong on the other side, and the blame that has come to us for action that has so far proved unnecessary is nothing to the blame that we should have earned, and rightly earned, if we had been caught unprepared. Governments, of course, make mistakes—

they would not be human if they did not—but I venture to think that most of our critics would have made at least as many. And may it not be that the fact of our having taken such precautionary measures has been one of the causes deterring the enemy from offensive action that he might otherwise have taken?

There is another wider consideration suggested by the way things have gone. The Germans' only chance of winning was to win a quick war by cashing in on the advantage they possessed through long preparation, their fortifications in the West, their air strength, and their readiness to stop at nothing in the waging of war by sea. Yet they have hesitated to launch this great offensive on land or in the air—not certainly because of any tender feelings for you and me, but simply for the reason that makes the bully hesitate to hit somebody who is likely to hit him back.

I have heard it said by men of responsibility and trained judgement that if the winter were to pass without a great land offensive by Germany, it would be the equivalent of a victory in a major campaign for the Allies. I am not competent to assess the value of that opinion, but I do know that we have made very good use of these last months. We have taken advantage of them to push on with our production, to land our ever-growing Expeditionary Force in France, and, above all, to co-ordinate every side of our effort with that of the French. The financial and economic agreements we have made with France are unprecedented, and open up a new chapter in the relations between our two countries. We hope that the close system of collaboration that these arrangements represent may in time find a basis even broader, and may lead to such free but close association in the economic and financial spheres between the nations of Europe as may hold out in future the best hope of peaceful reconstruction.

On land the French Army stands, as ever, the bastion of Western civilization. Here also we did not, as last time, wait until nearly four years had gone. Unity of command was realized from the very first day of the war, and, as a measure of the recognition we in this country give to the valour and military efficiency of our French Allies, our troops since the war began have been under the command of the French commander-in-chief to use and to send where he thinks fit.

Meanwhile the Germans have been concentrating their efforts on the forms of warfare that they have made particularly their own, by indiscriminate warfare at sea against British, Allied, and neutral shipping alike, and by unrestricted use of submarine and mine. But, in spite of every breach of international law, Germany seems to me to have gained astonishingly little by it. At the outset of the war the advantage, so far as our merchant fleet was concerned, was with the enemy. At a time when we still hoped and prayed that hostilities might yet be averted, the U-boats were taking up their stations on the ocean routes, lying in wait for our unarmed and unsuspecting merchant shipping. Some time had of necessity to elapse before our ships could be marshalled and the convoy system and other methods of defence could be brought into operation. Since this has been organized, something like 6,000 ships were convoyed to the end of December with a loss of only twelve ships—one in 500. To-day the oceans of the world have been swept clear of German ships. Over 140,000 tons of enemy shipping have been scuttled or run aground to avoid capture.

The first naval battle of the war—that of the River Plate—has been rightly called 'one of the finest naval actions in all British naval history'. The self-destruction of one of the enemy's much-vaunted pocket battleships and the events which led up to it have, like the most gallant action of the *Rawalpindi*, shown once again to the world that British sailors, even when outclassed in relative strength, will not hesitate to close with and engage the enemy. We often hear reference to Sir Richard Grenville's fight in the *Revenge*, and I have often said to myself: 'Did Sir Richard think that his action in facing what seemed to him and his ship's company a hopeless task, was going to be a well of inspiration for generations and generations of his fellow countrymen still unborn?' That is the worth of gallantry whenever it is shown.

And so, conscious of this inferiority at sea, and, as one may suppose, disheartened by the failure of the U-boats, Germany, in defiance of all the laws of humanity and in breach of international law, has resorted to the weapon of indiscriminate and unnotified mine-laying. In doing so, the German Government showed an even more callous indifference than before to the lives of non-combatant passengers and crews. You know that such mine-laying has imposed upon us heavy losses, and has caused us great anxiety. But I am happily able to tell you to-day that measures have been adopted and are daily being developed, which the Admiralty are confident will effectively cope with this new menace. Up to date, the net decrease in British sea-going vessels, suitable for carrying cargo or passengers, after allowing for replacements by new building, and transfers from other flags, represents considerably less than 1 per cent. of the total of such vessels when the war began, and no less than 11 million tons of British shipping is daily trafficking to and fro on the ocean highways.

And all the time the inexorable grip of British sea power is tightening on Germany. It is impossible to give complete statistics of this, but I may give you two or three examples of the effect of our contraband control. In the first two months of the war German imports from three countries whose trade has to cross the Atlantic fell to 7 per cent. of the figure for the same months of 1938. Germany's imports from two neighbouring countries were only slightly over half of those for the same period of 1938. In these first four months we have stopped something like half a million tons of contraband destined for Germany and vital for Germany's war needs. While we know that Germany is making a great effort to increase her trade in the Balkans, Scandinavia, and Russia, her capacity to export depends in large measure on the sea-borne supplies that we are steadily and increasingly denying to her. For that reason there can be very little prospect of her succeeding to any very great extent in increasing her trade in those directions.

While, therefore, it would be dangerous and wrong in any way to underrate the organized strength of the enemy or the severity of the ordeal that that strength is bound to impose upon ourselves and our Allies, I cannot doubt that the factors which will ultimately prove decisive are on our side. And if so, what kind of thing is in our minds to do when the war is over? What kind of a peace is it at which we aim?

Our peace aims, as distinct from our war aim, which is to win the war, have been clearly defined by the Prime Minister. We must insist upon the restoration of liberty to small nations that Germany has cruelly deprived of it, and, profiting I hope by experience of the past, we shall do our utmost to secure Europe from a repetition of this disaster. We seek nothing for ourselves. We have said publicly that if we could once again feel security that a German Government would respect its undertakings and honestly co-operate in trying to build, instead of destroy, European peace on terms of live-and-let-live for all nations, we would not seek a vindictive peace or one that would deny to Germany her rightful place among the nations. The only reason why peace cannot be made to-morrow is that the German Government have as yet given no evidence whatever of their readiness to repair the damage they have wrought upon their weaker neighbours, or of their capacity to convince the world that any pledge they may subscribe to is worth as much as the paper on which it may be written.

I spoke just now of the ordeal which this struggle is bound to impose upon those who are playing their part on the home front, and it is vital that we should realize that the home front in its own way is not less important, even if its duties are for the time being less dangerous, than any other. The land front against Germany in the west stretches from the Shetlands to Switzerland, and every yard of that front must be held with equal resolution. The holding of it is going to demand heavy sacrifices from us all. Service on the home front means sacrifice. It means willing and cheerful compliance with war-time restrictions, which, whether by releasing shipping or saving financial strain, may help our war effort. It means cutting out all but absolutely necessary expenditure. It means lending to the State every penny we can. It means changes in industry to meet the great demands of war production. It means hard and unremitting work for everyone in the country.

The campaign for war savings is a great national effort,

and it is of the highest importance to the State that that campaign should be a success. It has made a good beginning, but a steady and continuous effort will be needed throughout the war. One important way, I may mention in passing, of sustaining that campaign is to form groups for national saving, the money saved by these groups being put at the disposal of the State. Many new groups are needed, for example in places of employment, and I would like to appeal to employers and employees in the whole country to do anything they can to give practical help in that especially valuable way.

All this, and perhaps more, will be demanded of us at home. I have no doubt whatever that our people will wish to pay whatever price is necessary to secure the causes for which we are engaged, in which they know are bound up all the things that make life worth living. And I feel that once they are convinced of its necessity, so far from grudging the necessary sacrifice, those on the home front will be only anxious to share more equally in its burden with those who, on sea, and land, and in the air, are in the actual fighting line.

Many here have personal experience of this from the last war. There is no one whose imagination is so dull as to be unable to picture to himself something of what these men are doing for us and for our cause each moment of the day. The sailor, whether in the Royal Navy or the indomitable mercantile marine and fishing fleets, under the never-ending strain of sudden danger; the soldier on night patrol or raiding party; the airman facing all the forces of nature over sea and land to fight his way over enemy country on some special mission—when we compare with these such sacrifice and discomfort as we here at home in our several duties have so far been called upon to face, surely our only feeling can be one of how little it is that we can give.

And therefore let us give what we can, and give cheerfully, in the spirit of these examples. Above all, let us think of sacrifice as of something that gives strength and dignity to the cause in which it is made, and let us not forget that our cause will only earn victory if those who passionately believe in it are resolved to spend themselves in its behalf.

50

THE CHALLENGE TO LIBERTY

27 February 1940

[The following address was delivered by Lord Halifax in the Sheldonian Theatre at Oxford to the University of which he is Chancellor. It has been printed as a separate pamphlet by *The Times* as *A Conflict of Youth* and by the Oxford University Press under the title here given to it.]

IN addressing you, members of Oxford University, I suppose that I assume in your eyes a dual personality—that of Chancellor of the University and of Foreign Secretary. This evening I propose to perform the feat, if indeed it is a feat, of welding this dual personality into one and speaking to you in all sincerity with single heart and mind. One of my predecessors, Lord Grey of Fallodon, in whose steps I should be proud to walk, combined, though not like Lord Curzon simultaneously, the two offices with which I am to-day entrusted. It was only after Lord Grey had retired from a public life which did honour to his country and to himself, that his University welcomed him back as Chancellor. I can imagine no better representative of our University, and I would that he were here now to speak to you in my place.

Lord Grey hated war. He did his utmost, in and before 1914, to avoid war with Germany, just as we, his successors, did our utmost to avoid war with Germany in 1939. When in spite of his efforts war came in the summer of 1914, Lord Grey, standing at the window of his room in the Foreign Office, used words which you will remember, but which you will allow me once again to quote, since they were so remarkable a forecast of what has happened since. 'The lamps are going out all over Europe; we shall not see them lit again in our lifetime.'

The similarity between 1914 and 1939 or 1940 is striking. We too hate war. We also observe, with deepening anxiety, the growing darkness in Europe. Our attitude towards those instruments of force to which we are compelled to have resort in defence of the highest things for which and by which we live; our views about war; both these are unchanged. Nevertheless I should be misleading myself and you if I were to suggest that there is no difference between the position in 1914 and the position as you see it to-day. The emotional experience of one generation must of necessity differ from that of the generation which preceded it. In 1939 I and others of my age could without much difficulty recapture that earlier experience of 1914, but I know that I should be profoundly mistaken if I were to imagine that the youth of to-day were entering upon this second European war in the same mood as that in which we entered upon the first. I will attempt to explain to you where, as it appears to me, lies the difference.

It is not only that now we know better what war means, and that the temper in which we face it is rather one of set determination than any feeling of approach to a great and unknown adventure. We in 1914 had been born and grown up in an atmosphere of peace. Those who came up to Oxford with me lived in a world that we then thought was stable and secure. That security was rudely shaken in 1914, but not sufficiently shaken for us to have any serious doubt that it would soon be put right or to think that, when the war was over, the old life would not return. You, in the light of what has happened since, may think that we were foolish and short-sighted. Perhaps we were. But every generation must, *sub specie aeternitatis*, be foolish and short-sighted, and you no doubt hold your own views about your elders. What exactly these views are I do not pretend to know, but I suspect that you see us as people who, though no doubt well-meaning, have made havoc of the world in which you now have to live. You probably regard us as having lived through, and perhaps as still living in, the years of illusion, while you have lived through the years of disillusion. I fancy that to us patriotism presented itself in simpler and more straightforward form than it does to you, and that for this reason the same appeals which moved us no longer have the same power with you. The poetry of Rupert Brooke, which rightly inspired us, has been replaced on your shelves by that of other poets of your own times, who bring you a harsher message.

We were sure, as I say, in 1914 that once we had dealt with the matter in hand the world would return to old ways, which, in the main, we thought to be good ways. You are not so sure. I admit and sympathize with the difference, but having made the admission let me add this. No generation has the right to lay the cause of all its ills upon the shoulders of its predecessor, for no one age-group of men has the monopoly of vision. We are all men and women of our particular time and particular environment. We are all subject to the limitations of human weakness and fallibility. Just as you may criticize us, those who come after will no less certainly criticize you.

I have quoted to you some words of Lord Grey which have proved indeed prophetic. Let me quote also some words which were written by a French Jansenist[1] in the seventeenth century and which are very similar:

> 'Il me semble que je suis né dans une église éclairée de diverses lampes et de divers flambeaux, et que Dieu permet que je les voie éteindre les uns après les autres, sans qu'il paraisse qu'on y en substitue de nouveaux. Ainsi il me semble que l'air s'obscurcit de plus en plus, parce que nous ne méritons pas que Dieu répare les vides qu'il fait lui-même dans son église.'

You may perhaps find in these French words deeper analysis of the present ills of Europe. You may think that Western culture is falling into darkness because it deserves no better fate. You may think indeed that these times earn the title of one of the most remarkable poems of our day and conclude that Europe is indeed 'the waste land'. I would go some long way with you in agreement with this judgement. I think that the existence of war in Europe to-day is a sign of failure, or of something more than failure, in our Western civilization. When I consider that we—who hate war—are driven to the use of force; that you are asked to be the instruments of this force, in maintaining against bitter and evil attack the first principles upon which European life has hitherto been based, the darkness that hangs over Europe seems to me something which Milton might have described

[1] Nicole, in a letter to Antoine Arnauld, 16 June 1692 (*Lettres du feu M. Nicole*, Lille, 1718, tome 2, page 191).

as darkness visible. Moreover, I am appalled—there is no easier word for it—by one fact above all. This 'waste land' in which we live, this European civilization in which the lamps are burning dim, has not been brought to its present pass merely by the mistakes, the pride, and the selfishness of an older generation.

What has, for example, been the driving force behind the Nazi movement in Germany? It has been German youth. Deliberately deprived, as they have been, of the elements of true judgement, it is they who made the movement and who still sustain it. Their point of view stands in stark opposition to yours. They do not understand your way of thinking. Your ideals mean nothing to them. They have their own ideals, which to our minds are distorted and deformed, but for which hundreds of thousands of them are prepared without a moment's hesitation to sacrifice their lives. There is what seems an impenetrable barrier dividing you from them, which somehow will have to be broken down if the youth of Europe is to avoid living always in this waste land, and if the European temple of civilization is to deserve and win a rekindling of the lamps.

The real conflict, therefore, to-day is not between age and youth, but between youth and youth. It is important that this should be fully appreciated, for it is the kernel of our future problems. I am not disquieted by the divergences between age and youth. They have been with us since the world began. They represent an inevitable difference of perspective, but there is nothing in them which postulates a fundamental conflict. If I were to see life as you see it, or if you were to see it as I do, I should feel that there was something wrong with one or other of us. But there is something sinister in the acceptance, by the growing generations in different countries, of standards of conduct in sharp contradiction to one another, for that does constitute a terrifying challenge to the very foundations of human thought and action.

But in this challenge also lies our hope; for as we move to meet it, we shall more truly measure both its nature and the weapons with which it can be countered. It was easier a century ago to run away from the truth than it is to-day, less difficult to avoid looking squarely at grim and dangerous facts. In Victorian times there was much to encourage the assurance in the steady improvement of man's lot that generally prevailed. Major European wars were rare, and when they occurred they were according to modern standards brief. Their scale in any case was not such as to disturb the whole frame of national life. Human comprehension and knowledge were extended in both spiritual and material spheres; the arts and sciences flourished; man's social sense was awake and active; there was a growing respect for the rights of the individual, for freedom of speech and conscience; there was an insistent demand that all men should enjoy equality of opportunity. Ignoring the precarious nature of all human progress, it was too lightly assumed that the good things thus reflected in our attitude to our fellow men had come to stay and that the clock would not be put back. I sometimes picture the Victorian, who had lived and died in the comfortable and comforting belief that we were marching in orderly fashion 'from precedent to precedent', returning to life to-day. He would be astounded no doubt by the material conveniences with which we had added to the ease of life, but he would be still more astounded by the moral retrogression of Europe and this devastating perversion of youth in Germany.

Do not let me overstate the case. I am far from thinking that the wounds inflicted on our civilization need be mortal. But I do think that we are fighting for its life; and inasmuch as that life finally depends upon the ideals that inspire it, I think we have no choice but to resist and defeat by force the attack to which those ideals—yours as well as mine—are now exposed.

I know that it is said by men of high principle that force in itself, if not an evil thing, has a value only negative. I think this is an exaggeration. Most true it is that force cannot of itself exorcize the evil spirits that enter and deprave the hearts of men. But when these evil spirits invoke force for the prosecution of their purpose, and the struggle is thus joined in the physical arena, it is only by force on the battleground thus chosen that the evil can be resisted. Nor can I doubt that if, under what I must hold to be a one-sided and mistaken interpretation of our Lord's teaching, we refrain on principle from replying in kind to the use of force, we may be surrendering to extinction the most sacred causes for which we stand to posterity as guardians and trustees. Thus force, by resisting the destructive power of evil and guarding the field in which good can work, can render positive service which can be given in no other way. As I see this problem which is to-day so tragically forced upon our thought, it is the spiritual motive, alike in national as in individual action, on which judgement has to be passed. Always it is the spirit behind the application of force which makes or mars its value. And we may assuredly hope that the same spirit, which gives the physical and moral courage to defend the menaced values of life to-day, will avail us when we come through the valley of dark decision to the work of reconstruction.

Here I come back again to the idea of 'the waste land'. I do not believe, as I have said, that civilization has yet foundered, but I am certain that there is an active force of evil which, unless we fight it, will rapidly reduce our civilization to a desert of the soul. That evil force is at work in a period of human history in which change has been so sudden as to bring grave confusion of thought to give more favourable conditions for the Devil's work. It is, of course, true that the world never stands still, but there are times when the flywheel races, and you and I live in such a time to-day. You have never lived in any other. Your world has been influenced, whether you acknowledge it or not, by what I must take leave to term the inhuman conception of the so-called economic man. There has been a tendency for great thinkers, who have analysed the social and moral values on which the human community has been built, to stress the need for finding the perfect system. There has been a tendency to explain all history and humanity in economic instead of in human terms. Christianity, on the other hand, has rather made its end the perfection of the individual, in the conviction that here, too, lay the secret of life for all society. And this emphasis upon the ideal system, instead of the ideal individual, has not helped the development of the human character. Yet fundamentally men to-day remain much the same men as they were yesterday. They may be better informed, but they are not necessarily wiser. They wish to emancipate themselves from artificial conventions, but they are not more free from the dangers and pitfalls which caused those conventions to be accepted.

We none of us, young or old, like to be called conventional. Such a description seems in some way to impugn our intellectual fibre and independence. And so, desiring to assert our independence, we are tempted to revolt against canons which reason has not yet made our own, regardless of the fact that some of them at least may have permanent significance. One consequence is that in many quarters to-day there is failure to distinguish between the necessary revision of conventions, which must inevitably recur in any intelligent community, and the recognition of the necessity for some rules—which if you like you may call conventions—for the guidance and protection of society. Here is indeed one of life's problems which each has to settle for himself, finding his own adjustment between the necessity for change which is the law of life and the restraint without which society cannot live. T. H. Green once said: 'That man is free who is conscious of himself as the author of the law which he obeys.' Conventions are after all but the warning signals of society which has from the beginning of history felt the need of protecting human frailty.

The substance of any conventional code, however, must derive from the appreciation by society of the principles of its own survival. These in turn emerge from moral principles which man has gradually come to apprehend, and which themselves are rooted in religious instinct. The danger that in revising traditional and outward forms we impair the substance is familiar enough. If this happens, man is adrift without bearings and without anchor; and, as we see to-day, in the vile savageries to which in this twentieth century he can revert, the descent from man to animal is easy.

And so it is that, if we are to keep our bearings as a nation, we must base ourselves firmly on social, moral, and religious standards. No country will be at peace with itself or with others on any other basis, for the world's disorder to-day is the reflection of turmoil and conflict in the minds of men. If, therefore, we are to recapture the secret of order for international society—and here I speak of all countries—we must as individuals strive to erect or maintain standards that will bring true freedom through the way of discipline. Your standards will not perhaps be the same in form as those to which the loyalty of those older than yourselves are pledged. But in substance I fancy they will not greatly differ. That, however, is something which you must work out for yourselves, answering directly your own needs. And Oxford, much as she may have changed, still retains her essential quality as the great clearing-house of ideals and ideas, where values may be tested and appraised in the free play of thought. Oxford will still mould you as you are assuredly moulding her; and in this double process I do not doubt that she will remain the inspiration of a vital part of English life.

Many of you—perhaps most of you—are preparing to take your place before long in the ranks of the fighting forces, and you have every right to put the question, 'What is it that we are to fight for, and what prospect is there that we shall in the end secure the better world for which the fight is waged?' I have done my best here and elsewhere—as have others—to weigh what is involved in the present conflict. Its issue, as I believe, will affect profoundly the whole future of mankind, for what is here at stake is whether the nations that desire peace must perpetually be faced with war, if they are not prepared to accept any settlement that force may seek to impose upon them. And so, except for those—a tiny fraction of our people—who would for whatever reason feel that we had been wrong to embark upon this war at all, I cannot conceive of doubt arising as to the duty of bracing our resolution until, so far as it may be humanly possible to do so, we have secured the world against a repetition of this ordeal.

As to the future, it is not possible for me or for any other man to answer with complete assurance. If once the doctrine of force could effectively be put to shame, the way would be open to concentrate the effort now mobilized for war upon the cause of improving the common lot of man. Some months ago, before the war, I said that 'British policy rested upon twin foundations of purpose. One was determination to resist force. The other was our recognition of the world's desire to get on with the constructive work of building peace.'[1] The implication of those words holds good to-day. To none of us is vouchsafed certainty as to what it may be in our power to do, and, were I to attempt to make such claim, you would rightly challenge my presumption. But what *is* within our power is to define clearly our direction and the spirit in which we shall try to work. If this and the purposes for which we strive are right, we can surely feel that we have done everything we can to make our endeavour worthy of the cost.

I constantly remember the story of the traveller who asked the peasant working in the fields how far it was to Carcassonne. 'How far it is to Carcassonne, Sir, that I do not know. But that this is the road to Carcassonne, of that I am sure; for those who return say always that at the end lies Carcassonne.' Our Carcassonne is the world of our desire. I do not know whether it will be an easier world, but what matters is that we should desire not an easier but a better world, and equip ourselves in body, mind, and spirit to create it. For it depends mainly on ourselves whether we are to be masters of our fate.

There is no reason, therefore, to be disillusioned about the future, however much you may feel disillusioned about the past. Hope is the oldest and wisest counsellor of mankind, for without hope it is impossible for men to apprehend the power of the other great Christian virtues of faith and charity, and these alone can be the bond of peace for all members of the human family.

I have said that the real conflict of ideas is between youth and youth, and that the beliefs of German youth, nurtured in Nazi doctrines, are in stark opposition to your own. We should gravely err if we were to rate lightly the strength and reality of their beliefs. The racial doctrine, as interpreted in

[1] Page 296, above.

the Nazi creed, may be, and in my view is, sheer primitive nonsense; and we are no more prepared to admit German superiority of race than we are concerned to assert our own. If that were all, it would not greatly matter, but when this doctrine is invoked in justification of the oppression of other races, it becomes a crime against humanity.

Not only does it deny the corporate claim to liberty of men and women organized in national societies, but it refuses the much more fundamental claim of men and women to the free expression of human personality, which rests upon the eternal value of every human soul. True pride of race may be tested by the behaviour of its possessors towards their own fellow citizens and towards others. It will forbid conduct to individuals of which they should be ashamed in their private lives. It is thus evidently something far removed from the ideal of a race which by the German philosophy of to-day is called to stamp out the civilization of another. Between these two conceptions there is a great gulf fixed. The German race, under its present rulers, is betraying both itself and the greater whole of which it is part, and to whose progress it might, and ought to, be making its own distinctive contribution. And the real tragedy of that betrayal, as it affects the German youth, is the enlistment of the honourable instincts of self-sacrifice and devotion in the service of a crudely materialist philosophy. Until these false creeds are abjured, and replaced by a wider toleration, they must continue to excite resistance. The future of humanity must not be left in the hands of those who would imprison and enslave it.

We may readily admit that we, like other men, have often fallen short of our professions. Our history has not been free from faults; it has taken time to establish in universal practice principles which have now won general acceptance. And there are things to-day within our body politic which we need to fight not less intensely, if with other weapons, than we fight the enemy without. But the broad record of the British race stands to be judged on facts that are incontestable. It is the fact that during the nineteenth century, when the power of this country was unchallenged, there was no nation in Europe that felt for that reason insecure, or that did not recognize our power to be an instrument of peace. The *Pax Britannica* has been no empty or self-righteous boast of purpose. It is the fact, too, that in every corner of the world where men of British race have established influence, there by immutable law of nature you find established the seed and plant of liberty. It is the trail by which is marked their progress, interpreted to all by the standards of good faith, respect for law, and equal justice. Most truly, therefore, of our people was it said:[1]

> 'Their country's cause is the high cause of Freedom and Honour. That fairest earthly fame, the fame of Freedom, is inseparable from the names of Albion, Britain, England.'

My message, therefore, to you to-day as Chancellor and Foreign Secretary is to be so proud of the race to which you belong that you will be as jealous of its honour as you are of its safety, and that you will fight for both with equal determination. The struggle will be arduous, it may be long, and it will certainly demand of our nation that it should withhold nothing that may contribute to our strength. Let us never forget that of all the resources at our command, the most powerful will be the quality of our resolution, fed by a true perception of the responsibility laid upon each one of us, and of the spirit in which that responsibility must be discharged.

In front of the Viceroy's House in New Delhi stands a column, on which are inscribed the words:

> In Thought Faith
> In Word Wisdom
> In Deed Courage
> In Life Service
> So may India be great.

No one of us could offer for our country and our Commonwealth any better prayer to-day.

[1] By Robert Bridges in the Preface to *The Spirit of Man*, 1916.